——————————— MURDER WAS NOT A CRIME ———————————

Ashley and Peter Larkin Series in Greek and Roman Culture

MURDER WAS NOT A CRIME

Homicide and Power
in the Roman Republic

JUDY E. GAUGHAN

UNIVERSITY OF TEXAS PRESS

Austin

Requests for permission to reproduce material from
this work should be sent to:
Permissions
University of Texas Press
P.O. Box 7819
Austin, TX 78713-7819
www.utexas.edu/utpress/about/bpermission.html

⊗ The paper used in this book meets the minimum requirements of
ANSI/NISO Z39.48-1992 (R1997) (Permanence of Paper).

Library of Congress Cataloging-in-Publication Data
Gaughan, Judy E., 1961–
Murder was not a crime : homicide and power in the Roman republic /
by Judy E. Gaughan.
p. cm. — (Ashley and Peter Larkin series in Greek and Roman culture)
Includes bibliographical references and index.
ISBN 978-0-292-72567-6
1. Murder (Roman law) 2. Homicide (Roman law) 3. Rome—
Politics and government—510–30 B.C. I. Title.
KJA3397.G38 2010
345.37'6302523—dc22
2009031649

To my parents
who taught me to love learning
and
to my daughter
who reminds me daily of its joys

CONTENTS

ABBREVIATIONS

MODERN SOURCES

Alexander, *Trials*	Michael C. Alexander, *Trials in the Late Roman Republic 149 BC–50 BC*
BIDR	*Bulletino dell'istituto di diritto Romano*
Broughton, MRR	T. Robert S. Broughton, *The Magistrates of the Roman Republic*
Elster, *Gesetze*	Marianne Elster, *Die Gesetze der mittleren römischen Republik, Text und Kommentar*
FIRA	*Fontes Iuris Romani Anteiustiniani*
Flach, *Gesetze*	Dieter Flach, *Die Gesetze der frühen römischen Republik*
Gruen, RPCC	Erich Gruen, *Roman Politics and the Criminal Courts, 149–78 BC*
Index	*Index: Quaderni camerti di studi Romanistici*
Iura	*Iura: rivista internazionale di diritto romano e antico*
Kunkel, *Untersuchungen*	Wolfgang Kunkel, *Untersuchungen zur Entwicklung des römischen Kriminalverfahrens in vorsullanischer Zeit*
Labeo	*Labeo: Rassegna di diritto romano*
Mommsen, *Staatsr.*	Theodor Mommsen, *Römisches Staatsrecht*
Mommsen, *Strafr.*	Theodor Mommsen, *Römisches Strafrecht*

RE	*Paulys Real-Encyclopädie der classischen Altertumswissenschaft. Neue Bearbeitung*
RS	M. H. Crawford, et al., *Roman Statutes*
Santalucia, *Studi*	Bernardo Santalucia, *Studi di diritto penale romano*
SDHI	*Studia et Documenta Historiae et Iuris*
ZSS	*Zeitschrift der Savigny Stiftung für Rechtsgeschichte, Römanistiche Abteilung*

ANCIENT SOURCES

Appian *BC*	Appian, *Civil Wars*
Appian *Mith.*	Appian, *The Mithridatic Wars*
Ascon.	Asconius, Clark edition
August. *de lib. arbit.*	Augustine, *On Free Will*
Aul. Gell. *NA*	Aulus Gellius, *Attic Nights*
C. Th.	*Code of Theodosius*
Caes. *BC*	Caesar, *The Civil War*
Caes. *BG*	Caesar, *The Gallic War*
Cato *Orig.*	Cato, *Origins*
Cic. *ad Att.*	Cicero, *Letters to Atticus*
Cic. *ad fam.*	Cicero, *Letters to His Friends*
Cic. *ad Herr.*	Cicero, *Rhetoric to Herrenius*
Cic. *ad Quint. Frat.*	Cicero, *Letters to Quintus, his Brother*
Cic. *Brut.*	Cicero, *Brutus*
Cic. *Cat.*	Cicero, *Against Catiline*
Cic. *de amic.*	Cicero, *On Friendship*
Cic. *de domo*	Cicero, *On his house*
Cic. *de fin.*	Cicero, *On the Ends of Good and Evil*
Cic. *de inv.*	Cicero, *On Invention*
Cic. *de leg.*	Cicero, *On the Laws*
Cic. *de leg. agr.*	Cicero, *On the Agrarian Law*

Cic. *de rep.*	Cicero, *On the Republic*
Cic. *de or.*	Cicero, *On Oratory*
Cic. *Deiot.*	Cicero, *On Behalf of King Deiotarus*
Cic. *in Piso*	Cicero, *Against Piso*
Cic. *in Vat.*	Cicero, *Against Vatinius*
Cic. *in Verr.*	Cicero, *Against Verres*
Cic. *Para. Stoic.*	Cicero, *Stoic Paradoxes*
Cic. *Part. or.*	Cicero, *Partitions of Oratory*
Cic. *Phil.*	Cicero, *Philippics*
Cic. *pro Balbo*	Cicero, *On Behalf of Balbus*
Cic. *pro Cael.*	Cicero, *On Behalf of Caelius*
Cic. *pro Clu.*	Cicero, *On Behalf of Cluentius*
Cic. *pro Corn.*	Cicero, *On Behalf of Cornelius*
Cic. *pro Mil.*	Cicero, *On Behalf of Milo*
Cic. *pro Rab. perd.*	Cicero, *On Behalf of Rabirius on a Charge of Treason*
Cic. *pro Rosc. Am.*	Cicero, *On Behalf of Roscius of Ameria*
Cic. *pro Sest.*	Cicero, *On Behalf of Sestius*
Cic. *pro Tull.*	Cicero, *On Behalf of Tullius*
Cic. *Top.*	Cicero, *Topics*
CIL	*Corpus of Latin Inscriptions*
Codex *Iust.*	*The Code of Justinian*
Collatio	*Collection of Jewish and Roman Laws*
de vir. ill.	*On Illustrious Men*
D.	*Digest of Justinian*
Dio	Cassius Dio
Diod. Sic.	Diodorus the Sicilian
Dion. Hal.	Dionysius of Halicarnassus
Gaius	Gaius, *Institutes*
Festus	Sextus Pompeius Festus
Florus	Lucius Annaeus Florus
Just. *Inst.*	*Institutes of Justinian*

Livy *Ep.*	Livy, *Epitomes*
Livy *Per.*	Livy, *Summaries*
Lydus *de Mag.*	Lydus, *On Magistrates*
Macrob. *S.*	Macrobius, *Saturnalia*
Orosius	Orosius, *Against the Pagans*
Oxyr. Per.	*Oxyrrhincus Papyri*
Paul. *Sent.*	Julius Paulus, *Opinions*
Plaut. *Amphit.*	Plautus, *Amphitryon*
Plaut. *Aul.*	Plautus, *Pot of Gold*
Pliny *Nat. Hist.*	Pliny the Elder, *Natural History*
Plut. *C. Gr.*	Plutarch, *Life of Gaius Gracchus*
Plut. *Marius*	Plutarch, *Life of Marius*
Plut. *Numa*	Plutarch, *Life of Numa Pompilius*
Plut. *Quaest.*	Plutarch, *Questions*
Plut. *Poplic.*	Plutarch, *Life of Publicola*
Plut. *Rom.*	Plutarch, *Life of Romulus*
Plut. *Sulla*	Plutarch, *Life of Sulla*
Plut. *Ti. Gr.*	Plutarch, *Life of Tiberius Gracchus*
Polyb.	Polybius
Ps. Ascon.	Pseudo Asconius, Clark edition
Ps. Sall. *in Cic.*	Pseudo Sallust, *Against Cicero*
Quint. *Decl. Mai.*	Quintilian, *Major Speeches*
Sall. *Cat.*	Sallust, *Catilinarian War*
Sall. *Hist.*	Sallust, *Histories*
Sall. *Iug.*	Sallust, *Jugurthine War*
Salv. *de gubern. dei*	Salvianus, *On the Government of God*
Schol. Gronov.	*Gronovian Scholia*, Orelli, ed.
Schol. Bob.	*Bobian Scholia*, Stangl, ed.
Sen. *de Clem.*	Seneca, *On Clemency*
Serv. auct. *Ecl.*	Servius the Author, *Eclogues*
Suet. *Iul.*	Suetonius, *Life of Julius Caesar*
Suet. *Tib.*	Suetonius, *Life of Tiberius*

Tac. *Ann.*	Tacitus, *Annals*
Val. Max.	Valerius Maximus
Varro *de Ling. Lat.*	Varro, *On the Latin Language*
Vell. Pat.	Velleius Paterculus
Zonar.	Zonaras, *Epitome of Cassius Dio*

PREFACE

The impetus for this book lies in a peculiar state of affairs I discovered some years ago in the process of researching and writing my dissertation: the Romans seem to have had a murder law during the monarchy but not during the republic.

When I set out to write the dissertation, I intended to explore the nature and development of Roman public law by examining the treatment of one crime over the course of the republic. I chose the crime of murder because it seemed that not much research had been done in that area. I quickly discovered, however, that there did not seem to be any such thing as murder actionable via public law during the Roman republic. I also soon discovered that the same did not seem to be true for the monarchy, when such an offense does seem to have been actionable. Immediately, no doubt, some of my more skeptical readers are thinking that any evidence I have for the monarchy, or indeed for the early centuries of the republic, is going to be unreliable. This fact has concerned me all along through this research.

Yet, it did not make sense to me simply to dismiss all alleged evidence about the monarchy, especially when that evidence seemed so alien to later Roman practice, and there did not seem to be any particularly good reason for the Romans to have fabricated it. The anomaly kept pestering me. I kept asking myself why would murder have been a matter for the government to handle during the monarchy and then subsequently not its responsibility during the republic? My contemplation of this question converted my research from the evolution of public law into the exploration of the nature and growth of republican government as revealed by the treatment of homicide. This book represents my conclusions.

The nature and quality of the evidence require the unorthodox approach of asking why something did not exist. I realize that this is a perilous approach to antiquity, yet I risk it because I believe the results help to dispel strongly held and misplaced assumptions. The first of these is the notion that murder is necessarily a crime in a civilized society. This notion results in the assumption that the Roman government necessarily had jurisdiction over this crime, as so many modern governments do. This assumption, in turn, results in a misconception about the character of Roman republican government and the extent and nature of its power in the community of Rome. I risk the unorthodox approach to the evidence because by laying aside these erroneous assumptions, a more accurate picture of the Roman republic, and the nature of political power within it, can be presented.

ACKNOWLEDGMENTS

I have had the remarkable good fortune throughout my academic career to have consistently worked with scholars who took their pleasure in the acquisition of knowledge and the advancement of intelligence, not in the dance of one-upmanship. The places where I found these remarkable people start with my undergraduate work at San Francisco State University under the tutelage of Richard Hoffman, through my graduate years in the Group in Ancient History and Mediterranean Archaeology at Berkeley, and later among my colleagues in the History Department (and throughout the College of Liberal Arts) at Colorado State University, and at the annual conventions of the Association of Ancient Historians. Because of my remarkable good fortune in this regard, the number of people to whom I owe a debt of gratitude for the production of this manuscript is far greater than the number of names included here.

Some friends, mentors, and colleagues have made this book better than it would have been without their assistance, some by reading drafts, others by formal and informal conversations. These contributors include Michael Alexander, Shadi Bartsch, Courtenay Daum, Alison Futrell, Tobi Jacobi, Elizabeth Leake, Kathleen McCarthy, Andrew Riggsby, Jennifer Ross, Raphael Sealey, the anonymous readers assigned by the University of Texas Press, and the staff of the press, especially Jim Burr, Leslie Tingle, and Nancy Bryant, and Sheila D'Amico who not only gave birth to me but who edited many portions of the manuscript.

I have spent many a summer ensconced in the Robbins Collection of Roman and Canon Law at Boalt Law School on the campus of the University of California at Berkeley. I have benefited not only from the financial assistance provided by the Robbins Collection and the use of the resources available there but also from the assistance of its director, Laurent Mayali, and that of the generous and helpful staff.

To three people in particular I owe the greatest debt both personally and academically. My graduate school colleagues and great friends Beth Severy and Eric Orlin always challenge me intellectually while at the same time providing unending support. The same can be said for my mentor Erich Gruen, whose constant support—in many guises—was indispensable for the completion of this project. Their encouragement of my labors and critiques of the fruits of those labors have made me a better scholar and a relatively sane human being.

Any errors or weaknesses in the monograph are my own. All translations are my own, unless otherwise indicated.

MURDER WAS NOT A CRIME

INTRODUCTION

During the Roman republic murder was not a crime. In other words, the "killing of a human being by another with malice aforethought" was not "an act done in violation of those duties which an individual owes to the community and for the breach of which the law has provided that the offender shall make satisfaction to the public."[1] Indeed, the republican Romans had neither the capacity nor the inclination to make the essentially private act of malicious and intentional homicide an offense actionable by the government. This fact is closely linked to the nature and evolution of political power in Rome, in large part because the right to kill is embedded in two key definitions of power: *patria potestas* (the power possessed by a Roman father over his children, which included the *vitae necisque potestas,* the power of life and death) and magisterial *imperium* (the power to command, which included the power to kill Roman citizens).[2]

In this book I explore the relationship between homicide and power, with special emphasis on political power, from the beginning of the monarchy (753 B.C.E.) through the dictatorship of Lucius Cornelius Sulla (79 B.C.E.). The treatment of homicide, as revealed in this investigation of legislation, trials, punishment, assassinations, proscriptions, and the *vitae necisque potestas,* is a reflection of the extent and nature of the power of Roman government. This means that when the treatment of homicide changed, it was symptomatic of a change in the extent of political power possessed by the republican government. Change in the extent of political power usually coincided with a change in the structure of government. These changes largely revolve around the extent of the centralization of authority in the government. Roman republican government had little interest in controlling murder because the government was too decentralized to have its power challenged by an act of murder. For most of the republic, the government did not have the capacity to involve itself in matters that were not of primary interest to its security and stability.

In some respects the argument here echoes the theoretical approach of Max Weber, who saw control of violence as a defining element of the modern state. Weber's work was not the starting point for this book, however, but his was a theory that I discovered along the way that paralleled the theory that I was beginning to form based on the ancient evidence. In addition, I would argue that a book about homicide is not necessarily a book about violence. While in many respects, homicide, especially murder, is an act of violence, the act of taking another life is distinct from all other forms of violence, largely because of its irreversible result.[3]

TERMINOLOGY

Because this book is specifically about homicide and political power, and because the power of the government was often articulated through legislation, a large part of this book is concerned with Roman law, particularly the sphere and development of Roman public law.[4] Therefore, the argument of this book requires some preliminary remarks about legal terminology, both modern and ancient.

The study of Roman law is a complicated matter. As a result, scholars try to discuss it in language that has meaning for themselves and their contemporaries. While the use of comprehensible language is an admirable practice, in the case of Roman law, certain ubiquitous catchwords have resulted in a misrepresentation of the state of affairs, in particular by ascribing a deceptively familiar institutional structure to what were fluid practices. In republican Latin no words existed that can be literally translated as *murder, crime, criminal courts,* or *criminal law.* Thus, when scholars use such words to discuss Roman law, they end up attributing to the Romans concepts that were alien to them or, at the least, that one should not assume they possessed.

To begin this discussion of terminology, it is necessary to point out a confusion found in the English language. Although murder and homicide are often used interchangeably by lay persons, technically and legally they are two different acts. *Homicide* means simply "killing a person." This includes any kind of killing; thus, killing in battle or execution by the government, as well as murder, fall under this heading. *Murder* is a subset of homicide, and I use it in this study to mean intentional and malicious killing. The word *homicide* will be used simply to mean "taking a life."

The Romans not only had no legislation prohibiting murder, they had no word for murder. Even so, many words in Latin that mean "to kill" are often translated as murder: *caedere, interficere, interimere, occidere, necare,* and *iugulare.* Each of these, however, could mean either justifiable or unjustifiable homicide.[5] None of these words is used as the title of a standing public court, although any of them might have been employed if the Romans chose to promulgate a murder law.[6] The English word *homicide,* too, derives from the Latin word *homicidium,* which first appears in Cicero but is otherwise unknown in the republic and was never proscribed by law.[7]

In examining what words the Romans did use, it is essential to keep in mind the dangers of attributing to them notions alien to their culture. Mommsen, for example, wrote, "In classical Latin there was no simple expression for murder; the recent and not fully established word *homicidium,* the murder of a person, is first introduced late. Temporarily in the classical legal language, the terms bandit (*sicarius*) and poisoner (*veneficus*) were combined to mean murderer."[8] This is not accurate. The Romans used poisoner and bandit to mean poisoner and bandit, not to mean a word that did not exist for them, especially during the republic.

Mommsen is not the only scholar who has recognized the absence of a word meaning murder,[9] but the real significance of this absence needs greater attention, for it contributes to the evidence that the Romans were not interested in having killing per se actionable in their public courts or even regulated by law. This is true of the earliest republican laws on record right through Sulla's legislation, promulgated during his dictatorship in 81–79 B.C.E. In any statutes relating to homicide, the words the Romans used were not primarily concerned with the act of homicide.

The other significant problem of terminology is that of "crime." Offenses that modern scholars call crime were tried in Roman public courts, but I am as resistant to using the word *crime* as I am to using the word *murder,* because the word *crime* did not exist during the republic either. Crime (*Verbrechen* in German, *delitto* in Italian) finds no parallel in Latin. The modern terms imply a morally wrong offense actionable by law with a specific punishment attached to it. While many Latin words are often translated as "crime" — *maleficium, scelus, facinus, peccatum* — none of them has the same associations with law, and all are better rendered as "sin," "bad deed," or "offense."[10]

Just as the word *crime* is unrepresented in Roman republican vocabulary, so too is the term *criminal law* absent. Crimes falling under the rubric of modern criminal law (*Strafrecht* in German, *diritto penale* in Italian) share three elements: they are a matter of concern to society at large, prosecution of them occurs in a specific venue, and conviction for being found guilty of committing them earns a specifically prescribed punishment. Take, for example *Black's Modern Law Dictionary*'s entry under the heading "criminal law": "The substantive criminal law is that law which for the purpose of preventing harm to society, (a) declares what conduct is criminal, and (b) prescribes punishment to be imposed for such conduct."[11] Because criminal law, *Strafrecht,* and *diritto penale* are modern terms used as classifications for laws regulating crime, and because, as has already been mentioned, republican Latin had no word for "crime," one should not assume that the Romans had criminal law in our sense of the term.

Do the elements of modern criminal law mentioned above nevertheless apply to Roman public law? According to Roman jurists of the third century C.E.[12] and later, the developed *ius civile* (law for Roman citizens) was divided into *ius privatum* (private law) and *ius publicum* (public law). The acts under discussion in this work did not fall under the rubric of private law, and so the *ius publicum* is of concern here. *Ius publicum,* according to modern scholars, includes constitutional and criminal law. This modern construction—for it is not an ancient one—does more to hinder our understanding of Roman law than to contribute to it. Barry Nicholas, in his *Introduction to Roman Law,* perhaps the standard textbook on Roman law in the English language, writes,

> The Romans themselves made a distinction between public law and private law. The former was concerned with the functioning of the state, and included in particular constitutional law and criminal law; the latter was concerned with relations between individuals.[13]

While public law included elements that would be considered constitutional or criminal in the modern world, the Romans themselves did not make this distinction because they had neither a constitution nor crime.[14]

Because these terminological issues are more than simply matters of vocabulary, this discussion brings us back to the claim of the title of this work: Murder was not a crime. This apparently anachronistic phrase is meant to evoke the vast gulf between modern conceptions of the power and responsibility of governments and the republican Roman conceptions that are explored in this book. More concretely, the phrase means that the republican Roman government did not take cognizance of the malicious and intentional killing of one human being by another. That is, legislation prohibiting murder appears in no law either of the *ius publicum* or of the *ius privatum*.

"Murder was not a crime," however, does not mean that the Romans lacked concern for the unjustified taking of human life. The question of whether an offense was considered morally wrong by members of a society is different from asking how action was taken once an offense had been committed. Indeed, evidence exists that the Romans believed that intentional (though not malicious) killing was wrong under some circumstances because according to the *ius privatum,* it was right under other circumstances.[15] If killing was justifiable in some circumstances, then it must have been implicitly considered wrong in others. Furthermore, while murder was not regularly actionable in any venue of public law, and murder was not regulated by Roman private law,[16] Roman citizens had recourse to other methods of dispute resolution that did not require government action.

The difficulty for this study is that direct evidence for the treatment of homicide-related offenses in any of these alternate venues is scant or nonexistent. Nevertheless, during the republic, disputes could be resolved through vendetta, formal and informal arbitration, and mechanisms within families. Inferences about how these methods of dispute resolution played a role specifically in homicide are considered in subsequent chapters. Still, although the nature of our evidence limits the amount that can be said about how homicide was dealt with in these private venues, it does allow us to explore the nature of political power in the Roman republic by determining why murder was not the regular responsibility of the government, which brings us to the question of the sources.

SOURCES

Much of the material for this book is found in scattered references in the writings of historians, annalists, orators, and lexicographers and in infrequent passages in the compilation of the *Digest* and other late imperial law codes and legal texts. The sources for homicide and legislation about homicide in the Roman republic are generally not interested in the ordinary capacity of the Roman government in the area of public law; rather, the authors recorded stories because they determined the stories had some moral, historical, anecdotal, or other significance. This means the stories in the extant record probably do not represent the norm but illustrate the most sensational events. The bias of the sources for sensationalism is problematic but not insurmountable. The sources also contain another type of bias that has potentially serious implications for this study: their bias towards events of political interest and of interest to the upper classes.

I will be arguing throughout this book that the Romans from the founding of the republic through the dictatorship of Sulla did not have the capacity for, or interest in, dealing with homicide through any official institutions or magistracies or by means of legislation. Moreover, homicide—when it appeared—was peripheral to offenses that required direct government involvement in part because the act of homicide did not directly affect the government or those governing. Ideally, such an argument would be formulated based on a secure knowledge of what happened to nonpolitical acts of homicide and nonelite perpetrators of homicide.[17] Because of the nature of the sources, however, we simply do not know what happened to ordinary Romans who killed other ordinary Romans under, relatively speaking, ordinary circumstances.[18]

ORDINARY CRIMES

Many scholars of Roman public law often make mention, in passing, of murder under a modern rubric of so-called ordinary crimes,[19] but there is little evidence of ordinary crimes actionable in public venues, nor is there any evidence that the Romans had a conception of ordinary crime or that murder would have been counted under such a rubric. It is unlikely that the absence of ordinary crime is simply a product of the nature of the sources.

This conclusion is based in part on something that has been observed by every student of the Roman republic: the government had little in the way of institutions or magistrates whose primary responsibility was to manage violent behavior of its ever-expanding citizen body. This absence is dramatically represented in times when public safety is at issue and the Romans function in an ad hoc manner in their attempts to reestablish internal stability; Roman republican government barely had the institutions and individuals in place to act in the face of internal threats to public safety.[20] If institutional mechanisms were sparse for acts that threatened public safety, how much more limited were they for acts that did not threaten the security or stability of the *res publica*?

A potential threat to my claim that ordinary crime was, to all intents and purposes, not a concern of the government, and therefore a hitch in the argument that murder was not a crime in the Roman republic, is the existence of two sets of minor magistrates, the *quaestores parricidii* and the *tresviri capitales*. If any officials functioned in a capacity where they dealt with nonpolitical offenses or with homicides by nonelite offenders, it was these men. Both sets of officials will be discussed in greater detail in Chapter Four. Suffice it to say here that the earlier officials, the *quaestores parricidii*, might represent an interest by the Romans of the early republic in having the government play some role in the maintenance of public order through the suppression of ordinary crimes. Unfortunately, what we are told about them is both excessively little and contradictory. Mostly what can be said is that they probably existed at some point in early republican history, that they had the responsibility over *parricidium* (which may, at this period of Roman history, have been kin-killing, or culpable homicide, or simply an act worthy of the punishment of death[21]), and that they then either ceased to exist or ceased to maintain the responsibility. Some modern scholars have conjectured that these officials simply functioned as arbiters of disputes with no coercive or executive power, sort of a service offered by the government for the resolution of private disputes but not a means for the government to take over the responsibility for the resolution of such disputes or for the punishing of wrongdoers.[22]

About the *tresviri capitales*,[23] who probably came into existence around the beginning of the third century, we are blessed with at least a little contemporary evidence, though the implications of that evidence have been the subject of much debate, and conclusions must remain tentative. It seems likely that these men were not judges of citizens.[24] Among their responsibilities was the supervision of government executions[25] and of the prison in the forum. Most of the occurrences of such executions that are described in the sources are of capital and elite offenders.[26] Of greater significance for the discussion here is the role of the *tresviri* as some kind of officials to whom one could report an "ordinary" act of criminality.

What are the implications of this: is it that the Romans were interested in official, government-generated suppression of ordinary crimes? If so, the introduction of a mere three minor officials who had the primary responsibility for the prevention of fires (especially at night) and who were the supervisors of executions does not indicate a particularly great or strong interest in the active suppression of crime. Furthermore, the *tresviri* do not seem to have acted preemptively. In other words, complaints and even perpetrators were brought before them by private individuals; they did not actively seek out offenders,[27] nor would they have had any law to assist them in determining criminal behavior when they saw it.

7

With this complex and somewhat chaotic job description, it is difficult to see how the *tresviri* can represent an interest on the part of the government in a serious attempt to deal with ordinary people and ordinary crimes. There were simply too few of them, and they had too much to do.[28] No other venues seem to have had any regular capacity to deal with ordinary perpetrators and ordinary crimes, especially those, like homicide, that would most likely require the death of the perpetrator. The *tresviri* will be considered at greater length in Chapter Five, where I explore the capital judicial sphere of institutions and magistrates of the Roman republic.

This book is primarily arranged chronologically, beginning with the exploration of the treatment of homicide during the monarchy and the implications of Numa's murder law. In Chapter Two an examination of the ideological power possessed by the *pater familias* to kill his children and other dependents will reveal an important element of the decentralized power of the Roman Republic. Chapter Three explores the treatment of homicide in the early republic and the limitations of the power of institutions of the government to condemn citizens to death. In Chapter Four the specific kinds of offenses that become actionable by the later republic illustrate that murder was not a crime. The capital jurisdiction of institutions and officials of the government, and the limited employment of capital punishment, is the subject of Chapter Five. The assassinations beginning in the mid second century that reflect the tension of the expanding empire and increasing size and complexity of republican government are explored in Chapter Six. Finally, in Chapter Seven we will see the relationship between homicide and power revealed in the *hostis* declaration and the proscriptions. In this chapter, the exploration of Sulla's homicide-related legislation will reveal that even as late as 79 B.C.E., murder was not a crime.

ONE

KILLING AND THE KING

According to Roman tradition, the second king of Rome, Numa Pompilius, a man with a reputation for justice and piety, promulgated a law that prohibited murder.[1] One reason for the promulgation of the law during the monarchy is that the monarchs were trying to establish their own power in the face of what had preceded them, and one means of doing so was to control the power to kill. The kings arrogated such power for themselves and they defended, limited, or prohibited it in others. In addition to the self-interested motive of establishing and centralizing power, the kings also needed to ensure the stability of the kingdom. That stability was ensured by the maintenance of a good relationship with the gods, which an act of homicide could jeopardize. Thus, a murder law existed during the Roman monarchy because it served to establish and preserve the power of the king, and it served to keep the community safe.

A caveat is necessary here. No primary literary evidence about the monarchy exists, and references to this period by Roman authors writing centuries later are awash with legend and folkloric motifs. Later in this chapter, some reasons are provided regarding why some of the evidence might be taken seriously. The primary reason for including the discussion of the monarchic murder law in this book, however, is that it was the reported presence of a murder law in the monarchy and the apparent absence of one during most of the republic that began my thinking about the particular relationship in Rome between homicide and power. Even with the problematic nature of the sources, I ask more skeptical readers to consider the possibility that the distribution of power in the monarchy may indeed explain the existence of the attested murder law.

Five main points explored in this chapter reveal the intricate connection between the murder law of King Numa and the nature of monarchic power. First, the sources say that during the monarchy murder was regulated by law. Second, the nature of power in the monarchy was centered in the hands of one individual. Third, the tradition credits the second king of Rome with the promulgation of the law. If accurate, this would mean that the law was promulgated at a time when monarchic power was still being established, and thus the timing lends further credence to the idea that the law itself reflects the nature of that power. Fourth (relevant not only for this chapter but for the book as a whole), in Rome forms of power were frequently defined by the right to kill. Fifth, the king had jurisdiction to try and to punish offenders in cases of intentional homicide. In other words, the king claimed for himself the right to kill.

THE *LEX NUMAE*

Each of these issues will be addressed extensively below, but first, an examination of the law itself is appropriate. The *lex Numae* proclaims,

> si qui hominem liberum dolo sciens morti duit, paricidas esto.[2]

> If anyone knowingly with guilty intent kills a free person, let him be [a?] *paricidas.*

The law itself is quite simple; the difficulty for modern scholars, unlike the Romans living under Numa's rule, results from not knowing what the word *paricidas* means.[3] But even though we know neither the specific derivation of the word nor its precise meaning, it is probably safe to say that in Numa's law, *paricidas* indicated a person subject to a capital penalty. Another one of Numa's laws suggests this meaning, for it states that in cases of unintentional homicide the life of a ram is to be sacrificed in place of the life of the killer:

> in Numae legibus cautum est, ut, si quis imprudens occidisset hominem, pro capite occisi [agnatis] eius in [contione] offerret arietem.[4]

> It is the concern of a law of Numa that if anyone unintentionally killed a person, in the place of his head he would offer a ram to the agnates of the victim in [an assembly].

If the spilling of blood must occur to satisfy an unintentional homicide, then, a fortiori, blood spilling must occur in cases of intentional homicide.[5] Furthermore, this law on unintentional homicide states explicitly that the ram takes the place of the head, presumably of the killer himself (or herself).[6] Punishment for killing *dolo sciens* ("with guilty intent"), as opposed to *imprudens* ("unintentionally"), was death.

That a murderer suffered capital punishment means that not only did the king regulate murder, but he also claimed the right to kill for himself; at the same time that others' power was being restricted, the king's was being increased. For this statement to be accurate, two things need to be true. First, there must have existed a relationship between the right to punish with death and the restriction on committing murder. Second, the right of capital punishment must have belonged to the king.

The relationship between the king's power to use capital punishment and the law prohibiting murder is not as tenuous as it might at first appear. This is especially true if the limitation on murder can be viewed as a limitation on the right of individuals to execute capital punishment. Before power to execute capital punishment belonged to a central power, private individuals or families presumably had this responsibility. A person taking vengeance on another might not have fallen under Numa's classification of a person who killed *dolo sciens,* and so the relationship between the king's right to kill and the limitation of others' rights is not direct. Nevertheless, the existence of the law still suggests an infringement on the rights of individuals, because the government still plays a role in deciding whether an act deserves retaliation.

SOURCES

The claim that capital punishment was the king's responsibility requires more attention, but before turning to this issue, it is necessary to consider the quality of our sources on the regal period. My argument relies primarily on two different kinds of literary evidence: alleged quotations of the *leges regiae* ("laws of the kings") on the one hand and the legend of Horatius on the other. Although both the legends and the laws are reported by authors living several hundred years after the events they claim to report, the *leges regiae* have greater claim to authenticity. Two reasons exist for this: one is that the *leges* often retain the archaic language in which they were originally written, and the other is that the content of the laws fits well with archaic Rome. J. D. Cloud expressed the former argument, with specific reference to the *lex Numae* on murder:

The wording and content almost guarantee the substantial authenticity of the law: what forger would have been capable of inventing a word like "paricidas," a type which is almost unique in Latin? As for the content, it is equally hard to believe that any forger of the late republic could have concocted a law which fits an early date so well and is at the same time alien from late republican jurisprudence.[7]

Despite Cloud's belief in the antiquity of the law, he rejects the attribution to the period of the monarchy.[8] Alan Watson, however, argued that the *leges regiae* are accurately attributed to the kings, at least with regard to private law. He bases this argument on the distinctly different content of the *leges regiae* as compared with the content of republican laws.[9] His argument has two important implications here. First, he has shown that there is good reason to accept the authenticity of the *leges regiae* as a whole. Second, as will be seen later in this chapter, his argument, though he does not explicitly state it, suggests precisely the shifting nature of power between monarchy and republic that I am claiming is the explanation for the existence of the *lex Numae* on murder. Much more will be said of this below.

The most important piece of evidence for the theory proposed in this chapter is the existence of the monarchic murder law itself; thus, the main idea of the argument rests on evidence that has some claim to authenticity. The upcoming, more subtle discussion on the nature of regal power in regard to homicide takes as its starting point an analysis of a legend that appears in the far-from-contemporary historians Livy and Dionysius of Halicarnassus. Livy and Dionysius cannot have been accurate reporters of events that happened hundreds of years before their lifetimes, and the fantastic and legendary stories in their histories cannot be read as actual reports of events.[10] Nevertheless, their interpretations of an event that they claim took place during the monarchy bring up some reasonable ways to envision the nature of power and its relationship to homicide during the monarchy. This is especially true when that scenario supports what little evidence is available.

HORATIUS

For example, Numa's law implies that capital punishment was the king's responsibility or at least that the king created a means of controlling when and how and whether a murderer would be punished. The trial of

Horatius,[11] to which we now turn, shows a possible way to envision how the power of the king was executed. In the complex legal maneuverings in the story, although others had the right to try and to punish, the king had the ultimate right and responsibility.

According to legend, during the reign of Servius Tullius, Publius Horatius and two of his brothers did battle on behalf of Rome against the three Curiatii, the champions from the neighboring town of Veii. The victors in this combat would bring victory in war to their people. Only one of the Horatii survived, and he single handedly defeated the three Curiatii. Horatius, having thus brought victory to Rome, returned home where he met his sister. When she saw him carrying the spoils of the Curiatii, one of whom—unfortunately—was her betrothed, she began to mourn for the dead. This act infuriated her brother, who stabbed and killed her with the very same sword he had used to kill the enemy. For this act he was accused and brought before the king.[12]

The subsequent events in the story include many elements of jurisdiction overlapping: that of the father, the assembly, the *duumviri perduellionis* ("two men with jurisdiction in matters of treason"), and, supreme among them all, the king. That the king had the ultimate power in this case is suggested both by the report that the matter was brought to the king's attention[13] and by the king's subsequent decisions. These decisions included his decision not to try the case himself, his appointment of specific officials to do so, his directions to those officials to convict Horatius, and his recommendation to Horatius to appeal their decision.[14] The king was thereby giving his approval both to the conviction and to the lenience, and avoiding responsibility for either.

Let us consider the process more closely. The king chose not to try the case. The first implication of this is that he had the right to do so. The second implication is that he recognized that any decision he might make would have serious political repercussions for himself. This shows that, despite the king's power to act, he also had to answer to the community at large. Although neither could act completely independently of the other, the king was ultimately responsible. The appointment of the *duumviri perduellionis* to try the case shows that the king could use intermediaries to condemn someone to capital punishment, but the fact that he made the appointment (an act that would have been done by the senate or an assembly in the republic) means that the greater power lay with him.[15]

It is worth exploring the circumstances of the appointment of the *duumviri* in the story in order to consider a possible scenario for the use of officials by the monarch, even though this story provides the only evidence that the *duumviri perduellionis* existed during the monarchy. Evidence of other officials extant during the monarchy is more abundant.[16] These are the so-called *quaestores parricidii*. The same passage of Festus that preserves Numa's murder law makes reference to these officials; indeed, the law itself appears under this heading:

> Parrici<di> Quaestores apellabantur, qui solebant creari causa rerum capitalium quaerendarum.[17]

> Those men were called *parricidi quaestores* who used to be chosen for the sake of investigating capital affairs.

That the *quaestores parricidii* originated during the period of the monarchy is not explicitly stated in the Festus passage. The jurist Pomponius, however, places them more firmly in the monarchic period.[18] In addition, Ulpian, in his book *On the Duty of Quaestors*, writes that *quaestores* were created earlier than all other magistracies, perhaps as early as Romulus and Numa but certainly as early as Tullus Hostilius, the third king of Rome.[19]

The precise job of these officials is not discussed by any ancient source that makes reference to them, and although some interesting conjectures have been made, they are not particularly relevant to this discussion.[20] What is relevant is how the *quaestores* were selected for the job and the fact of their existence. All of the references to them suggest that they were elected by the people. This differs from how the *duumviri* are selected in the story of Horatius. The ancient authors who reflect the tradition that the *quaestores parricidii* were elected, however, also mistakenly consider these *quaestores* to be identical with the *quaestores* who were regular republican magistrates whose job was to assist consuls and who had various financial responsibilities.[21] The true explanation for how the *quaestores parricidii* were selected is out of reach, but it is at least possible that the notion that they were elected came about because later republican *quaestores* were elected and not because the monarchy allowed such an election to take place.

Regardless of how they were created or what their precise role was, the very existence of the *quaestores parricidii* is important because it shows that during the monarchy, the issue of homicide was of such great importance to the king that he not only drafted laws but he also created particular officials to facilitate the resolution of issues to which the laws almost certainly gave rise. With the creation of the *quaestores parricidii*, the government was indicating that it would take some control of matters of homicide, even though the extent of that control remains unclear in the historical record.

Curiously, the *quaestores parricidii* do not make an appearance in the Horatius legend. Horatius' killing of his sister, Horatia, may be a homicide, but in some versions of the story the act is considered treasonous. The appointment of officials in charge of treason cases for an act of homicide further indicates a strong relationship between killing and monarchic power. Evidence of this relationship receives reinforcement from Livy, who states that the charge against Horatius was *perduellio* (treason), despite the suggestion of some ancient authors that it was parricide (the killing of a relative).[22] Livy's version has provoked much discussion about how Horatius' act of homicide could be considered *perduellio*. In an article on the death of Horatius' sister, Alan Watson argued that Horatius was guilty of this crime because *perduellio* can be an act against an individual as well as an act directed against the state per se.[23] Ogilvie, in his commentary on Livy, argued that Horatia herself was guilty of treason by virtue of having mourned an enemy. Thus, when her brother killed her, he superseded the power of an individual and infringed upon the king's power.[24]

Ultimately, neither of these arguments is disprovable, but if my theory is correct, a simpler explanation will suffice and will support the underlying notions of each scholar's argument: one that an act of killing an individual can be an act of *perduellio,* and the other that the authority of the king was being infringed upon. I suggest that Horatius' killing of his sister was an infringement upon the authority of the king not because she had committed treason but because the right to kill ultimately belonged to the king.

Although Horatius was ultimately acquitted, he was required to perform certain expiatory acts. In one of these acts of expiation, his subordination to the power of the king is made explicit. In the context of Horatius' submission, Dionysius gives the following explanation of the yoke:

ἔστι δὲ Ῥωμαίοις νόμιμον, ὅταν πολεμίων παραδιδόντων τὰ ὅπλα γένωνται κύριοι, δύο καταπήττειν ξύλα ὀρθὰ καὶ τρίτον ἐφαρμόττειν αὐτοῖς ἄνωθεν πλάγιον, ἔπειθ' ὑπάγειν τοὺς αἰχμαλώτους ὑπὸ ταῦτα καὶ διελθόντας ἀπολύειν ἐλευθέρους ἐπὶ τὰ σφέτερα.

It is a custom of the Romans, when enemies deliver up their arms and submit to their power, to fix two pieces of wood straight up in the ground and fasten a third sideways on top of them, then to lead the captives under this, and after they have passed through, to set them free to return to their own homes.[25]

The practice of going under the yoke for defeated enemies is a sign of submission to the greater power of Rome. This act, listed among the acts of expiation, resembles much more an act of submission. This could well be submission to the king's power, especially because it is in Dionysius' version of the legend that the king orders the expiatory acts to be performed. Horatius' submission to a greater power suggests that he needed to be humbled after committing a deed beyond his power.

Before his acquittal and his performance of the expiatory acts, however, Horatius is said to have gone through an extensive legal procedure. First, as we saw, he was brought before the king, who appointed *duumviri* to convict him.[26] Then Horatius appealed the decision of the *duumviri* and was brought before the assembly. Thus, in addition to the jurisdiction of particular officials subordinate to and appointed by the king, the Horatius legend attributes to the assembly some power in these matters. But, although a judicial appeal was made to the assembly in this story, the assembly did not have greater power than the king. Two factors support this. First, the assembly's acquittal on appeal was encouraged by the king, who suggested it in the first place. Even before the trial, the king had already given his approval to an acquittal. Second, and this explains also the appointment of *duumviri* to convict, the appeal was not the appeal of a decision of the king but the appeal of the decision of the *duumviri*. In other words, the appeal could occur only because it was not the king's decision that was being appealed.

The Horatius legend shows judicial jurisdiction in the sphere of homicide possessed by the assembly, the *duumviri perduellionis* and, primarily, the king. One more character in the story has a role to play: Horatius' father. Both Dionysius' and Livy's versions show the father making some claim to having the power to make a decision about Horatia's homicide, but the judicial strength of that power is implicitly denied. Dionysius, who presents the most elaborate account of the legend, says that Horatius, after killing his sister, went immediately to his father, who approved of what he had done. Indeed, the father was so much in agreement with the homicide that he even went so far as to refuse burial and other rites to his daughter.[27] But then others brought the matter before the king. When Horatius himself was brought before the king, his father supported him by saying that Horatius' homicide was a punishment of which he himself approved, and not a murder.

Thus, Horatius' father seems to have functioned as a witness in the public case rather than as a judge of his own family's actions, despite his claim that being the judge was his right.[28] The same can be said of Livy's version of the story when the father testifies before the assembly on behalf of the son. In the process, he claims that the right and responsibility for punishing the son was his own and that he considered his son to be innocent: *ni ita esset, patrio iure in filium animadversurum fuisse*[29] ("if that had not been the case, by his paternal right he would have punished his son").

Thus, in the story, paternal power is made impotent in the face of the overriding interests of the community and the involvement of the institutions of the government. This is the case even when both the victim and the culprit were children of the same father. What the actual power of the father was during the monarchy is difficult to gauge. As will be discussed in the next chapter, the *ius vitae necisque* ("the right of life and death") possessed by the Roman *pater* may not have entered Rome until the reign of the Etruscan kings or even later. Yet it is hard to envision a Roman *pater* without this authority. Indeed, later Roman authors and their Greek contemporaries could not envision Rome without paternal power as a key ingredient, and so Dionysius credits the first king of Rome with giving to the *pater familias* power over his son for his whole life: the power to scourge, to chain, to compel forced labor, and to kill.[30]

THE POWER OF THE KING

How and why the king might have defined paternal power is suggested by Dionysius' discussion of another *lex* that he credits to Romulus. Romulus is said to have provided that a woman might be judged and executed by her husband along with other adult male relatives under certain conditions, in particular adultery and drinking wine.

ἀμφότερα γὰρ ταῦτα θανάτῳ ξημιοῦν συνεχώρησεν ὁ Ῥωμύλος,

For both these acts, Romulus conceded that they punish with death.[31]

The idea of Romulus "conceding" this power suggests a useful way to view this regulation. The advent of monarchy must have compelled a negotiation of the balance of power between the already extant private authority and the newly existing public authority, the king. Private authority probably was not defined in such absolute terms as *patria potestas* or the more specific *ius vitae necisque* but existed as an undefined yet understood power that belonged in some form to the family, whether headed by a *pater* or the broader conception of relatives in the *gens* or clan. Romulus, to establish his newly created position in the community, might have had to delineate spheres of power more clearly.[32]

In ensuring that the form of power was defined by his supremacy, Romulus restricted the rights of husbands and male relatives in the sphere of homicide, and he may have defined that power for fathers as well. His successor, Numa, took this notion of limiting relatives' rights further by promulgating laws on intentional and unintentional homicide,[33] which could then leave decisions about such things as guilty intent (*dolo sciens*) in the hands of the king rather than in the hands of individual families or *gentes.*

Whatever the degree or the definition of paternal power in the monarchy, the alleged participation of Horatius' father brings to light an important point: the king was not the sole holder of authority—authority in the community was far more complex than that—but his power was superior to others. When Romulus regulated the father's right to kill, he did not do so in a vacuum. Any newly established monarch has to take into consideration the response of his subjects to his assertion of authority, just as, in the Horatius legend, Servius Tullus took into consideration the potential backlash from the community should he punish Horatius. Nevertheless, this monarchic power was defined in part by the king's power to kill and to regulate others' killing.

Another indication of the king's superior power was his apparent right to practice summary execution, which is implied because it would be explicitly forbidden to republican magistrates. I speak, of course, of the *provocatio* (appeal) legislation.[34] Although at their inception the highest republican magistrates were granted monarchic-style *imperium* (the power, among other things, to kill Roman citizens), they were simultaneously limited in that right by the citizens' right of *provocatio.* The fact that the right of killing was so explicitly limited for republican magistrates implies that those in charge before the republic existed, namely the kings, did have the right to kill. The distinction between the republican magistrates' power and those of the king is laid out by the late jurist Pomponius. Pomponius shows how magisterial power, that is, the power of republican magistrates—unlike the earlier monarchic power—was limited by appeal to the people.

qui tamen ne per omnia regiam potestatem sibi vindicarent, lege lata factum est, ut ab eis provocatio esset neve possent in caput civis Romani animadvertere iniussu populi.[35]

Lest, however, they [the consuls] should gain in all respects the royal power, a law was passed that from their decisions there should be an appeal and that they should not be able to inflict capital punishment on a Roman citizen without the order of the people.

The transition from monarchy to republic, then, caused a shift in the perception of the kind and extent of the power that should be possessed by members of the government. Understanding this shift requires a further understanding of the relationship between power and homicide in the monarchy itself. How might the kings, particularly Romulus and Numa, the first two kings, have been able to claim such power in the sphere of homicide? On what grounds did they assert it? One possible interpretation of why a Roman king might have passed homicide laws was that he was fulfilling his role as middleman between the community and the gods. Most commentaries on the *leges regiae* point out that the laws show a remarkable connection with religion and religious sanctions. This connection contrasts sharply with early republican legislation (especially the XII Tables) in which the religious element is nearly absent.[36]

The element of religion appears both in the legendary trial of Horatius and in Numa's law on unintentional homicide. Both suggest that a killing required expiation of guilt through the shedding of more blood. As we saw above, although acquitted, Horatius was nevertheless required to perform certain expiatory rites.[37] Dionysius puts in the words of those accusing Horatius the idea that the community might suffer at the hands of the gods from an unexpiated act of homicide. His suggestion that the blood guilt might pollute the community is also reflected in the laws. The law attributed to Numa on unintentional homicide shows that even unintentional killing had potential religious ramifications. For, it is widely agreed, the sacrifice of a ram is meant to be not only a prevention of possible retaliation (in light of an evolution from a feud-based society) but also an atonement for the blood of the dead victim.[38]

The requirement of expiation may be one key to understanding why this murder law was promulgated by a king in the early monarchy and in particular by Numa, who is alleged to have had a particular interest in the Romans' relationship with their gods.[39] Expiation was a way to satisfy the gods. Because part of the king's power was based upon keeping peace with the gods, and because a homicide could provide a danger to the *pax deorum* (lit., peace of the gods) and therefore to the community, the kings' responsibility was to see to it that expiation was accomplished. If the king could control not just the acts of expiation but the original act of killing, so much the better.[40] Whether the gods were a means to achieve his earthly authority or his earthly authority was derived from them, the result was the same.

The preservation of the *pax deorum* is a sufficient motive for the creation of homicide laws, but it does not fully explain the state of affairs. Embedded in nearly all definitions and concepts of power in Rome is the right to kill. Because of this, the promulgation of a murder law must also be seen in relation to changing conceptions of power. Therefore, it is worth considering more carefully the person who is credited with promulgating the law and the circumstances of that promulgation.

Although even scholars who believe that some evidence about the monarchy is credible generally do not accept the accurate attribution of a law to a particular king, it is striking that the murder law is credited to Numa, the second king of Rome. The attribution to Numa suggests that his accession was a crucial time for clarifying issues of relative power. According to tradition, the murder law was promulgated early in the monarchy when the institution of monarchy itself was being created. An especially sensitive time in the creation of a new institution or system of government is when power passes to the successor; the first person in charge often seems to get much accomplished by virtue of his (or, elsewhere, her) own personality. This is particularly true of ancient monarchies in which the personality of the founder is crucial to the creation of the government.[41] The first successor is left with the task of stabilizing the new power relationships created by the change in government. In Numa's case, this task could have included the promulgation of murder legislation. The timing of the law and the name of the promulgator, as handed down in the ancient sources, support the idea that establishing monarchic power was the reason for the law.

Another means of exploring the importance of power in the promulgation of this law comes in trying to explore the hierarchical structure of Rome in the monarchy and early republic. Why would a society that had once created a murder law cease to have one? The answer, I theorized, was to be found in the nature of the different governments: somehow, the monarchy required a murder law and the republic did not. In the monarchy there was a single locus of power, while in the republic there were many. That the difference in where power lay had an impact on the structure of society as well as the rules and regulations that governed it is implied by the argument set forth a few decades ago by Alan Watson, already alluded to above. Arguing in favor of the accurate attribution of the *leges regiae* to the kings, Watson made some interesting observations about the differences in two areas of private law between the monarchy and the republic: *patria potestas* (paternal power) and the patron/client relationship. By examining the laws from each period, Watson demonstrated that in the shift from monarchy to republic, "the bonds of *patronatus* [patronage] loosened, the *patria potestas* increased in strength."[42] Watson's conclusions have serious implications for this study.

The reason for their respective social structures was that a monarch could have ultimate control in a society in which the patron/client relationship had greater strength because he would be at the top of the patronage pyramid. The power of individual *patres,* so central to the republican world, could not serve the king nor the idea of monarchy. At the head of a society based on *patria potestas* is the *pater;* at the head of one based on the patron/client relationship is the king: one head, one decision making power. Although the extent of the differences between the republic and monarchy is difficult to gauge, during the monarchy, the power of the *pater familias* relative to the power of the *patronus* was less than in the republic. With the creation of the republic, when the single, individual decision-making power of the king disappeared, the power of individual *patres* increased.

In addition to the shift of power to individual *patres,* the institutions of government themselves were far from centralized during the Roman republic. Power was distributed in the private realm among *patres* and in the public realm among various magistrates, the senate and the assemblies of the republic.[43] During the republic, it was no longer true that one individual was responsible for the *pax deorum.* If the theory proposed above about the motivation for the promulgation of a murder law—the centralization of power under a single individual and the preservation of the *pax deorum* by that individual—is correct, then once the monarchy was brought to an end, the murder law was no longer required. Indeed, as we shall see in Chapters Three and Four, murder became no longer actionable through mechanisms of the government in the republic.

During the monarchy, the primary locus of power existed in the person of the king, and during the monarchy, murder was an actionable offense punishable by death. The monarchic government, by virtue of the promulgation of law, expressed its control of this sphere. During the early republic, no new law about intentional homicide was created, although remnants of the old murder law may have existed in the form of unintentional homicide laws and laws about justifiable homicide. The reason for the presence of the law in the monarchy was that the king's power, based on the sanction of the gods, required the king to control the spilling of blood. His control lay in the promulgation of legislation on intentional and unintentional homicide. His control was also facilitated by the creation of officials with particular jurisdiction in homicide offenses. Furthermore, the king's power was defined in part by his own ability to kill; the king had *imperium* unrestricted by *provocatio*. When the monarchy was no longer in existence and this central power had vanished, the law ceased to be relevant and so fell into disuse. Eventually, it became a mere sidebar in an antiquarian's interest in the definition of an obscure official position.

TWO

POWER OF LIFE AND DEATH

Pater *and* Res Publica

Through the course of the Roman republic, power was diffused both within the institutions of government and beyond them. In many ways, managing and providing stability for an ever expanding and ever more complex *civitas*[1] was beyond the capacity of republican government alone. The limited capacity of republican government will be considered in more detail in the next two chapters. Suffice it to say here that institutions outside the government compensated for its limited power and scope. One of the most important and pervasive of these nongovernmental institutions was to be found within the Roman family. The father in a Roman family had many legally defined powers over those subject to him. Among these was the *vitae necisque potestas* or the power of life and death: the *pater* had the legal right to kill those under his *potestas*. Although the *pater*'s power to kill was limited to those within his own family, and thus was a tool for the management of the family, it was also a tool used by the father for the benefit of the *res publica*.

THE PURPOSE OF PATERNAL POWER

My argument that the *vitae necisque potestas* had a role to play beyond the confines of the family has been inspired in part by recent scholarship that has shifted our understanding of the role of the *pater* and of the function of *patria potestas* (paternal power) in the Roman family. The picture of an authoritarian father with absolute rights over other members of the family and household, which *vitae necisque potestas* implies, has been brought into question by recent studies of the role and perception of the *pater* in the family. In Roman literature and art, it has been argued, the *pater* is often illustrated more as a nurturing figure than as an authoritarian one.[2] This interpretation suggests that the exercise of paternal power was not a term particularly applicable to social history; it did not have much direct relevance to a father's practical function in the family. In the legal sphere, however, *patria potestas* defined precise authoritarian rights; an important right among these was financial control of the family's resources. According to Roman law, the *pater* owned all of the property acquired by any of his descendants regardless of their age. The term *pater familias* ("father of the family") may thus best be understood as owner of an estate.[3] Although the estate-holding aspect of paternal power is important for understanding family law, it does not explain the peculiar aspect of the father's power under consideration here, namely, the *vitae necisque potestas*. As a result, it leaves open the question of the purpose of this particular aspect of paternal power.

The question of the purpose is further emphasized by the apparent limitation of the use of *vitae necisque potestas* in republican history. The actual capacity of fathers to exercise the right of life and death has been brought into question because so few cases exist of it being employed against adult children, and those cases that do exist often imply some limitation on the right. Thus, Yan Thomas could claim of the power of life and death that it was "de la sorte une définition abstrait du pouvoir."[4] The question remains, however, what was the purpose of this abstract definition of power if it did not simply serve to intimidate and control the members of the family? In this chapter I will show that the father's ideological right to kill and the nature of the limitations placed on it demonstrate that the *pater* played, and was meant to play, an integral role in the functioning of the republic, in particular to work alongside the institutions of the government to secure the stability of the community.

This responsibility of the *pater* to the community is not just applicable to *patres* of the elite classes, as one might assume, given the socioeconomic hierarchy of republican government that required an incredible amount of wealth to be a senator and magistrate, and given the nature of the political system of the early republic, which—tradition tells us—is a struggle between those with political power and those without it. Although no examples exist in the sources of cases of lower-class fathers exercising their right to kill adult children, neither does any source suggest that the right of life and death did not extend to all *patres*. Quite the contrary, in fact, as seen in an early legal formula used for *adrogatio*, a form of adoption:

> Velitis, iubeatis, uti L. Valerius L. Titio tam iure legeque filius siet, quam si ex eo patre matreque familias eius natus esset, utique ei vitae necisque in eum potestas siet, uti patri endo filio est.[5]

May you wish and may you command that Lucius Valerius be the son of Lucius Titius both by law and by statute, just as if he had been born of the father and mother of that family; and that the *vitae necisque potestas* over him [Lucius Valerius] be his [Lucius Titius'], just as it is a father's over his son.

If the right of life and death belonged exclusively to the upper classes, then some extant source would contain some record of this limitation. Instead, like Aulus Gellius, sources that make reference to this paternal power consistently assume that the power belongs to all Roman fathers.[6]

Because the importance of the father to the success of the republic was expressed through the authority he possessed over life and death, drafting of murder legislation could conceivably have limited the father's ability to play such a role. Because, ideologically, the power to kill belonged to *patres,* and because each *pater* was meant to play an integral role in the running of the *res publica,* it would have been contrary to the interests and security of the *res publica* to promulgate a murder law. Support for the integral role of the *pater* to the *res publica* is found in (1) the extent to which the term is used to define Roman-ness rather than father-ness; (2) the origins of the term and the possible timing of its entry into Rome; and, most particularly and extensively, (3) the legends and examples of its use, which illustrate the relationship between family and *civitas.*

Scholars who study paternal power have noted that this power is a means by which the Romans claimed to be distinct from other peoples. The commonly referenced passage from Gaius is instructive in this regard.

Item in potestate nostra sunt liberi nostri, quos iustis nuptiis procreavimus. Quod ius proprium civium Romanorum est (fere enim nulli alii sunt homines, qui talem in filios suos habent potestatem, qualem nos habemus) idque divi Hadriani edicto, quod proposuit de his, qui sibi liberisque suis ab eo civitatem Romanam petebant, significatur. Nec me praeterit Galatarum gentem credere in potestate parentum liberos esse.[7]

Likewise in our power are our children, whom we have begotten in lawful marriage. This right is characteristic of Roman citizens (for hardly any other humans have as much power over their sons as we have), and this is indicated in an edict of the divine Hadrian, which he proposed concerning those who were seeking from him the right for themselves and their children to become Roman citizens. Nor has it passed me by that the clans of the Galatians believe that their children are in the power of the parents.

Although Gaius does not specifically mention life and death, for us to assume that Gaius was not including *vitae necisque potestas* in his "*talem . . . potestatem*" would be disingenuous. This is particularly true because his reference to the Galatians brings to mind Caesar's information: *Viri in uxores, sicuti in liberos, vitae necisque habent potestatem.*[8] ("Men have the power of life and death over their wives just as they have over their children.") Caesar reports the power of life and death as a specific power possessed by the Gauls.

The edict by the emperor Hadrian saw *patria potestas* as a means of describing citizenship for these petitioners. Although this is clearly not a source from the republic (both Hadrian and Gaius date to the second century C.E.), the implications of the statement provide important insight into understanding one ideological function of the *ius vitae necisque,* the right of life and death. Hadrian uses the term to explain a quality of Roman citizenship. In addition to Hadrian, Gaius himself makes the right a peculiar quality (*proprium*) of the Romans, even though he is forced to acknowledge that it is not.[9] Furthermore, the emphasis here is not on how the power sets the father apart from other members of the family, but how such power sets him apart from non-Romans.[10] Thus, though the father's *potestas* does not describe citizenship in a direct legal sense, it is a means of identifying and distinguishing the Roman citizen male: what characterizes the citizen is that he is one who possesses *potestas.*[11]

Because the *pater* does not primarily function as an authoritarian figure in the Roman family and because his *potestas* can be used as a means of defining citizenship, it is reasonable to conjecture that *vitae necisque potestas* places the *pater* as much in the *civitas* as in the *familia.* This idea is further substantiated by the origin of the term. Raymond Westbrook expanded on a notion that Reuven Yaron proposed several decades ago, that the particular phrase *vitae necisque potestas,* although it had no comparable phrases in Latin, had precedents in Near Eastern law codes. Two points presented in Westbrook's article are particularly relevant here: (1) Near Eastern texts ascribe this power to Near Eastern kings and (2) the term may have entered Rome in the later part of the monarchy.

The investigation, begun by Yaron in 1962, arose out of the observation that the "*vitae*" ("of life") in the phrase had no parallel in Roman laws and that it did not seem to serve a purpose. The power over death made sense, but how did a *pater* have the power over life?[12] Yaron's investigation led him to propose that a possible source, or at least a reasonable comparison, existed in ancient Near Eastern law codes as a means of defining the monarch's power.[13] Following in Yaron's footsteps, Westbrook, after providing abundant evidence of the use of this duality of killing and giving life as a mechanism of the judicial obligations of monarchs in many Near Eastern civilizations, posits a time frame for the reception of Near Eastern law codes in Rome, namely, when the Etruscan kings ruled. Although there are some reasons to accept this date,[14] it must be acknowledged that the timing of the reception is largely conjectural. If Westbrook is correct, however, the possibilities are intriguing. In particular, if the Romans originally encountered the term as a means of defining monarchic power,[15] how did the term come to define paternal power?

After the expulsion of the kings, the Romans chose to distribute power among leaders in the new government to avoid too much centralization of power and a re-introduction of monarchy. For example, they provided for annual terms, joint magistracies and veto power.[16] The new magistracies, however, were not the only loci of power created with the dissolution of the monarchy. The power of life and death was not granted to magistrates, but was granted to all male Roman citizens when they became *patres*. The power of Roman *patres* increased with the change in the political system.

A comparison of the *leges regiae* ("laws of the kings") with republican laws provides further evidence that power possessed by *patres* underwent a shift at the same time that the shift in governmental authority occurred. In the previous chapter, I discussed Alan Watson's observations about the increase in the power of the *pater* in the republic relative to power of the *pater* in the monarchy.[17] By combining Westbrook's hypothesis regarding the timing of the introduction of this *vitae necisque potestas* into Rome with Watson's thesis, we can posit a real attempt on the part of early Romans to decentralize power in the new republican government not just via the newly created magistracies but via the enhanced power of the *patres*. Though the absence of any reference to Roman kings holding this power is problematic, it is interesting to ponder further whether this gave the *patres* a vested interest in the success of the new government because it gave them responsibility to ensure the functioning of that government. If individual *patres* are to have a share in the power of governing, they are more likely to be committed to the government's success.

Whatever the origins of the term (and it must be observed that the reconstruction of the origins is uncertain[18]), the notion that *vitae necisque potestas* was a tool enabling *patres* to work in conjunction with the government is suggested repeatedly and quite dramatically by its execution, and the stories of its execution, in republican history. The observation that this power was used in the service of the *res publica* is not a new one. For example, Thomas wrote, "Tuer son fils est presque toujours sacrilège, sauf lorsqu'un père incarne l'État ou que l'État est mal représenté par un fils."[19] The fact that examples or stories of the use of *vitae necisque potestas* show it being used in the service of the state, however, should not be read as a way of saying the state was superior to the individual family to the detriment of the latter (that the state was strong, and the *patres* were weak). Rather, it should be read as a way of saying that this power was a representation of the father's responsibility to the community more than (or at least as much as) being a sign of his power within the family itself.

POLITIES

A useful way to conceptualize the role of the *pater* is to borrow the term "polity" from our colleagues in political science. As described by Yale Ferguson and Richard Mansbach, "A polity (or political authority) has a distinct identity; a capacity to mobilize persons and their resources for political purposes, that is, for value satisfaction; and a degree of institutionalization and hierarchy (leaders and constituents)."[20] These are characteristics both of the Roman family and of republican government.[21] Ferguson and Mansbach go on to point out that individuals belong to cooperating as well as to competing polities: "*At any given moment,* there exist numerous actual and potential political forms that attract and sometimes compete for human loyalties. . . . In every historical context, human beings are subject to crosscutting pressures arising from multiple identities."[22]

The father of the family, in his position in the polity of the family, had a responsibility to that family, in particular, perhaps, as the successful manager of the estate[23] but also as ensurer of its political and social success. But the *pater* in his position as a citizen of the polity of the *res publica* also had an obligation to preserve and protect the *res publica*. Although paternal power could be exercised on behalf of either, these two polities, ideally, would mutually benefit from his use of that power. Examples of the employment of his right to kill his children, however, in apparent incongruity, usually demonstrate his obligation to the larger polity of the *res publica* more than to his family. *Vitae necisque potestas* often places the father firmly in the polity of the *res publica*.

That a father owed supreme loyalty to the *res publica* is evidenced by a legend about the first generation of the republic. Brutus, the liberator who helped oust the kings and subsequently shared the first consulship in republican history, killed his sons for trying to help those same kings return to power in Rome.[24] Because Brutus was a consul when he put his son to death, this legend has been read as a lesson that magistrates must place their role as magistrates ahead of their role as fathers. Indeed, William Harris suggests that "these legends [of magistrates killing their sons] contributed to the prestige which magistrates so obviously needed in the Roman state in order to get their orders obeyed."[25] The first-century C.E. moralist Valerius Maximus also draws a distinction in this regard. Of Brutus' decision to take action he writes, "*Exuit patrem ut consulem ageret.*" ("He put off the father to play the consul.")[26] I take this to mean that Valerius thought he had to deny his feelings as a father to conduct his business for the state, but it might be more accurate to say that Brutus acted in support of the state both as a magistrate and as a father. The lesson, that the *res publica* should take precedence over the *familia,* may be not only a lesson for and about magistrates with *imperium.* The lesson could also have been directed toward fathers more generally.[27] If necessary, they should willingly sacrifice their individual families for the good of the community as a whole.

In his attempt to demonstrate an extremely limited exercise of *vitae necisque potestas* in Rome, Harris also states that Brutus killed his son not by virtue of *patria potestas* but by virtue of magisterial *imperium.*[28] The distinction that Harris makes, however, may be an insufficiently complex view of the situation. The very fact that Brutus is consul and *pater* at the same time is suggestive. Brutus' ability to be consul is contingent upon his ability to be a responsible *pater.* Further proof of this is that the senators of Rome were also called *patres.*[29] This characterization of the senate shows that the *res publica* ideally was to be administered by the heads of its individual families and therefore that the family and *res publica* were inextricably connected. It would be going too far to say that childless men were ineligible for the consulship, but an irresponsible father might have found it difficult to earn that position.

The legend of *vitae necisque potestas* employed against the demagogue Spurius Cassius reinforces the interpretation that *patres* should willingly sacrifice their children for the good of the *res publica,* regardless of the magisterial position of said *patres.* Spurius Cassius had been consul three times and victorious in battle over the enemies of Rome.[30] Indeed, his success and popularity were his downfall, for people started to suspect him of seeking *regnum,* that is, of trying to become a king, an act punishable by death. Spurius Cassius was brought to task for this offense.

Livy, Dionysius of Halicarnassus, Valerius Maximus, and Cicero all preserve parts of the story. Two different versions arise of how the matter was treated: one that he was tried in a public venue,[31] and the other that he was tried and convicted by his father with a *consilium*.[32] The existence of different versions of the story is not of as much concern here[33] as the existence of a story in which a *pater* who was not a magistrate killed his son, Spurius Cassius, for what was clearly an offense against the *res publica* and not a private act. That the father acted on behalf of the *res publica* is further supported by the claim—in both versions where the father executes his *potestas*—that he waits for his son to leave office. Thus, the father respects the consulship per se and ensures the stability and power of that office by delaying his punishment of his son until the latter has given up that office.

Even though Spurius Cassius' father was not a magistrate, he, like the consul Brutus, stood firmly in the polity of the *res publica* and met its needs by executing his son. The killing of the son seems to indicate that the family's needs are in competition with the polity of the *res publica,* but it is striking that, although the fathers are presumably heartbroken and the reader is supposed to empathize with them, there is never any hesitation on the part of *patres*. This leads to the possibility that the needs of the community are in line with the needs of the family; the idea of a *pater* working on behalf of both polities comes across more clearly in the most famous legend of a father killing his daughter.

The legend of the killing of Verginia suggests that ideally the desires of the family and the desires of the government would not be in conflict. In this case, paternal power was exercised for the good of the family and for the good of the *res publica.* According to Roman tradition, the decemvirs, magistrates created in the middle of the fifth century to draft the XII Tables, did draft the laws but then began to behave tyrannically. The most dramatic sign of this was when the most powerful of the decemvirs, Appius Claudius, in lustful disregard for justice, besotted by the beauty of a young virgin, Verginia, tried to claim that she was not a free woman but was a slave so that he might take possession of her and do as he pleased. Verginius, the young woman's father, to save her from the ignominy of mistreatment at Appius' hands, killed his daughter.[34] Presumably he did this by virtue of his *potestas,* because he held no magistracy endowed with *imperium.* He stabbed her with a butcher's knife to save her from a fate worse than death.

Verginius' motive, then, was the protection of his family. The major consequence of this act of homicide, however, was that because of their excessive abuses of power, illustrated so dramatically by Appius' actions, the decemvirs were compelled to resign their position, and the regular republican magistracies were reinstated. Verginius' act had the effect of saving her (in however brutal and hopeless a manner) and the *res publica*. The employment of *vitae necisque potestas,* then, in this legend, not only served the ends of the family but also brought about the ultimate good for the community as a whole: the restoration of the republic.

To talk about a single polity of government with regard to the story, however, is inaccurate, for, on the one hand, there is the government that is restored at the end of the story—with regular republican magistrates whose decision-making power was subject to checks and balances—and, on the other hand, there is the government in place when Verginia is killed: that of the decemvirs from whose decisions there is no appeal and whose power is potentially limitless.[35] The relationship between paternal power and each of these two forms of government is significant. The decemvirs, in the opinion of the authors who record the stories of their existence, were not a republican office;[36] their very existence (and certainly their behavior) was a threat to the republic.[37] It is not coincidence that the Romans envisioned a threat to the republic as a threat to the power of the father and the internal sovereignty of the father in his family, because the father was an important ingredient in the success of the republic. The legend of the removal of the decemvirs from power suggests that the relationship between these two polities was ideally envisioned as symbiotic.[38]

IUS VITAE NECISQUE

In addition to demonstrating the ideological symbiosis between republican government and paternal power, Verginia's story brings up two important elements that require discussion: one has to do with the nature of the evidence; the other is the difference in the use of *vitae necisque potestas* to kill sons and its use to kill daughters. The preponderance of the evidence for the killing of adult sons appears in traditional Roman legends, which means that this power has a strong ideological hold on the Romans.[39] This hold is significant because as much as the actual execution of *vitae necisque potestas* on behalf of the polity of republican government, it has an impact on the Roman treatment of homicide and, in particular, on the absence of murder legislation in the republic.

The drafting of a murder law would necessarily involve a definition of culpable homicide. If the father had not only a right but even a responsibility to kill on behalf of the republic, then republican government would have been unlikely to promulgate a law regulating killing directly. If *patres* had been implicitly shorn of this power by the state defining what was an actionable homicide offense, then not only would the power of each individual family have been weakened, the power of the father himself would have been as well. This would hold true even if the father were not such a central player in maintaining the stability of the *res publica*. The *pater*'s employment of his power on behalf of the *res publica*, however, suggests that the weakening of paternal power would necessarily also have been a weakening of the *res publica* itself, so drafting such legislation would have affected the ability of the government — not just the ability of the *pater* — to function. The flexibility inherent in the absence of legislation best served the republic.

The second element brought up by the story of Verginius killing his daughter has to do with gender. Three characteristics of the right to kill and gender show the integral role of the *pater* in the functioning of the republic. These characteristics are (1) that daughters tend to be subject to death at the hands of their fathers on account of sexual misbehavior, (2) that the institutions of republican government avoid punishing women with death if they can avoid it, and (3) that women can be killed by relatives who are not *patres*. Because these characteristics reveal a distinction between the domestic sphere and the public sphere, an exploration of them serves to highlight the relationship between the family and the *civitas* as well as the obligation of the father to each.

In almost every example where a father kills a son with impunity he does it in response to a son's public acts.[40] On the surface, the same is not true for daughters. Among the acts for which daughters receive death at the hands of their fathers is sexual misbehavior. For example, Pontius Aufidianus killed his daughter who had had sex with a slave,[41] and P. Atilius Philiscus killed his daughter for *stuprum*.[42] One reason daughters but not sons might be killed for more private acts is that sons have the potential to stand more directly in the polity of the *res publica* than daughters. A woman's private actions are punishable by her father because, unlike a son, she is not destined to become a *pater* or a *civis* in her own right. In these cases, the father may employ *vitae necisque potestas* to ensure his own and his family's honor.

On the other hand, female chastity may not be as much of a private act as it appears at first. Indeed, there is good reason to believe that female chastity was requisite for the stability of the *res publica*. That Vestal Virgins functioned as scapegoats in times of crisis is already well understood: they were subject to ritual capital punishment if they broke their vows of chastity.[43] Such scapegoating, however, was not limited to the priestesses of Vesta. "Female sexuality under male control was the basis of and paradigm for keeping society under control."[44] If women failed to live up to the paradigm, they threatened more than their own family honor, though that, too, was at stake; they threatened the security of the community.[45]

This does not mean that the capital punishment of women was always only about their sexuality. When women engaged in public acts that were harmful to the *res publica,* they could be subject to a punishment of death. For example, many women were executed during the so-called Bacchanalian conspiracy for their participation in the more injurious acts alleged against the cult followers of the god Bacchus:

Qui tantum initiati erant et ex carmine sacro, praeeunte verba sacerdote, precationes fecerant, [in] quibus nefanda coniuratio in omne facinus ac libidinem continebatur, nec earum rerum ullam, in quas iureiurando obligati erant, in se aut alios admiserant, eos in uinculis relinquebant: qui stupris aut caedibus violati erant, qui falsis testimoniis, signis adulterinis, subiectione testamentorum, fraudibus aliis contaminati, eos capitali poena adficiebant. Plures necati quam in vincula coniecti sunt. Magna vis in utraque causa virorum mulierumque fuit. Mulieres damnatas cognatis, aut in quorum manu essent, tradebant, ut ipsi in privato animadverterent in eas: si nemo erat idoneus supplicii exactor, in publico animaduertebatur.[46]

Those who had only been initiated and who, with the priest before them saying the words of the sacred songs, made prayers in which was contained an irreligious conspiracy in every bad deed and libidinous desire but they had not committed through themselves or others any of these things which they had been obligated by oath, these they left in chains. Those who had been defiled by debaucheries or slaughters, and those who had contaminated themselves by giving false evidence, forging seals and wills and [committing] other fraudulent practices, these they subjected to capital punishment. More were killed than were thrown into prison; there was a great force of men and women in each case. They handed the condemned women over to their cognates, or to those in whose *manus* they were, so that those men might punish them in private; if there was no suitable person to exact punishment, they were punished in public.

Despite the government's direct involvement in their trial and conviction, these women were turned over to their families for capital punishment.[47] Precisely why this was the case is unclear. One hypothesis assumes that the women were punished by family members because in most forms of Roman execution the culprit is stripped naked.[48] It seems likely that the Romans could have found a different way to deal with the problem of propriety (i.e., the women could have been executed with clothes on) had they been so inclined, and one is forced to wonder about those women who were killed publicly.

The question of the motivation of the Romans in assigning domestic punishment for these women has been an understandably problematic one for modern scholars, and the answers proposed often have to do with issues of modesty and propriety.[49] Modern scholars, however, may err in seeing this as what should not happen — the women were not supposed to be punished in public — rather than as what should happen — the women were supposed to be punished by their families. If we take cooperation between the domestic sphere and the *res publica* as the norm, then the issue is less problematic. Furthermore, that it is the norm seems to be the assumption of the ancient authors who express no difficulty whatsoever with the venue of the punishment. If one looks at this event as what was supposed to happen rather than what was not supposed to happen, then the position of the women in the family and the community is illuminated. That officials of Roman government chose a domestic venue for punishment reinforces the theory that the family could and did take responsibility for the security of the community as a whole.

The conviction of the female worshipers of Bacchus by government officials and their punishment by members of their individual families suggest that even when women were acting against the *res publica,* they were still firmly in the polity of the family whenever possible. The events of the Bacchanalian conspiracy also suggest that members of the government (in this case, the consuls) recognized that the family had the responsibility and the capacity to help secure the stability of the *res publica* in a great crisis. If this notion of the family as an active and participating element in the security of the *res publica* did not exist, then the consuls would have just had the women killed publicly, as they did with those women who had no family members who could kill them.

Furthermore, this was a perilous moment in time, and what the Romans needed, in the face of sacrilege, debauchery, and murder (or at least the panic resulting from rumors of these activities), was substantial restoration of order that went beyond simply convicting the guilty. Valerius

Maximus' general emphasis on morality notwithstanding, his statement is provocative:

> Lateque patens opprobrii deformitas severitate supplicii emendata est, quia quantum ruboris civitati nostrae mulieres turpiter se gerendo incusserant, tantum laudis graviter punitae attulerunt.[50]

> The disgrace of the wicked deed spread wide, but it was corrected by the severity of the punishment because, however much the women had inflicted on our shamefaced *civitas* by conducting themselves scandalously, that is how much weighty praise their punishment brought.

Valerius here is talking about the severity and not the circumstances of the punishment, but one can perhaps apply his same interpretation of these events to the venue of the punishment. If Bauman is correct that "the Bacchanalian movement had been condemned as a combination of organized sex and malpractice threatening both religious and social stability,"[51] then the reaffirmation of these women as belonging to the polity of the family and being put in their place is of even greater import. The restoration of order in the republic included the relegation of women back into the private sphere, but this was more than a simple gender correction, it was reestablishing balance in the *civitas* by reestablishing families as strong individual units and as units that owed allegiance to the community as a whole and to the *res publica*. The reaffirmation of stability required both the women to be placed securely in the polity of the family and the families to be working on behalf of the *res publica*.

The Bacchanalian conspiracy is important not only because it shows the cooperation between the domestic and public spheres but also because it reveals the consequences, both practical and ideological, of absent fathers. Later in the second century, two other women, whose fathers were presumably no longer alive, were put to death by other relatives. In 154 B.C.E., Publilia and Licinia, women of senatorial status, were brought before the praetor and charged with poisoning their husbands. Some of their relatives took over the case, convicted them, and put them to death.[52] The absence of fathers among the female Bacchanalian conspirators and in the case of Publilia and Licinia shaped both the practical treatment of these culpable women and, seen with a wider lens, may have shaped the entire circumstances of their involvement in these affairs.

The practical consequences should be considered first. Because there were no fathers present in either event, there was also no one in any of the families who possessed *vitae necisque potestas*.[53] The technical right to kill belonged exclusively to *patres familias*. Nonetheless, these women were put to death. In the Bacchanalian conspiracy, we might be free to claim that officials of the republic, who themselves had the capacity to kill, either implicitly or explicitly granted that right temporarily to male family members other than the father, but because *imperium* was not transferable in other instances, this seems unlikely at best. Furthermore, the case of Publilia and Licinia does not allow this interpretation.

In this case, rather than the magistrate requesting that the families punish the women, the relatives paid a surety to the praetor with the intention of taking on that responsibility.[54] Both Valerius and Livy's epitomator record the case. Valerius says that these two women *propinquorum decreto strangulatae sunt*[55] ("were strangled by the decree of their relatives"), and the epitome of Livy records:

> De ueneficiis quaesitum: Publilia et Licinia, nobiles feminae, quae uiros suos consulares necasse insimulabantur, cognita causa, cum praetori praedes uades dedissent, cognatorum decreto necatae sunt.[56]

> About a *quaestio* on poisoning: Publilia and Licinia, noble women who were being charged with having killed their consular husbands, *cognita causa*, when the guarantors gave surety to the praetor, they were killed by decree of their cognates.

Both Livy's epitomator and Valerius Maximus state quite clearly that a decision was made by the relatives: this was not simply, as the execution of the Bacchanalian women appears to have been, the family implementing a decision of the magistrate. The *cognita causa* in Livy causes some confusion because it can apply both to the preliminary phase of the trial in which the praetor appoints a judge (*iudex*) and to the part of the trial in which the *iudex* makes a decision.[57] This confusion is alleviated by Valerius Maximus' claim that the relatives paid the surety and dealt with the matter themselves because they did not want to await a long trial.[58] The decision to execute and the act of execution belonged to the relatives.

Unfortunately, it is not clear by what right the relatives took action, nor indeed is it clear who these relatives were. While clarity on the specific family members would be helpful in understanding family law, relationships, and hierarchies of power, given our limited sources for these incidents, it is difficult to see how agreement will be reached on the precise people involved.[59] Two observations, however, are revealing about this incident. First, the Romans' desire to keep women in the polity of the family and out of the public sphere was so strong that they were willing to use any family member available to achieve that goal. This was true both when the magistrates themselves sought assistance from the family and when the family was the initiator of the change of venue. The second revelation is that the Romans were not as fixated on the procedure as modern legal historians want them to be. There was little need to follow precise legislation when the community was largely in agreement. What mattered was that stability was restored and that these women were placed back into a domestic jurisdiction, not that they were executed according to a clearly defined legal authority.

That being said, the absence of fathers in the reports of these cases does merit consideration. We are told of no Bacchanalian conspirator who was turned over to a father, though husbands, cognates, and anybody who had the ability to execute were mentioned. The absence of fathers in the story is no accidental omission. This is not to suggest that Livy consciously left fathers out of the story but rather that the concept of the failure of fathers en bloc in such a threatening crisis was too abhorrent for the Romans to consider. The failure would have been the inability of fathers to prevent their daughters from disrupting the stability of the *res publica*. Where a group of women at any stage of their lives, or a group of young men could be responsible for subversive behavior[60] —so long as they were subsequently corrected—fathers could not. The ideology of the father in control of his family was requisite for the feeling of security of the *civitas,* and even the possibility of such an egregious failure was incomprehensible, in part because it would suggest that such a failure could be repeated.

Just as daughters differ from sons in the extent of their connection to the *res publica,* so too do sons differ from fathers. Where daughters will belong exclusively to the domestic sphere (though the family itself might change) throughout their lives, sons are in training for their future positions as *patres* and thereby as the primary connection between family and community. One of the most striking illustrations of both the role of sons and the evolution of this role over a man's lifetime comes in two stories about the same character, Titus Manlius Torquatus.[61] The first concerns Torquatus as a young man: His father is about to be brought to trial by the tribune of the plebs for his harshness in his treatment of soldiers (especially during a levy) and his harshness in his treatment of his son. According to Livy, Torquatus came to the bedroom of the tribune and threatened him with a knife.[62] Torquatus compelled the tribune to swear an oath that the tribune would not put Torquatus the elder on trial. Thus, the son Torquatus protected the father against the desires of governing officials.

The story grows more interesting. By threatening homicide against an official of the government, Torquatus, despite his lack of a distinguished career, was that year elected the second of six military tribunes.[63] The message: when the son shows himself to be capable of extreme loyalty to the family and to the *pater,* he becomes capable of military commands on behalf of the *res publica.* In Roman legend, then, a son's loyalty to his father is an indication of his fitness to become a contributing Roman citizen in his own right.

The second story concerns Torquatus as a father: When faced with the choice between son and fatherland, Torquatus chose fatherland over son. Ignoring a direct order not to engage the enemy in single combat, Torquatus' son returned victorious from just such an engagement, carrying the spoils of his enemy. Torquatus put him to death.[64] Thus, when he was a *pater* Torquatus protected the desires of the state—in particular the rigors of military discipline—against his son, though as a son he had protected his family against the state. Scholars argue that he killed his son by virtue of his *imperium* as a dictator, that is, that this did not technically fall under *vitae necisque potestas.* While this claim is probably correct, that he grew up to be a magistrate is a reflection of his obligation to the *res publica,* and his actions in that role while he was also a *pater* reconfirm his commitment as a *pater* to the *res publica.*

The role of *pater* and the role of magistrate complement each other, as they did with the first consul, Brutus. Furthermore, the extension of the responsibility of *patres* beyond the sphere of the family meant active participation in the *res publica.*[65] For elite men, this responsibility meant holding magistracies that further reinforced the obligation. It also meant that as magistrates, they had double authority to kill sons.

This discussion of *patres* and magistrates reintroduces the question of the relevance of class to this discussion. As discussed at the beginning of this chapter, although no examples exist in the extant sources of lower-class fathers exercising their right to kill adult children, *vitae necisque potestas* was not limited to fathers of certain classes but was considered the right of all Roman citizens. A lower-class father would not have had the power of a magistrate in the *res publica* as a whole, but he would still have had the power of a father and could conceivably have used this to benefit the *res publica.* Unfortunately, the absence of evidence for the actions of lower-class *patres* makes further pursuit of the class issue impossible.

So far, the act of fathers killing adult sons has been seen in the didactic legends from Rome's glorious past, and in these legends, the triad of father, son, and *res publica* is illuminated. Like Torquatus, Spurius Cassius' father shows that allegiance to the state is the responsibility of the father. In this case, the father/son dichotomy holds true even though it is the son who was the magistrate. Such legends suggest that it is the father's obligation to enforce the family's obligation to the *res publica,* and *vitae necisque potestas* is the means of defining that responsibility (though it is not the sole manifestation of it). This notion appears not only in the literary genre of didactic legend but also in an interesting historical incident in the first century B.C.E.

In the year 63 Cicero reported to the senate that Catiline was attempting to kill him and take control of the government. Ultimately, the troubles came to such a pitch that Cicero, as consul, was granted a *senatus consultum ultimum* (*scu*), a "final decree of the senate"[66] requesting that the magistrates do whatever was necessary to preserve the *res publica.* Cicero then went on to kill citizens without a trial, and his colleague in office took up weapons against the conspirators who had managed to field a small army before they were finally defeated. In this threat to the republic, Aulus Fulvius, who was a supporter of Catiline against his father's wishes, was killed by his father for participating in the conspiracy. Valerius Maximus explicitly states that the killing of Aulus Fulvius was on behalf of the *res publica.*

> A. Fulvius, vir senatorii ordinis, euntem in aciem filium retraxit . . . :
> . . . medio itinere abstractum supplicio mortis adfecit, praefatus non se Catilinae illum adversus patriam sed patriae adversus Catilinam genuisse.[67]

> Aulus Fulvius, a man of senatorial rank, dragged back his son who was going into battle [with Catiline]: he subjected his son (dragged back in the middle of his journey) to the punishment of death, having said that he had not generated him for Catiline against the fatherland but for the fatherland against Catiline.

This historical incident reflects that same relationship among father, son, and *res publica* that the legends of Torquatus, Brutus, and Spurius Cassius suggest. If the son acts against the *res publica,* then the father's obligation to the *res publica* takes precedence. Valerius' report of this event, however, goes even further. Not only did the father kill the son to protect the *res publica,* but he reportedly created the son in the first place for that purpose.[68] In other words, the very act of producing male progeny could be envisioned—as it was, at the very least, by Sallust—as an act meant to benefit the *res publica.*

A similar connection between *res publica* and *familia* can be found in an incident that occurred nearly eighty years earlier between Decimus Silanus, governor of Macedonia, and his biological father, Titus Manlius Torquatus.[69] Silanus had already been adopted out of Torquatus' family and therefore was not legally subject to his biological father's power. Nevertheless, when he was about to be investigated by the senate for official misbehavior, his biological father took action:

> Nam cum ad senatum Macedonia de filio eius D. Silano, qui eam provinciam obtinuerat, querellas per legatos detulisset, a patribus conscriptis petiit [Torquatus] ne quid ante de ea re statuerent quam ipse Macedonum filiique sui causam inspexisset. Summo deinde cum amplissimi ordinis tum etiam eorum qui questum venerant consensu cognitione suscepta, domi consedit.[70]

> For when Macedonia, through legates, brought complaints to the senate concerning his son Decimus Silanus, who had held that province [in 141], [Torquatus] requested from the conscript fathers [i.e., senators] that, before they decide anything concerning that matter, he himself be allowed to look into the case of the Macedonians and of his own son. Then with the greatest agreement of both that most ample order and even of those who had brought the complaint, he undertook the investigation at home.

That this was a matter of concern for the *res publica* as a whole is illustrated not only by the nature of the offense—misbehavior of an official in his official capacity as governor of a province—but also by the embassy that came from Macedon to the senate to make its complaints. Nevertheless, both the senators and the Macedonians saw fit to make way for Torquatus' request to look into the matter. After two days of investigation, Torquatus reportedly declared,

> Cum Silanum filium meum pecunias a sociis accepisse probatum mihi sit, et re publica eum et domo mea indignum iudico, protinusque e conspectu meo abire iubeo.[71]

Because it seems to me proven that my son Silanus accepted money from our allies, I judge him unworthy both of the *res publica* and of my *domus* [house], and I order him to leave my sight immediately.

Torquatus here draws a parallel between his own *domus* and the *res publica* by showing that when the *res publica* suffers by the act of his biological son, the family also suffers. Silanus takes this matter so seriously that the following day he commits suicide.[72] Silanus, by his act of suicide, redeems both himself and his father. Torquatus can once again be revealed as a prominent *civis*.[73]

Torquatus here has the approval of the senate to look into the matter. The senators recognize that the *pater* can contribute to the stability of the *res publica*, even though this was not the normal practice for maladministration of a province.[74] Perhaps an even more striking indication of the importance of paternal power in the preservation of the *res publica* is that because Silanus was adopted, he was not under the *potestas* of Torquatus. Still, the senators agreed that Torquatus could investigate the matter before they themselves looked into it. One must, perhaps, wonder whether Torquatus required the approval of the senate to take action, but it seems more likely that the only reason senatorial approval was provided was that Torquatus seems to have first found out about the charges when the Macedonian legates came before the senate. Otherwise, given his eagerness to investigate the matter himself, he probably would have acted on his own accord first if he had heard the news privately.

The question of the role of the senate in granting authority to the father may also have arisen in the case of Aulus Fulvius. Some have seen the Catilinarian incident as similar to the Bacchanalian incident of the second century in that the father killed his son under the auspices, if not under the direction of, magisterial authority. Dio implies that the killing of Aulus Fulvius was connected with the *quaestiones* of the consuls,[75] but there is no other cause to connect the killing of Aulus Fulvius explicitly with the *scu*. Rather, the father seems to be acting on his own in his killing of his son to protect the *res publica*.

An even more compelling indication of the relationship between family and *res publica* is the idea of symbiosis between these polities. Sallust claims that Catiline's conspiracy included a plan for *filii familiarum* (sons of families) to kill their parents. Catiline ordered that at the same time that fires were to be started in twelve important parts of the city, and Cicero and other victims were to be assaulted, *filii familiarum, quorum ex nobilitate maxuma pars erat, parentis interficerent* ("sons of families of whom a great part were from the nobility, would kill their parents").[76] The attribution of general parricide may merely be vicious propaganda against Catiline, but it does seem to suggest that Catiline, or at least his defamers, recognized that the security of the *res publica* depended upon the stability of families within the *res publica*. Sallust sees that a successful attack on the republic required not only an attack on the consul and the physical buildings of the republic but also on the families. This suggests that he recognized the importance of families to the stability of the republic as a whole; an attack on them was a disruption of the functioning of the *res publica,* thereby providing Catiline an opportunity to further weaken the latter. If, as this reading of Sallust implies, Catiline could have gotten sons to kill fathers, then the members of the family who owed the most allegiance to the *res publica* and whose responsibility it was to see that the other members of the family paid allegiance as well would have died. Thus, the plans for the ruin of the republic required plans for the ruin of individual families as well.

In addition, one wonders whether Fulvius the Elder had also heard these rumors of planned parricides and decided to kill his son not only to preserve the republic but also to preserve his own family. It may be a stretch to think of Fulvius as employing *vitae necisque potestas* to prevent his son from committing an act of parricide, but the contemplation of this possibility reveals a contribution that could be made by a father in a place where the government had little authority. In Roman law, attempting to commit a crime was not an actionable offense. Because the father's jurisdiction was not technically part of the legal system,[77] the father had far more flexibility to defend against potential offenses than the government of the republic had.

Another occasion of a father acting in response to an attempted offense, where the government might have been incapable of acting, was Lucius Gellius' acquittal of his son for attempted parricide:

> L. Gellius, omnibus honoribus ad censuram defunctus, cum gravissima crimina de filio, in novercam commissum stuprum et parricidium cogitatum, propemodum explorata haberet, non tamen ad vindictam continuo procucurrit, sed paene universo senatu adhibito in consilium expositis suspicionibus, defendendi se adulescenti potestatem fecit; inspectaque diligentissime causa, absolvit eum cum consilii, tum etiam sua sententia. Quod si impetu irae abstractus saevire festinasset, admisisset magis scelus quam vindicasset.[78]

L. Gellius, having completed all the offices up to the censorship, although he considered that the most serious charges concerning his son, that he had committed adultery against his stepmother and had planned parricide, were almost certain, still he did not immediately punish him, but with nearly the entire senate summoned into a *consilium*, after the suspicions were exposed, he granted for the young man the power to defend himself and, with the case most diligently inspected, absolved him both with the *consilium* and even by his own opinion. But if he had been diverted by the passion of anger and had hastened to be severe, he would have committed a greater wickedness than he would have punished.

The capability of the father to bring a son to task for contemplating a misdeed and for actually committing one shows a practical application of paternal power in the republic, for although the *stuprum* had allegedly been committed, the other accusation, the planning of parricide, had not. The father was able to act in situations in which the laws of the republican government did not allow action. The father had greater flexibility in his prevention of misdeeds because he could investigate attempted offenses and not only accomplished ones. In Roman law, attempt was not actionable.

In addition to the greater flexibility provided by domestic jurisdiction, the *consilium* summoned by L. Gellius brings up two other important aspects of *vitae necisque potestas* as it relates to the father's responsibility to the *res publica*. The first aspect is the responsibility of the father to act justly in the employment of this power, as is reflected in Valerius' observation that L. Gellius made the right choice in not acting on his passions but rather in making careful examination of the offense and in applying an appropriate response at the conclusion of his investigation. The second aspect is the responsibility of the father not only to behave responsibly but also to appear to be behaving responsibly.

Because the employment of *vitae necisque potestas* was supposed to benefit the *res publica,* the right came with profound responsibility. The responsible employment of the right to kill and to give life has a long history. In many Near Eastern civilizations, the right to kill and to give life was "used to describe the dual right of rulers to condemn to death or to pardon a person guilty of a capital offence."[79] This quality, stated in the negative, is that the power was not arbitrary.[80] That the power of life and death was not meant to be an arbitrary execution of power, suggests that a great responsibility was borne by those who wielded it.

This is further implied by a passage from Cicero, which suggests that the Romans found the power to be problematic when misused: *Sunt enim omnes, qui in populum vitae necisque potestatem habent, tyranni, sed se Iovis optimi nomine malunt reges vocari.* ("For all are tyrants who have the power of life and death over the people, but they prefer to be called kings in the manner of Jove Optimus.")[81] Unfortunately, a large lacuna precedes Cicero's statement here, and so any context for his discussion of the power of life and death is lost. Nevertheless, this quote suggests that this power in the wrong hands was tyrannical and therefore bad (the *in populum* implies that the tyrant wielded the power specifically against the people). In another instance, however, Cicero implies that the power of life and death when possessed by responsible *patres* was a useful tool. Cicero, in attacking his personal enemy, Clodius, makes reference to Clodius' father as "*patrem tuum, civem optimum, clarissimi viri filium*" ("your father, the best of citizens, son of a most illustrious man") and then goes on to say, "*Si viveret, qua severitate fuit, tu profecto non viveres*"[82] ("He was of such severity, if he were living you really would not be alive"). The implication is that the father would have been justified in killing such a badly behaved son. Thus in the hands of a good citizen of an illustrious family, *vitae necisque potestas* could be a useful tool.

That the father had to be just and responsible in his application of *vitae necisque potestas* is further indicated by the dire consequences that the father could suffer if he misused it. Q. Fabius Maximus Eburnus[83] was punished for killing his son for a sexual offense.

Isdem temporibus Q. Fabius Maximus filium suum adulescentem, rus relegatum, cum duobus servis parricidii ministris interfecit ipsosque continuo servos in pretium sceleris manumisit. Die dicta Cn. Pompeio accusante damnatus est.[84]

At the same time, Q. Fabius Maximus, with two slaves as his helpers in parricide, killed his youthful son after he had relegated him to the country. He immediately freed those very slaves as a reward for their wicked deed. Being brought to court and accused by Cn. Pompeius, he was condemned.

This is a remarkable case, for the father was brought up on charges, although it was technically his legal right to kill his son. Because it would be hard to imagine that the advocate on his behalf did not at least attempt to include the father's legal right to kill his son among his arguments, one can only assume that this was an insufficient argument to result in his acquittal, which begs the question, why was he condemned? Our knowledge of the event is limited. Modern arguments suggest that it was the manner in which the father executed the son that was problematic: Not only did the father call no *consilium* by which he might have conducted formal investigation into his son's acts, but there appears to have been no thoughtful consideration of the matter at all. The young man seems to have been simply an unwitting victim of an attack by slaves (whom his father then freed).[85] He used his power in an irresponsible way and paid for that misuse with his condemnation in a public trial and exile.[86]

The father's conviction substantiates the notion that *patria potestas* was no arbitrary power granted simply to an individual in charge of the family. It was a power granted to a responsible person who would be looking out for the good of those in the family and for the good of the *civitas* as a whole. If he acted in a way that the *civitas* did not approve, the consequences could be dire. It was not a means created for the father to have control above and beyond that of the *res publica;* rather, the power of the father was a mechanism of control in a society in which both courts and enforcers were few and far between. His power was never meant to be opposed to the society but rather to enforce and reinforce societal norms. Thus, when the actions of the father did not fit in with societal expectations, the father lost his right of life and death because he used it improperly.

Another example occurs in the first generation of the empire, when a certain Tricho was attacked for killing his son. The sources do not inform us of the reason for this killing. What we do know is that the society, or some members of it, did not approve, and they expressed their disapproval by beating the father.

Trichonem equitem Romanum memoria nostra, quia filium suum flagellis occiderat, populus graphiis in foro confodit; vix illum Augusti Caesaris auctoritas infestis tam patrum quam filiorum manibus eripuit.[87]

Within my memory the people in the forum stabbed Tricho, a Roman knight, with their writing styluses because he had flogged his son to death; Augustus Caesar's authority barely rescued him from the hostile hands of as many sons as fathers.

The *civitas* thus had social means as well as legal means to punish a *pater* for killing someone who was technically inside his jurisdiction. In fact, it was a more powerful figure in society, namely, Augustus, who prevented the imminent killing of Tricho. For *vitae necisque potestas* to serve its function as a solid foundation ensuring communal stability, its execution always required just cause.

The father needed to have just cause for his action, but what precisely defined "just cause" is not entirely clear. It seems likely that the Romans themselves did not define the limits of *vitae necisque potestas* precisely enough to indicate when it went wrong because the expectation would have been that the father should know the limitations. Despite the absence of regulations regarding the employment of *vitae necisque potestas,* some actions taken on the part of the father could help ensure that his contemporary Romans would consider him to be acting justly. The most important of these actions would have been the use of a *consilium* (an informal gathering of friends and relatives to act as advisers when important decisions needed to be made), as in the case of Lucius Gellius. The *consilium,* however useful it might have been in ensuring the support of the community for one's actions, was not a requirement.[88]

Gellius' use of the *consilium* demonstrates the need for responsible action on the part of the *pater,* but the particular composition of his *consilium* shows another obligation of the father, that he demonstrate that he is behaving responsibly, that he is capable of representing his family to the community at large. Gellius invited practically the entire senate to join his *consilium.* This fact and the outcome of the case suggest that this was meant to be a public acknowledgement of a good son, rather than the punishment of a bad one.

The decision on what course of action should be taken was Gellius', but he chose to allow many public decision-makers into his domestic sphere. We should keep in mind, of course, that the senators were the peers of Gellius, and many, no doubt, his *amici* and *clientes* (friends and clients), but Valerius' means of describing them as "almost the entire senate" should not be disregarded. Gellius might have been motivated by self-preservation in the way he chose to conduct this investigation.[89] If he had refused to take any action against his son, or if he had acquitted him among just a small *consilium,* his peers might have suspected him of not taking proper action. By inviting so many senatorial members to participate in the decision-making process, he precluded them from ruining his reputation as a responsible *pater* and a responsible senator. This domestic decision-making process was a public show that demonstrated not only the innocence of the younger Gellius but also, and maybe even more importantly, the competence of the elder Gellius. The latter demonstrated that he had raised a moral son and also demonstrated that he was in control of what was happening in his own family. Such control and responsibility would have necessarily also reassured the community that he was capable of responsible participation in the *res publica*.

EVOLUTION OF PATERNAL POWER?

The *consilium* called by Gellius took place some time after 70 B.C.E. in the last decades of the republic, while the first example discussed in this chapter was the legend of Brutus, dated to the founding of the republic over four hundred years earlier. This spread of time leads to the final consideration of this chapter, namely, the issue of chronology. So far the discussion has been largely synchronous, yet the period of the republic lasted some five hundred years and encompassed myriad changes. Many scholars who take up the issue of chronology are concerned with the question of morality, and wherever they date changes in the system, they credit those changes to changes in moral attitudes of the Romans.[90] Yet I have been arguing that we should see this aspect of paternal power as an expression of political might. If change occurs, it occurs because of changes in the nature of power, not changes in morality. Massive political changes did take place over the course of the republic. Thus, Ferguson and Mansbach's exploration of the effect of change on polities is a useful tool for talking about possible changes in the father's right of life and death:

> Conquest, proselytism, diplomacy, changing economic and social ties, and additional mechanisms of global intercourse may lead to an expansion or retrenchment of the number of persons and/or space over which polities exercise authority. Change will also take place in the number and/or range of issues in which polities engage and in the weight of their authority over specific issues.[91]

This is a particularly logical statement, because it suggests that change in one aspect of political activity necessarily has an effect on other aspects. The expansion of Roman military, political, and economic activities beyond central Italy and eventually across the entire Mediterranean basin had an impact on how the Romans governed themselves internally. The continual increase in the size of government to facilitate the management of the growing territorial empire also shaped the judicial sphere of republican government. The third century B.C.E. appears to have been a period of particular vitality in the expansion and increased sophistication of the judicial activity of the government, and by the mid second century, in the year 149, the Romans established their first standing public court (*quaestio perpetua*). In the following year, Macedon became the first Roman province in the Greek east, and within three years, the Romans defeated Carthage for the third and final time, and created a province on the continent of Africa.

The timing is not coincidental. The growth of the territory over which the government of the republic was responsible necessitated an increased size and resulted in an increased complexity of that government. Further discussion of political and judicial power exercised by the institutions of government will be the subject of the next three chapters. The question here is whether the shift in the "range of issues" and the "weight of authority" exercised by republican government had an effect on the capacity of the polity of the family.

Did the increase in power possessed by the government have an impact on the extent of power that a *pater* could wield? None of the *quaestiones perpetuae,* and no legislation, directly inhibited paternal power. Furthermore, no murder law was drafted, and few laws regulating specific kinds of homicide were. Nevertheless, the increased criminal judicial jurisdiction of the government may have had an impact, however indirectly, on the extent of power that a *pater* could wield. The issue is complicated by the government itself being made up of multiple polities. The *quaestiones perpetuae,* for example, may be an indication of a movement, begun in the previous century, away from the power of the assemblies of citizens (themselves an official polity) toward greater control by the elite classes.[92] This in turn may indicate a decrease in the power of individual citizens. If this is so, then the power of the *pater,* especially as I have been illustrating him, as the quintessential *civis,* might necessarily have been increasingly limited.

Two incidents discussed by William Harris and his interpretation of them require further exploration. As related above, sometime shortly after his praetorship in the year 141 B.C.E., Decimus Iunius Silanus was investigated by Torquatus, his biological father, for peculation during his term as governor in Macedonia and was ultimately banished from his father's sight.[93] Four decades later, probably in the year 102, M. Aemilius Scaurus told his son—who had deserted the consul on the battle line—that he never wanted to see him again. Both Silanus' and Scaurus' sons committed suicide. Of these events, William Harris writes, "At Rome, Cases 8 and 9 [Silanus and Scaurus respectively] make it plain that by the second century B.C.E. at the latest there were those who thought the father's power to kill his son should not be put to use."[94] Although there may be some cause to warrant this interpretation, both cases exhibit peculiar circumstances that allow different explanations for the suicides.

Silanus' case has already been considered above in the observation of the symbiotic relationship between *res publica* and *pater,* but here it is necessary to consider further the nature of the relationship between Torquatus and Silanus and the outcome of this event. The day after Titus Manlius Torquatus banished his son from his sight, Silanus committed suicide. What concerns us here is whether the suicide of Silanus represents an anxiety on the part of the father to exercise his right to kill. Harris suggests that the father expected the suicide and used it as "a deliberate attempt to avoid direct responsibility for death."[95] In other words, has there been a shift— especially with the advent of so many changes in the power of government—in Roman attitudes about the right of the father to kill? The matter between Torquatus and Silanus could indicate Torquatus' reluctance to take responsibility for killing his son, as Harris further suggests, thereby indicating that in the same decade that the Romans had established their first standing criminal court (and had finally defeated Carthage and had created a province in European Greece), fathers were hesitant to employ their right to kill. And indeed, Torquatus might have intended and expected that the result of his decision, his son would commit suicide.[96]

The major problem with this interpretation, however, is that Torquatus did not have *potestas* over his son.[97] Torquatus may just not have been interested in testing the willingness of the Romans to continue to see him as having the moral right to act in a capital matter in regard to a son no longer in his power. Another possibility is that he might have hoped to give Silanus the opportunity to redeem himself by putting into his hands the power to kill himself on behalf of the *res publica* and on behalf of the family, one final lesson in filial and civic responsibility.

Although the interpretation of the incident between Torquatus and Silanus is clouded by their nonlegal relationship, the activities of the Aemilii Scauri provide a clearer indication of the impact of the expansion of the government's activities on the *vitae necisque potestas* possessed by a Roman father. Aemilius Scaurus the younger had been among a group of equestrians who deserted the consul (probably of 102) in a battle against the Cimbri.

M. vero Scaurus . . . filio suo misit qui diceret libentius se in acie eius interfecti ossibus occursurum quam ipsum tam deformis fugae reum visurum: itaque, si qui modo reliquum in pectore verecundiae superesset, conspectum degenerati patris vitaturum: recordatione enim iuventae

suae qualis M. Scauro aut habendus aut supernendus filius esset ad-
monebatur. Quo nuntio accepto iuvenis coactus est fortius adversus
semet ipsum gladio uti quam adversus hostes usus fuerat.[98]

But Marcus [Aemilius] Scaurus sent a letter to his son saying that he
would rather himself see the bones of his dead son in battle than to see
him guilty of so disgraceful a flight; therefore, if there was any remainder
of shame still in existence in any way in his breast, he would avoid the
sight of his father from whom he had degenerated. For, recalling his own
youth, it was brought to mind for him what sort of son Marcus Scaurus
should either have or spurn. When this letter had been received, he [the
younger Aemilius Scaurus] made use of his sword more bravely against
himself than he had against the enemy.

Valerius' use of the term *"degenerati"* is profound. Aemilius the younger
can no longer consider himself a part of the *genus:*[99] he has de-generated.
If Aemilius used such strong language in his letter, then he, too, could very
well have intended the outcome to be his son's suicide, though it is important to note that in this instance the *pater* apparently did not conduct an
investigation, call a *consilium,* or even make a decision in the presence of
his son. He simply sent a letter, and with this simple yet powerful tool, the
elder Aemilius compelled the younger to commit suicide.

It is worth considering what choices were available to the father in the
face of his son's behavior. He could have chosen to do nothing, but such
a choice would have diminished his prestige, both because his family's
honor was diminished by the son's actions and because he would have
been seen as negligent in his duties as father. He would also have left the
field open for his son to be investigated and punished by someone other
than himself, again demonstrating that he had shirked his responsibility.
He could have investigated the matter more formally and convicted the
young man and put him to death, but a recent and serious precedent might
have influenced him to take an alternate course.

The precedent, as well as Aemilius' (the father's) possible reaction to it,
shows how the expansion of the government's power and range of interests
could have had an impact on the activities of a father's employment of *vitae
necisque potestas.* As related above, two years before Aemilius banished his
son for betraying the *patria* and the consul, Q. Fabius Maximus Eburnus
was tried in a temporary public court on the charge of parricide for killing
his son.[100] These events should be considered together because Eburnus
and Aemilius Scaurus were not only contemporaries (they held the consul-

ship, respectively, in 116 and 115) but also political enemies.[101] One must wonder if Aemilius considered his options in light of the consequences faced by Eburnus. In particular, he might have felt that if he employed *vitae necisque potestas* so recently after Eburnus' conviction and exile, that he, too, might fall victim to his political enemies.

Although these incidents hint that the expanding polity of republican government was beginning to infringe upon the father's power to employ his *ius vitae necisque,* the evidence is not unequivocal. For example, on the one hand, Eburnus was convicted of parricide, and neither Aemilius Scaurus nor Torquatus directly killed his son. On the other hand, Eburnus' conviction probably came about because of the method of his execution rather than because of the act itself, while Torquatus was not a legal *pater,* and Aemilius Scaurus did not conduct an investigation. What the consideration of these incidents suggests is not a clear-cut delineation of paternal power and the power of the mechanisms of the government or even a clearly delineated moment of change. The ambiguity in these examples is not simply a consequence of the limitations of our sources. Rather, it illustrates the actual ambiguity with which the Romans lived and their approach to change.

What may be happening in the last decade of the second century is a negotiation between the two polities brought about by the expanding responsibilities of the government. That Eburnus' trial did not put an end to the employment of a father's right to kill is illustrated by Fulvius' killing of his son during the Catilinarian conspiracy. What is even more striking about Fulvius' act is that it takes place not only after the *quaestiones perpetuae* have been around for eighty years but also after the dictator Sulla's conflation of the previously extant homicide-related legislation into one law instituting a single court. In addition, Pompey's parricide law of the mid first century reflects the ongoing power of the *pater* by giving a list of relatives whose relationship to their killer would constitute parricide. Sons and daughters are not on this list. Furthermore, late republican authors still see the right of the father to kill his sons as paradigmatic. It is unlikely, however, that the Romans made a conscious decision to keep paternal rights in place in the face of the expanding government. Rather, it is more likely that the option of change did not occur to them because to diminish a man's paternal rights would be to make a man no longer Roman.[102]

This ambiguity about the extent of paternal power had been a characteristic of this power since its inception. I do not mean to argue that the

Romans intentionally set out to establish an ambiguous system but rather that the fluidity of paternal power and of the ability of the *civitas* to interfere with it served a purpose. It allowed for the *res publica* to be truly a public affair, with responsibility for its success resting on the shoulders of individual *patres*. It also allowed for interference by the community, over time represented more and more by the official institutions of the government, but never completely replaced by those institutions, in a father's execution of his rights. This balance of power and of responsibility is what allowed for stability among the Romans for centuries with such a minimal bureaucracy.

The actual execution of *vitae necisque potestas* may have been practiced seldom, but its ideological strength and method for understanding the role of individual citizens to the community as a whole and to the *res publica* remained potent for centuries. The stability of the family and the stability of the *res publica* were intertwined, and a primary element of this connection was the power a Roman father possessed to kill his own children. *Vitae necisque potestas* was a stabilizing force for the republic. The right of fathers to kill and the ideological hold of this right on the Romans would have made it difficult for the Romans to promulgate legislation against murder. The limitations of paternal power in this regard needed to be fluid to accommodate unusual circumstances, such as the conspiracy of Catiline. Drafting of murder legislation might have restricted, either explicitly or implicitly, the flexibility of this paternal right and in doing so could have jeopardized the stability of the republic.

THREE

KILLING AND THE LAW,
509–450 B.C.E.

According to Roman tradition, when the Romans ousted their kings and established annual magistracies, the chief magistrates retained the political powers of the kings; among these was the right of summary execution. These magistrates, in addition, carried symbols of royal power in the *fasces,* a bundle of rods and axes bound together, signifying the chief magistrates' right to scourge and kill citizens. Then, in the second year of the fledgling republic—the tradition continues—the consul Valerius limited the magisterial authority of summary execution by promulgating a *provocatio* law whereby Roman citizens could appeal to the people from capital and corporal sentences of magistrates. At the same time Valerius passed a law removing the axes from the *fasces* when they were carried within the city. Thus, he limited the actual right to kill at the same time that he removed the visible symbol of that right. The right to kill and the simultaneous limitation of that right remained a characteristic expression of the power possessed by chief magistrates throughout the republic as well as a characteristic expression of the relationship between magistrates and citizens.

The Roman tradition about *provocatio* and the *fasces* reveals two important themes of this study: the right to commit homicide is a means of defining supreme power, and the supreme power does not belong exclusively in the hands of a centralized institution of the government. The sixth and fifth centuries B.C.E. saw the creation of some of the formative ideology of the relationship between citizens and their government: the relationships among the evolving institutions of the government; the founding of republican magistracies and other institutions; the beginning of the struggle for power between plebeians and patricians, which put its indelible mark on these institutions; and the publication of laws shaped how the government functioned. Any study of these formative years is hindered by the scant or nonexistent primary evidence and the skepticism with which one must view the later sources. Nevertheless, what evidence there is suggests that murder was not a crime because the nature of power in the early Roman republic required that it not be. What follows is a reconstruction and analysis, based on the available evidence, of the nature and development of political power as it is revealed in the treatment of homicide in this period.

THE FIRST PLEBISCITE

A homicide-related plebiscite from the early republic reflects the struggle for power that took place between plebeians and patricians. Furthermore, the treatment of homicide shows the extent to which the power of governing officials was limited by its diffusion to citizens more generally. Finally, the absence of a murder law in the XII Tables means that in the middle of the fifth century, murder was not a crime.

That control over the act of homicide (either committing it or punishing it) is a display of power is revealed in an early plebiscite, indeed in what might be the first plebiscite ever. The second-century C.E. antiquarian Festus, in his book *On the Meaning of Words,* defines the term *homo sacer* (lit., sacred person) as follows:

> At homo sacer is est, quem populus iudicavit ob maleficium; neque fas est eum immolari, sed, qui occidit, parricidi non damnatur; nam lege tribunicia prima cavetur, "si quis eum, qui eo plebei scito sacer sit, occiderit, parricida[1] ne sit."[2]

> But a *homo sacer* is he whom the people judged guilty of an evil deed, and it is not right for him to be killed, but, whoever kills him is not condemned as a parricide; for it is the concern of the first tribunician law, "If anyone will kill him who was made *sacer* by this plebiscite, he is not to be [treated as] a parricide."

By means of this first plebiscite, the plebeian assembly stakes claim to power by insisting that it has the right to determine when someone is subject to the penalty of death. The insistence is evident in the double claim to authority within the plebiscite. The initial claim is that the assembly has the right to make a person *sacer* in the first place. By virtue of this designation, the person becomes the property of the gods and becomes a potential sacrificial victim.[3] This means that the killer of the *homo sacer* does not legally commit malicious and actionable homicide but kills with impunity.[4] That the plebiscite defines *sacer,* a term whose meaning was almost certainly familiar in the early republic, suggests that the plebiscite is not simply a claim to power but is a demand for power. The plebeians are saying that they have the right to determine who deserves the designation *sacer*—and so who can be killed with impunity—and also they reserve for themselves the right to determine at least one category of actor who is to be free from capital punishment, namely, someone who killed a person made *sacer* by the plebiscite. Thus, the assembly insists on the right to determine when a person can be subject to death and when a person cannot.

Not only does this double claim to power feel peculiarly insistent, the double authority actually claimed in the plebiscite also reflects, ironically, a certain degree of impotence. The regulation suggests that the assembly can order no executive action itself; it cannot actively kill someone condemned by its decision. Instead, it must resort to removing any human protection from the offender. This inability to guarantee death directly by a capital sentence shows an attempt to assert authority by the plebeian assembly and simultaneously shows the impotence of that assembly.

Festus' introduction of the quote provides an explanation for the impotence. He refers to this plebiscite as *"lege tribunicia prima."* The most obvious translation is that this is "the first regulation passed by the plebeian assembly." Because the plebeian assembly was created early in the Struggle of the Orders as a concession to the plebeians, who had temporarily seceded from Rome in the hopes of acquiring greater protection from the patrician government and a greater voice within it, one should expect the early decision-making both to be directed toward the acquisition of power and to reflect the limitation of that power. It would be preferable to have more context to be certain of this interpretation, and here we are not as lost as one might reasonably expect, given the nature of Festus' work. What is basically a dictionary usually presents information entirely out of context, but it is striking that immediately preceding the excerpt quoted above, Festus is defining the *"mons sacer"* as the sacred mountain where the plebeians seceded from the patricians and created the offices of tribunes of the plebeians.

The similar context of this entry could be coincidence, because the author is merely trying to define the meaning of *sacer,* but it seems probable that his use of the plebiscite to define the term *homo sacer* is made not just because of the connection of the vocabulary but also because of the proximity of the events to the secession and the creation of the tribunate.

It seems likely that in his source for this information, he found *sacer* in the plebiscite alongside his evidence for *mons sacer* in the secession of the plebs.[5] This context strengthens the interpretation of *prima,* suggesting that this was not just any plebiscite but was the first plebiscite, which would mean that control over homicide was a primary mechanism for staking a claim to political power.

PROVOCATIO

Furthermore, this conclusion is supported by the first legislation of the republican *comitia centuriata* (assembly of all Roman citizens organized by centuries). Cicero remarks,

> Publicola . . . legem ad populum tulit eam quae centuriatis comitiis prima lata est, ne quis magistratus civem Romanum adversus provocationem necaret neve verberaret.[6]

> Publicola . . . brought a law before the people, which was the first law proposed before the *comitia centuriata,* that no magistrate kill or lash a Roman citizen in the face of *provocatio.*

The attribution of this legislation to the founding of the republic is unanimous among the ancient authors who mention a date for the earliest *provocatio* legislation. According to Cicero, Livy, Dionysius of Halicarnassus, Valerius Maximus, Plutarch, and Pomponius, during the first year of the republic, Valerius Publicola introduced *provocatio* (commonly translated as "appeal").[7] Thus, the tradition of the limitation of magisterial rights as being a founding element of the republic was so pervasive that it is reflected in a philosophical treatise, two histories, a moral treatise, a biography, and a legal treatise, publications spanning the mid first century B.C.E. to the mid second century C.E. If the attribution is correct, then just as the plebeian assembly began its assertion of power by claiming rights connected with homicide, so, too, had the assembly of the entire citizen body by its first act asserted its right to control homicide. While the right of *provocatio* and the *sacer* classification are not precisely parallel, both provide the respective assemblies power over the life of a Roman citizen.

Interpreting *provocatio,* however, especially as it existed at the beginning of the republic, is problematic. Superior magistrates, by virtue of their *imperium,*[8] had the executive power of the earlier kings to condemn and punish Roman citizens. This right, according to our sources, was tempered by *provocatio,* but many modern scholars have rejected the tradition of the *provocatio* law of 509 entirely[9] and claim that the attribution for it (along with the subsequent laws of 449[10]) is anachronistic. The charge of anachronism in Roman literature is not an unjust one, but the rejection of the *provocatio* law of 509 seems unnecessary. Some reasons for this have been expressed elsewhere;[11] here I will consider instead what the *provocatio* law might indicate if it is accurately attributed. The existence of *provocatio* legislation at the founding of the republic reflects the renegotiation of power that resulted from the end of one form of government and the beginning of another.

The successful transition of power from one individual to many would have benefitted from the support of ordinary citizens, regardless of whether the end of the monarchy was the sudden break envisioned by later Romans or a gradual transition. Monarchy brings with it a certain amount of stability and consistency. The new political system divided authority among many, and limited office holding to an annual position. Such a potentially unstable system could have provoked anxiety on the part of the majority of Romans, who could not have counted on their patrons holding office continually. Yet the support of these ordinary Romans, or at least their tacit acceptance, would have made for a smoother transition from monarchy to republic. A good way to acquire the support of the masses was to ensure their protection from arbitrary behavior and physical harm.[12]

The creation of *provocatio,* however, was not simply motivated by a desire to protect and thereby placate ordinary Romans. The elite themselves benefitted from *provocatio.*[13] Even among the highest echelon of Roman patricians, men spent the majority of their lives not holding official magistracies. The promulgator of the law was not limiting only his own power; he was limiting the power of his peers, who, while they held office, would have had the legal power to command obedience and to punish even members of their own class. To successfully wield that power, a magistrate would have required the acceptance of his power by his peers as well as by his political inferiors. Thus, the second motive for the promulgation of the law at the beginning of the republic would have been to ensure that members of the office-holding class were guaranteed protections while they were not holding office,[14] and officials could not abuse their temporary political dominance.

The idea of limiting the power of the individual magistrate for the benefit of the elite patricians at this time of a shift in the structure of political power can also be seen in the simultaneous, at least according to some of our sources, promulgation of a law prohibiting a return to monarchy and subjecting to death anyone who tried to institute such a return.[15] The law against seeking *regnum* (kingship) would have been of at least as much concern—and probably greater concern—to the elite as to the average lower-class Roman. The elite would have had the most to lose in a return to monarchy: their own access to supreme power, even if only temporary. The right to kill someone seeking *regnum* meant that the elite could be assured that a position of power obtained by a political enemy would not give that man permanent access to such power. The applicability of *provocatio* to all citizens, however, does suggest that the people as a whole had a vested interest in the nature of power possessed by the magistrates and that the elite patricians could not proceed without at least taking these interests into account.[16]

If protection and a smooth transition were the motives for the creation of the *provocatio* law, the consequence was the delineation of a power structure among the institutions and people of the early republic. Understanding that power structure, however, depends upon the questions, What authority did the *populus Romanus* have in the sphere of *provocatio,* and Was the authority built into the early institutions of the republic? Even if one could conclusively prove the existence of *provocatio* at the dawn of the republic, the precise nature of this right at this time is impossible to know, and various reconstructions seem plausible. Was it simply a call for help, or was it an official judicial procedure?[17] The small size of Rome and the public quality of magisterial activity could have meant that a good percentage of the population would have been present when a call for help was heard. If this call was an instantaneous appeal to the crowd, was the crowd's opinion, in some informal way, binding on the magistrate, or did the appeal for help lead to a formal appeals hearing of the *comitia centuriata*? Was the practice of *provocatio* informal because law had yet to become the complicated institution that it was to become, or was the practice entirely formal because it might have been dependent more upon ritual than expediency?[18] Because any of these scenarios seem possible, precise conclusions about the relative power of republican institutions cannot be drawn.

The importance of *provocatio* in the eyes of later Romans, however, is indisputable, and its consequences for the concepts of political power in Rome were profound. The Romans never completely took away the right of a magistrate to kill, and possibly from the very start of the republic, never allowed a magistrate to completely possess that right. This made for a curious notion of power in the republic: the simultaneous absolute power of punishment and the superiority of the people as a group over that arbitrary power. It was the tension between *imperium* on the one hand and the limitation of *imperium* by *provocatio* on the other that defined the magistrate's power in the republic. It was the magistrate's *imperium* combined with the right of a people en masse to overrule it that helped to define the relative power of government institutions in the republic.

THE XII TABLES

So far, this chapter has been concerned with the right to kill and the limitation on that right for officials of the government or citizens functioning in their role as part of the government, but regulations about homicide also existed for Romans as private citizens. The extant XII Tables—the body of law published in the mid fifth century B.C.E. that was perceived by later Romans as the foundation of their legal system—do not include any law regulating murder, though they do include laws on justifiable and unintentional homicide. It is a mistake to assume that the existence of these other laws meant there also existed a murder law.[19]

Because the nature of the XII Tables seems to have been somewhat random, and the work is not a lawcode in any comprehensive sense, for the modern legal scholar to assume that a law was included simply because its existence would create a comfortable perception of completion and balance is a mistake.[20] The inclusion of the law on unintentional homicide does not imply that a law on murder was also included, especially because it seems possible that the Romans published in the XII Tables those acts that were the most contentious or whose consequences lacked consensus.[21] Furthermore, in contrast to modern scholars,[22] no Roman author makes explicit reference to what modern historians see as the complementary nature of an unintentional homicide law and an intentional one. Finally, despite the admittedly scattered and fragmented references to the unintentional law, it seems quite unlikely that an intentional homicide law in the XII Tables would have left not a single trace in the sources of the last couple of generations of the republic, when acts of intentional homicide were almost certainly regularly on the minds of Roman authors.[23]

An examination of the unintentional homicide law and of other references to homicide in the XII Tables will result in the following conclusions. Although the XII Tables incorporated no murder law, the customary consequence for someone who committed intentional and malicious homicide was death. Importantly, for understanding political and private power in archaic Rome, death was not meted out by institutions of the government but by the relatives of the victim.

The majority of our knowledge of this law comes from two passages in the writings of the great late-republican orator Cicero, who, in his speech *pro Tullio,* quotes a regulation of the XII Tables:

> Quis est cui magis ignosci conveniat, quoniam me ad xii tabulas revocas, quam si quis quem imprudens occiderit? . . . nam lex est in xii tabulis: si telum manu fugit ma . . .[24]

> Who is there for whom it is more fitting to be pardoned—since you recall the XII Tables for me—than whoever without forethought, kills anyone else? . . . For a law is in the XII Tables: if a weapon flies from the hand m . . .[25]

Unfortunately, here the manuscript breaks off, and so nowhere is the law quoted directly in an ancient source. Cicero, however, makes reference to this law also in his treatise *Topica.* The translation of the second sentence is literal (and the italics are mine) to highlight the difficulty of interpretation.

> Nam iacere telum voluntatis est, ferire quem nolueris fortunae. Ex quo *aries* subicitur ille in vestris *actionibus:* si telum manu fugit magis quam iecit.[26]

> For to throw a weapon is an act of will, to strike someone when you will not have intended is an act of fortune. From that, that *ram* is thrown under in your *actions:* "if a weapon flies from his hand more than he throws it."

There are two issues of interpretation: the *aries* and the *actionibus.* Literally the *aries* means ram, but is the meaning here literal? Lewis and Short's *Latin Dictionary* uses this very passage to illustrate an alternate meeting of *aries,* as buttress or prop, used literally that way by Julius Caesar, but used, supposedly, figuratively here.[27] *Aries* can also mean battering ram. These figurative meanings, however, ignore the possibility that the context makes the literal meaning the most likely one.[28] The regal law on unintentional homicide, quoted and discussed in Chapter One, states that a person who committed unintentional homicide should offer a ram (*arietem*) in the place of his own life.[29] Because Cicero was talking here about a law on unintentional homicide, *aries,* as meaning the actual animal, seems likely. In his commentary on the *Topica,* Tobias Reinhardt argues rightly in favor of this literal translation.[30]

His argument also depends on the translation of *actionibus* in its precisely legal context as "actions in law."[31] The word *actiones,* however, appears in the *Topica* with other meanings. It is used in a general way in contrast to cogitation,[32] and Cicero also uses it to refer to a court case or specifically to a forensic speech.[33] The word *actiones,* however, also has a specific legal meaning in Roman procedural law of the early republic. The *legis actiones* were the "actions in law," the particular forms that had to be used to bring a case before the courts, and the forms were based exclusively in statutory law, which itself originates with the XII Tables.

Cicero may quite likely have intended the meaning of the phrase above to be, "From that [theory of intention], that ram is handed over in your actions in law." The use of the term *"vestris"* ("your") makes this the only possible interpretation because Trebatius, for whom the treatise was composed,[34] was a Roman jurist, an expert in the *ius civile,*[35] and because Cicero uses the second person possessive plural pronoun six times in the *Topica.* Furthermore, he uses it exclusively for the things connected with Trebatius' role as a jurisconsult and specifically not for things connected with his role as an advocate and orator.

> Ficta enim exempla similtudinis habent vim; sed ea oratoria magis sunt quam vestra; quamquam uti etiam vos soletis, sed hoc modo: Finge mancipio aliquem dedisse id quod mancipio dari non potest.[36]

> For fictitious examples of similitude have force, but that more in oratory than in yours (*vestra*); although that even you (*vos*) are accustomed to do, but in this way: Imagine someone gives a thing using *mancipatio* [the legal procedure for transfer of property], which is not able to be transferred by *mancipatio.*

Leaving the noun implied rather than stated in this excerpt serves to underscore Cicero's use of this particular possessive pronoun only for Trebatius' activities as a jurisconsult.[37] Thus, "in your actions" cannot refer to Trebatius' activities in the courtroom but only to his activities as an expert in the *ius civile* and thus only to the *legis actiones.* If Cicero refers to the *legis actiones* here, then he is referring to a *legis actio* that was founded on the

XII Tables, because we know from his speech for Tullius that this law was recorded in the XII Tables.[38]

The consequence for unintentional homicide in the XII Tables was the spilling of the blood of a ram, that is, the death of an animal. For intentional homicide, blood must also have been spilt. This is not a particularly disputed statement, but because this book is built on the notion that the Roman treatment of homicide differed from modern treatment, it is worth identifying the evidence that makes this statement true. That the blood spilt in retaliation for intentional homicide was human blood is suggested in part by the Romans distinguishing between the intentional and the unintentional act in the XII Tables. Whether or not the XII Tables included a murder law, the consequences for each offense must have been different; otherwise, there would have been no point in making the distinction.

The XII Tables also provided for *talio* (retaliation in kind, like "an eye for an eye").[39] Because *talio* existed at this time, it is easy to see how it would have been applied to intentional homicide, especially because death was also an acceptable punishment for other acts. Theft at night,[40] or theft of someone else's crops,[41] or theft where a thief used a weapon after he had been caught,[42] could have resulted in death for the perpetrator, as could arson,[43] false testimony,[44] defrauding a client,[45] and slanderous (perhaps magical) incantations.[46] If the Romans of the fifth century could envision a punishment of death for these acts, then they could have envisioned it for intentional homicide. That death was the consequence for intentional homicide is further suggested by the almost certainly correct belief that the ram's head was meant to substitute for the killer's.

Scholars of early Roman law are largely in agreement that the unintentional homicide law of the XII Tables, like the unintentional homicide law attributed to King Numa, required the handing over of a ram[47] and that the ram took the place of the killer. Earlier, the killer would have suffered the same fate he had meted out upon his victim whether his act was intentional or not. In other words, the system out of which this law was formulated was based on vengeance.

Partly, this belief derives from ancient statements concerning the act of handing over the ram. The passages that provide insight into the purpose of handing over the ram are not explicitly connected with the XII Tables. Nonetheless, the purpose of handing it over is illuminated by these passages. The *lex Numae* on unintentional homicide, whence the unintentional homicide law of the XII Tables probably originates, expresses this quite literally with the notion that the ram is handed over "*pro capite*" (in the place of [the killer's] head),[48] and this interpretation is further supported by Festus, with a citation from Antistius Labeo's fifteenth book *On Pontifical Law*:

> Subigere arietem, in eodem libro Antistius esse ait dare arietem, qui pro se agatur, caedatur.[49]

> "*Subigere arietem*," Antistius says in that book "is to give a ram who, would be killed in the place of himself who was accused."[50]

Though the specific context for Antistius' reference to this rule is unknown, and the Servius quote refers to a law of the regal period, the similarity of the regal law to the XII Tables suggests that the ram had the same purpose, to take the place of the killer. Because the ram was killed, the killer must also have been subject to death. Therefore, death was the consequence for someone who committed intentional, malicious homicide, although it was not articulated in the XII Tables.

Death was the standard punishment for the act. Nevertheless, the standard executor of that punishment was not to be found among the institutions or officials of republican government[51] but rather among the members of the family of the victim. This is evident from the apparent fact that the unintentional homicide law is grounded in the notion of vendetta, and the XII Tables are replete with acts of self-help. The complete picture of who gets to determine and execute a punishment is hampered by Latin's love of the passive voice, which means that in many instances the record contains no reference to the person responsible for carrying out the punishment. Nonetheless, sufficient clues exist to illustrate both the traces of vendetta and the prevalence of self-help that together reveal the weakness of republican government in the mid fifth century B.C.E.

The apparent transition from a vendetta system is implied by the *pro capite* of Numa's law discussed above.[52] Further evidence of the system of vengeance as a tool of the regulation of order in the early republic is seen in the law providing for *talio*. That the person who gets to enforce *talio* in the case of a broken limb is the victim is suggested by his ability to choose an alternative form of restitution:

> Si membrum rup(s)it, ni cum eo pacit, talio esto.[53]

> If he breaks a limb, unless he make peace with him, let there be *talio*.

The victim can break the limb of the perpetrator unless he settles for some alternative form of compensation. He seems to have three options here: make peace, break the perpetrator's limb, or punish the perpetrator in some other way. The decision for whether *talio* will be meted out is in his hands. The government plays no role beyond the promulgation of the law.

In addition to the traces of a system of vendetta in the legislation of the XII Tables, a substantial amount of self-help is built into these laws. For example, although the Tables provide for the existence of a judge, no official of the government exists who can compel a citizen to come to court. That rests in the hands of the individuals who wish them to appear.[54]

The experience of self-help is, of course, common among societies with no police force and minimal judicial institutions. In the case of Rome, the emphasis on self-help must have been augmented by the position of the father in the community, as discussed in the previous chapter.[55] Because the father was responsible for the behavior of the members of the *familia*, appeal to him would have been the first recourse for one seeking justice. This must have reinforced the private nature of justice.

COMMUNITY AND GOVERNMENT

Despite the prevalence of self-help as a form of justice, some offenses apparently did merit the particular interest of the community to such a degree that punishment became more than a private matter. For example, if someone stole grain at night, his punishment was not merely death but the sacrifice of his life to Ceres, a goddess of agriculture.[56] This ultimate religious sanction imposed on a grain thief suggests that the act was so severe that the community as a whole was imperiled by it.

This leaves us with a question: Could the act of intentional homicide have also endangered the community and been subject to religious sanctions? The religious sanctions against the ram (who serves not simply as restitution but as a form of expiation[57]) in the place of the unintentional killer suggest that the answer could be yes. If the death of the intentional killer was not simply punishment or revenge but also a form of expiation, the act might have been of concern to more than only the family of the victim; it would have been of concern to the community at large.

Community involvement, however, was not necessarily government involvement. Even under circumstances in which one might most reasonably expect a representative of the government to carry out a punishment of death, the identification of the punisher in the XII Tables is ambivalent at best. The three offenses that directly affected the government and were subject to a punishment of death were bearing false witness, accepting bribes while acting as a judge, and treason.

Bearing false witness must have resulted in severe consequences not only for the person against whom the false witness was perpetrated but also for the stability of the courts as institutions of the government. The stability would have been jeopardized even more in a case in which a judge accepted a bribe. If the courts could be cheated, then they could not be trusted. Thus, the Romans provided in the XII Tables a mechanism to ensure the integrity of the institutions that those self-same laws established, with the rule that anyone who bears false witness *e saxo Tarpeio deiceretur*[58] (is thrown from the Tarpeian rock) and any judge who accepts a bribe *capite poenitur*[59] (suffers capital punishment). Yet scholars are of a mixed opinion on the issue of whether hurling a culprit from the Tarpeian rock was a private or a public punishment,[60] and the *capite poenitur* was probably not the actual wording in the ancient law. The act of treason was an even more direct attack upon Roman government, and yet even in this instance, it is possible that the reference to the act as an element of the XII Tables is in error.[61] Thus, government involvement in carrying out punishments in the XII Tables was minimal at best.

Just as community involvement was not necessarily government involvement, so government was not synonymous with community. In fact, the tension between the two is suggested by the legislation of the XII Tables that prohibited an uncondemned man from being put to death; the legislation punished with death the official who took such an extreme action.[62] These regulations show the extent of the power of the government, the nature of that power, and its limits. Most striking perhaps is that governing officials drafted and published the laws, yet the laws limited the power of those very officials in the sphere of homicide. If even the lawgivers in early Rome, who held, or could have expected to hold, positions as magistrates showed a resistance to endowing those magistrates with the power to kill, then the Romans of the fifth century must have possessed a real fear of the potential arbitrary acts of officials of the government.[63] The government as an institution was not powerful enough to combat this fear.

The "government" is the actor in the previous paragraphs, but the government was never monolithic. The right to condemn a citizen to death was denied to magistrates but provided to the assembly.[64] Even though the assembly is an institution of the government, it is distinct from the magistrates, the senate, and later the standing courts in one significant way. The assembly was the government at its most diffuse, made up of the citizen-community as a whole. Only the community as a whole had the power to condemn a citizen to death. Thus, the death of a citizen could not be a decision of any mechanism of the government unless that mechanism was identified with the community. Representatives of the government, through any of its narrower configurations, had neither the capacity to kill, nor did its agents have the inclination to take on that capacity.

Although unintentional homicide got the attention of the lawgivers of the XII Tables in the last decade of the sixth and in the fifth century B.C.E., the Romans promulgated no murder law. Although the Romans granted the right to kill to high magistrates, they immediately limited that right by *provocatio.* The tension between the right to kill and the limitations on it remained a defining element of the power of these high magistrates throughout the republic. The absence of a murder law also remained a characteristic of republican Rome. In addition, no cases of unintentional homicide appear in the sources at all; when mention is made of the regulation on homicide in the XII Tables, it is not in the context of any contemporary law or judicial proceeding. This may, in part, be a product of our sources that are concerned almost exclusively with events that are dramatically great, morally reprehensible, or abhorrent to the civic body. Unintentional homicide seldom was such an event. On the other hand, the uniqueness of the law to early Rome may have had something to do with its religious nature (a remnant of the time when the officials in charge of law were the chief priests of Rome).[65]

Indeed, it seems entirely unlikely that the law on unintentional homicide had any long-term efficacy as law in Rome. Furthermore, the monarchic homicide law, if it did extend into the early years of the republic, which seems unlikely,[66] also had no impact on later laws or judicial proceedings. It is time, now, to turn to those proceedings to consider what did have an impact on them.

FOUR

MURDER WAS NOT A CRIME, 449–81 B.C.E.

If murder was not a crime, what was? Before the middle of the second century B.C.E., there were no crimes. This does not mean that before the middle of the second century the Romans experienced either total nihilistic anarchy or beatific peaceful relations, only that the mechanisms for dealing with disputes, even violent disputes, must almost always have been beyond the purview of the government. Social structures such as the *familia* and the patron/client relationship must have served as the mechanisms for the resolution of myriad disputes. There also were additional methods of private arbitration when these more personal forms of resolution were unmanageable.[1] Although the precise mechanisms are unknown, what is known is that the government did not legislate regarding criminal acts until the middle of the second century B.C.E., when the legislation was tied to the creation of standing criminal courts, the *quaestiones perpetuae*.

The Romans' territory expanded more than exponentially during the period between the mid fifth century and the early first century B.C.E.; the changes resulted in an increase in the size and complexity of Roman government; and this complexity and size included, eventually, *quaestiones perpetuae* (the standing public courts that dealt with acts "done in violation of those duties which an individual owes to the community and for the breach of which the law has provided that the offender shall make satisfaction to the public"[2]). Nevertheless, murder still was not a crime. Certain offenses involving homicide did become actionable—at first irregularly and some, eventually, regularly—in Roman courts, but homicide per se was not the reason these activities were actionable in a public venue. The reason often had little to do with the act of one human being killing another.

THE GOVERNMENT'S SPHERE OF AUTHORITY

The concern about murder and unintentional homicide during the monarchy does not seem to have reappeared in the historical period of the republic. Instead, when Roman institutions began to take an interest in criminal activities (to some degree before the second century, but certainly during the second century), offenses that included homicide found their way into what eventually became a permanent system of standing courts. The reasons for the inclusion reflect Roman perceptions of the role of government and its responsibilities and limitations. Murder was not a crime because the judicial forces of the government did not involve themselves with the private activity of one Roman killing another, and because it was not an act intended to harm the *res publica*. Only specific kinds of killing, or killings that occurred under particular circumstances, became crimes because they did endanger the *res publica*.

The reasons for a public trial were often, no doubt, more complicated in each individual case than the limited descriptions in the sources will allow us to determine, but there are certain tendencies that reveal themselves. In particular, the *res publica* was threatened by the death of large numbers of victims, by acts of public violence (though not yet defined as such), and, in particular, by threats to the elite, who guided the *res publica*. These characteristics of actionable homicide reflect the personal nature of Roman political administration and the role of the government, which was primarily the protection, preservation, and success of the *res publica*.

In the period before the institution of the *quaestiones perpetuae*, starting in 149 B.C.E., the offense itself was not necessarily the determining factor for a public trial, yet some offenses appeared more often in the reports of public trials than others. For example, with regard to homicide-related offenses, *parricidium* (kin-killing) and *veneficium* (poisoning) seem to have been tried in a public venue. Each of these offenses has its own particular qualities that brought it to the attention of the community at large. Furthermore, an act of intentional homicide could fall under the rubric of another offense: *perduellio* (treason), and being a *sicarius* (a dagger-wielder) was of interest to the government at least as early as the beginning of the second century, though no trials are recorded in the extant record. Most of these became actionable in the standing courts instituted in the late second century and early first century. Each of these offenses is explored in this chapter to demonstrate how the concerns of the legislators and of those who might have presided over public courts reflect the values and concerns of the Roman government during the republic.

The argument that murder was not a crime must contend with two pieces of evidence that may seem to indicate otherwise. One of these is a reference to the judicial actions of L. Cassius Longinus Ravilla (cos. 127 B.C.E.):

> L. Cassius fuit, sicut saepe diximus, summae vir severitatis. Is quotiens quaesitor iudicii alicuius esset in quo quaerebatur de homine occiso suadebat atque etiam praeibat iudicibus hoc quod Cicero nunc admonet, ut quaereretur cui bono fuisset perire eum cuius morte quaeritur.[3]

> L. Cassius was, as we have often said, a man of the greatest severity. As often as he was a judge of some court in which the investigation was about a person who was killed, he urged and even commanded the jurors, the thing that Cicero now advises, to ask for whose benefit it was to destroy him whose death was being investigated.

Two parts of this passage seem to suggest a regular jurisdiction over homicide. One is that Cassius was often (*quotiens*) a *quaesitor iudicii alicuius* ("a judge of some court") *de homine occiso* ("concerning a killed person"). The other is that the "cui bono?" question was posed about the person whose death was being investigated.

The "cui bono?" question may be explained by this passage being an excerpt from Asconius' commentary on Cicero's speech on behalf of Milo. Milo was brought to trial in the year 52, on a charge of public violence that included the killing of Cicero's personal enemy Clodius. The implication of Asconius' report is that Cassius Longinus asked this question only in matters of homicide, but Asconius' implication may have been colored by Cicero's defense of Milo in which Cicero was attempting to justify the killing of Clodius. Cassius Longinus might have asked this question with regard to any kind of victim.

On the other hand, even if Cassius Longinus asked this question only about someone's death, this does not mean that there was a regular or even an irregular murder court. Indeed, as far as the evidence shows, there was never a standing court *de homine occiso*. It is possible that Cassius presided over the *quaestio inter sicarios* ("the court concerning brigands"),[4] but there is no reason to assume that either he or his contemporaries viewed this as a court *de homine occiso*. For Asconius, who lived during the first century of the empire, the perception of the *quaestio inter sicarios* may well have changed because of both the influence of the *lex Cornelia de sicariis et veneficiis* and the later creation of the *questiones de vi publica* and *vi*

69

privata[5] ("the court concerning public and private violence"), which must have taken over some of the jurisdiction that the *quaestio de sicariis* had earlier controlled. A further indication that Cassius was probably not presiding over a court identified as *"de homine occiso"* is that this was never the heading of a *quaestio perpetua* in Rome, and yet Cassius was presiding at a time when such *quaestiones* were being created.[6] If he had regularly presided over such a court, presumably the court itself would have been regular.

The one actual investigation that appears to contradict the claim that murder was not a crime was the unusual case of the killings in the Sila forest. In the year 138, multiple homicides came to the attention of the senate of Rome. Cicero remarks,

> Memoria teneo Smyrnae me ex P. Rutilio Rufo audivisse, cum diceret adulescentulo se accidisse, ut ex senatus consulto P. Scipio et D. Brutus, ut opinor, consules de re atroci magnaque quaererent. Nam cum in silva Sila facta caedes esset notique homines interfecti insimulareturque familia, partim etiam liberi societatis eius quae picarias de P. Cornelio L. Mummio censoribus redemisset, decrevisse senatum ut de ea re cognoscerent et statuerent consules.[7]

> I still remember something I heard at Smyrna from P. Rutilius Rufus when he said that when he was a young man, it came about that in the consulship of P. Scipio and D. Brutus, as I believe, the consuls were instructed by a *senatus consultum* to investigate a dreadful and huge affair. For in the Sila forest, slaughter had been committed, and famous people were killed and the slaves of the company were accused, and even some free men of that company, which had leased the pine-pitch factory from the censors P. Cornelius and L. Mummius, were accused. The senate had decreed that the consuls should investigate and pass judgment about this matter.

The accused were eventually acquitted with the help of the rhetorical eloquence of their advocate—Cicero's reason for reporting this event. Cicero's discussion of this trial provides important insight for understanding the nature of public involvement in the trial of offenses prior to the institution of most of the permanent courts.

Two different issues deserve attention: the reason for senatorial involvement and the nature of that involvement. Although the incident involved culpable homicides, the consuls were not assigned to investigate *de homine*

occiso. Consules de re atroci magnaque quaererent ("consuls were to investigate concerning an atrocious and great matter"). I am not suggesting that
this was the formal title of the investigation, only that the lack of a clearly
designated title suggests that the senate did not assign the consuls to investigate murder but rather to investigate the bizarre happenings, which is
not the same as suggesting that the act itself is a natural matter of concern
to the government.

The magnitude and the atrocity of this incident, we are told, compelled
the senators to send consuls to investigate. This incident was great and atrocious not simply because intentional homicide was alleged to have been
committed. Cicero points out two important elements in the case. First,
the victims were *noti homines* ("well-known people"). The involvement of
public officials, especially at the level of the senate and the consuls, would
not have occurred had the victims been of lower status. The status of the
participants in an offense was central to determining whether the offense
would have been investigated by an official *quaestio*. This in itself might
have been sufficient reason for senatorial involvement, but even more was
at stake here.

The *noti homines* were reported to have been killed by people of lesser
status, including freedmen and even slaves. This event was a disruption of
social order. The killing of masters by the slaves and former slaves demonstrated that the masters were not capable of retaining order; thus, it became necessary for a representative of the larger community to reestablish
order. Cicero also mentions that the company leased a pine-pitch factory
from the censors, and so the government of Rome was already directly
involved in the activities of this company and had a vested interest in the
success of its endeavors.

The combination of the disruption of social order, the high status of
the victims, the seriousness of the act, and the involvement of the victims
directly with the government all helped to bring about senatorial participation in this trial. The nature of the participation deserves attention. Once
again, Cicero's language sheds light on the issue. He reports that the consuls were to investigate "a dreadful and huge affair" and, in referring to the
case to be investigated he writes, "this matter." The charges are not defined,
probably because there were no specific charges alleged. The consuls were
supposed to investigate the matter, not conduct a trial on a specific charge.
This interpretation does not mean that they did not have the capacity to
judge and condemn or acquit, but merely that it was unnecessary to lay
a specific accusation because no law had been broken. The senate could
choose to order consuls or any other magistrates to investigate matters of

any sort that came to their attention; they did not require a specific accusation defined by law.

Thus, the apparent evidence that murder was the purview of the government does not really illustrate that fact at all. Instead, it shows that an act of murder could come to the attention of the mechanisms of the government under certain circumstances. Furthermore, such matters came to the attention of the public mechanisms because of the status of the victims and the perceived threat to the social order.

Threats to the security, stability, or success of the republic appear in each of the homicide-related cases that came to be tried in a public venue. These threats include direct public violence that puts the community of the city in danger, a disruption of social order, and the status of those involved (either as culprits or as victims), and they are the defining characteristics of cases that enjoy the attention of the institutions and officials of republican government. The inclusion of the status of those involved reflects also the peculiarly personal nature of Roman republican statesmanship with which, for good or ill, the government of the *res publica* operated.

DAGGER-WIELDERS

Among the perpetrators of acts involving homicide whom the Romans eventually came to try in standing public courts, the most obvious example of a threat to security and stability is the *sicarius* or dagger-wielder. That a man wielding a dagger with the intention of committing a theft or killing someone, would be of greater concern to the government than an ordinary murderer is not particularly surprising. Indeed, even though there was no such thing as a crime defined and regulated by law at the time, the comic playwright Plautus provides evidence that wielding a dagger was worthy of the attention of the institutions of the government even as early as the beginning of the second century B.C.E.[8]

> Euclio. Redi. Quo fugis nunc? tene, tene.
> Congrio. Quid, stolide, clamas?
> Euclio. Quia ad tris viros iam ego deferam nomen tuom.
> Congrio. Quam ob rem?
> Euclio Quia Cultrum habes![9]

> Euclio: Get back. What are you doing now? Hold! Hold!
> Congrio: Dimwit, why are you calling out?

Euclio: Because I am going to bring your name before the *tresviri*.
Congrio: Why?
Euclio: Because you have a knife!

Plautus, naturally, makes a joke of what could really be a threat to public safety by having a character plan to arrest a cook who is wielding a knife, but the point—for our purposes—is that the knife-wielder was perceived as a real threat to public safety long before a standing court was established that took cognizance of such an offense. This is evident because a primary responsibility of the *tresviri* was to help maintain public order.[10]

During the second century the Romans must have continued to perceive dealing with this threat to be an obligation of the government, for one of the earliest *quaestiones perpetuae* was that for the trial of the *sicarius*.[11] This statement should not be taken to suggest that the Romans originally created these standing courts based on an abstract sense of the danger to the *res publica*. It is clear from other sources that the standing courts, like many developments of Roman government, were inspired by particular incidents or circumstances and could even be used to make *ad hominem* attacks. Unfortunately, as with most of the early *quaestiones perpetuae*, the precise motive for the introduction of this court is unknown. Nonetheless, the creation and ongoing employment of the standing court to try the *sicarius* illustrates the growing belief of the Romans that the government should take cognizance of acts that threatened public safety.

Despite scholarly consensus, now, that the early *sicarius* court was no simple murder court, it is still treated as though murder were its primary interest. Because of this, it is worth reiterating the arguments that reveal this conclusion to be false. In 1969 J. D. Cloud expanded on Wolfgang Kunkel's argument against the claims of earlier scholars, including Mommsen, that the *sicarius* was a common murderer, and thus Sulla's *quaestio de sicariis* was a court with jurisdiction over the common murderer.[12] Cloud closely examines Cicero's speech on behalf of Roscius and concludes that "Cicero makes it clear that the sic[arius] is very different from the 'murderer' of Berger's definition: he is a gangster, forming part of a *societas*, who is a public nuisance, who kills or arranges killings for financial gain" and sometimes also for political motives.[13] Another one of Cloud's methods was to look at how often the word is connected to such words as *latrones* (bandits), *sectores* (cutpurses), and even *gladiatores*. The *sicarii* are also often referred to as being in crowds or mobs (*grex, multitudo*, even the more formal *societas*). His point is well taken; the *sicarius* is always associated with public violence or with the people who participated in it.

The *sicarius,* however, does not even have to be a killer at all, as Cicero clearly indicates in a hypothetical case in his *de inventione.* Although in this treatise Cicero is concerned with describing various mechanisms of legal procedure, these need not concern us. What is relevant in this passage is the nature of the offense that is considered actionable in the *quaestio inter sicarios.* The basic outline of Cicero's discussion is that one member of a band of men, men armed with the intent to do violence, cut off the hand of a Roman equestrian with a sword.

> Cum ad vim faciendam quidam armati venissent, armati contra praesto fuerunt, et cuidam equiti Romano quidam ex armatis resistenti gladio manum praecidit. Agit is cui manus praecisa est iniuriarum.[14]

> When, for the purpose of committing violence, a certain armed band came and armed men were ready against them, and one of the armed men, resisting a Roman equestrian, cut off his hand with a sword. He whose hand was cut off brings an accusation for *iniuria.*

The victim brings a charge of *iniuria* (injury), and the trial is to take place before *recuperatores. Recuperatores,* literally "recoverers," are a panel of judges, often for trials concerning property.[15] As is the practice in civil procedure, the two parties to the suit appear before the praetor (*in iure*)[16] and define the case which is to go before the judge or, in this case, before the *recuperatores.* During the *in iure* procedure, one of the supporting arguments for the defendant is,

> Non enim oportet in recuperatio iudicio eius malefici, de quo inter sicarios quaeritur, preiudicium fieri.[17]

> For prejudgment ought not to be made before a court of *recuperatores* about this malefaction, which should be tried *inter sicarios.*

In this case, the man who should be tried in the *quaestio inter sicarios* was not a murderer at all but one of a band of villains who wielded weapons. Two conclusions arise from this example: the *sicarius* was not necessarily a killer, and the *quaestio inter sicarios* was not necessarily a homicide court.

Indeed, not only was it not necessarily a homicide court, it was not even primarily concerned with homicide. The text of the law that created the first *inter sicarios* court is no longer extant, but the language of some extant versions of Sulla's later *lex de sicariis et veneficiis* shows what so many scholars pass over in silence: that the intent to commit homicide is not the only wrongful intent of the wielder of a weapon and that even the part of the law that mentions homicide was not primarily aimed at homicide.

> Marcianos libro quarto decimo institutionum. Lege Cornelia de sicariis et veneficiis tenetur, qui hominem occiderit: cuiusve dolo malo incendium factum erit: quive hominis occidendi furtive faciendi causa cum telo ambulaverit.[18]

> Marcian *Inst.* 14: Under the *lex Cornelia de sicariis et veneficiis,* someone is liable who kills a person, or by whose malicious intent a fire is made, or who walks around with a weapon for the sake of killing a person or committing a theft.

Note, first, that carrying a weapon with the intent to commit theft is a culpable offense equal to carrying a weapon with the intent to kill. The author of this law was not simply trying to make homicide an offense. Furthermore, to label the court established by this law a "murder court" is to present an entirely inaccurate picture of the purpose of the court and the law by implicitly excluding from its jurisdiction other culpable offenses. By placing that clause first, Marcian reflects the notion that homicide was the primary concern of the law, but his word order is anachronistic, as a comparison with Cicero and Ulpian shows.[19]

Cicero interprets the wording of the *lex Cornelia* slightly differently from Marcian:

> Etsi persapienter et quodam modo tacite dat ipse lex potestatem defendendi quae non hominem occidi, sed esse cum telo hominis occidendi causa vetat, ut, cum causa, non telum, quaereretur, qui sui defendendi causa telo esset usus, non hominis occidendi causa habuisse telum iudicaretur.[20]

> Most wisely and tacitly the law authorizes self-defense; it does not forbid killing a person, but [it does forbid] carrying a weapon with a view to killing, and consequently when the circumstances of the case and not the carrying of the weapon was being investigated, the one who had employed a weapon in self-defense was not held to have carried that weapon with a view toward killing a person.[21]

Cicero had his own agenda for emphasizing the aspect of the law that is concerned with public violence, but his explicit statement that the law does not forbid killing a person suggests that the law does not, perhaps, have the clause that was later inserted by the jurists. Otherwise, Cicero ran the risk of his opponents pointing out his error.

Indeed, evidence from Ulpian reinforces Cicero's wording even though he, like Marcian, includes the phrase *hominemve occiderit* ("or who will have killed a person"):

> ... cavetur ... praetor ... uti quaerat ... de capite eius, qui cum telo ambulaverit hominis necandi furtive faciendi causa, hominemve occiderit, cuiusve id dolo malo factum erit.[22]

> The praetor is responsible for investigating about the *caput* of the person who will have walked around with a weapon for the sake of killing or for the sake of committing a theft, or who will have killed a person, or by whose malicious intent this will have been done.

In addition to its confirmation of Cicero's claim, Ulpian's word order is thought to be more accurate than Marcian's: because he was writing in a time when murder was the primary purpose of the law, and it would have been illogical for him to create a word order that implied otherwise. The only logical explanations for his text are that the original law did not include the simple homicide clause at all or that the simple homicide clause came after the clauses about wielding a weapon.[23] According to the text of the only extant *sicarius* law, the culprit was primarily one who carried around a weapon with the intent to kill or steal, and according to the general usage of the term *sicarius,* this person put members of society at risk by that action. Thus, it is not particularly surprising that when the Romans began to institute standing public courts, they instituted one to take cognizance of weapon-wielding in the city of Rome.

The long-term interest of government institutions in violence of this sort may explain why the Roman authors themselves appear to have exhibited very little interest in the creation of a standing public court for the trial of people who were not serving in an official capacity.[24] Indeed, they seem to have had little interest in the standing courts at all. Nonetheless, now the state had both a law and a permanent public institution responsible for the suppression of the activity, however dangerous, of a private citizen, and yet murder was not a crime.

POISONING

The *sicarius* did pose a significant threat to the safety and security of the city of Rome and of its government; so, too, upon occasion, did perpetrators of poisoning. *Veneficium* had a long history as an actionable offense in Rome before the creation of the permanent court in the late second century. It may even have been actionable as early as the XII Tables, though the only extant suggestion of this is found in the *Digest* of Justinian from Gaius' book *On the XII Tables,* and all Gaius reports is that one should be careful in using the word *venenum* because it can mean medicine as well as poison.[25]

In the second half of the fourth century, however, the first of a few mass poisoning cases appeared in Rome. It seems likely that these mass poisoning cases had an impact on the development of the *quaestiones perpetuae,* but they also serve to illustrate why the government got involved in earlier periods in trials for poisoning, even though no law prohibited the act. The reasons include the importance of the people involved and the apparent threat created by the poisoners to the security of the *res publica.* This threat manifested itself in a different way for poisoning than for other offenses, that is, by the large numbers of people involved.

According to Livy, the first time *veneficium* was investigated publicly in Rome was in the fourth century. The reason this case ended up being investigated by the senators is that Rome was in peril. Livy recalls 331 B.C.E. as a *foedus annus* ("terrible year"). Pestilence was spreading in the city, and *primores civitatis* ("the leading citizens") began to fall ill. It was only when they became ill that an informer came to the aedile and claimed she would reveal the reason for the calamity. Having been granted immunity she told her tale.

> Tum patefactum muliebri fraude civitatem premi matronasque ea venena coquere, et si sequi extemplo velint manifesto deprehendi posse. Secuti indicem et coquentes quasdam medicamenta etre condita alia invenerunt. Quibus in forum delatis et ad viginti matronis, apud quas deprehensa erant, per viatorem accitis, duae ex eis, Cornelia ac Sergia, patricae utraque gentis, cum ea medicamenta salubria esse contenderent, ab confutante indice bibere iussae, ut se falsum commentam in conspectu omnium arguerent, spatio ad conloquendum sumpto, cum submoto populo rem ad ceteras retulissent, haud abnuentibus et illis bibere, epoto medicamento suamet ipsae fraude omnes interierunt.

Comprehensae extemplo earum comites magnum numerum matronarum indicaverunt; ex quibus ad centum septuaginta damnatae. Neque
de veneficiis ante eam diem Romae quaesitum est. Prodigii ea res loco
habita capitisque magis mentibus quam consceleratis similis visa.[26]

She then disclosed that the state was oppressed by womanly deceit and
that matrons were concocting these poisons, and if they wished to follow immediately, they would be able to catch them red-handed. They
followed the informer and found certain women brewing drugs, and
other drugs stored away. These concoctions were brought into the forum,
and some twenty matrons, in whose houses they had been discovered,
were summoned there by an appointed official. Two of their number,
Cornelia and Sergia, both of patrician families, asserted that these drugs
were salutary. On the informer giving them the lie, and bidding them
drink and prove her charges false in the sight of all, they took time to
confer, and after the crowd had been dismissed, they referred the question to the rest, and finding that they, like themselves, would not refuse
the draught, they all drank the drug and perished by their own wicked
practices. Their attendants, being instantly arrested, informed against a
large number of matrons, of whom around one hundred and seventy
were found guilty;[27] yet before that day there had never been a public
investigation concerning poisonings in Rome. Their act was regarded as
a prodigy and suggested madness rather than felonious intent.

That this case should have come to the attention of the entire senate is
not particularly surprising. The sheer number of people involved, both
victims and poisoners, indicates that the community should have been
concerned. This is generally true, but it may have been particularly true
in Rome, because the large number of poisoners implies a potential conspiracy, and the Romans were always greatly concerned about the possibility of conspiracy.[28] Thus, it may have been conspiracy to poison and not
only poisoning that brought about the public trial of those accused by the
attendants of the women present.

Another key element is that this event occurred at a time when the state
was in danger; thus, the actions of the accused were perceived to have
caused that danger or to have increased it. The threat to social order must
have seemed great because the pestilence was so widespread. The problem
is, as usual, the nature of our evidence. Naturally, the cases that are more
likely to be recorded in our sources, especially in Livy, who is our main
source for these poisoning cases, are those that pose a threat to the state.

The participation of women in this grand conspiracy, concocting probably what they thought were remedies, is another way in which this (and the trial in 180 discussed below) was a disruption of social order.

Of even greater importance than the numbers of women concocting poisons is that both the victims and the poisoners were of high social status. The poisoners—at least two of them—were of important patrician families. Furthermore, Livy reports that the informant did not come forward until *primores civitatis*[29] ("leading citizens of the state") became afflicted and died. This incident thus affected not only large numbers but also people well known to those making a decision to investigate the matter, that is, the senators.

The same two characteristics of the first trial were true for the trials in the second century as well. The next reported poisoning trial occurred in the year 184.

> Secundum comitia censorum consules praetoresque in provincias profecti praeter Q. Naevium, quem quattuor non minus menses, priusquam in Sardiniam iret, quaestiones veneficii, quarum magnam partem extra urbem per municipia conciliabulaque habuit, quia ita aptius visum erat, tenuerunt. Si Antiati Valerio credere libet, ad duo milia hominum damnavit. Et L. Postumius praetor, cui Tarentum provincia evenerat magnas pastorum coniurationes vindicavit, et reliquias Bacchanalium quaestionis cum cura exsecutus est.[30]

> After the election of the censors, the consuls and praetors departed for their provinces, except the praetor Q. Naevius, whom *quaestiones veneficii* detained for not less than four months before he could set out for Sardinia. A great part of these *quaestiones* he conducted beyond the city in the municipalities and rural communities, because this method seemed more convenient. If it is permitted to believe Valerius Antias, he condemned about two thousand people. And the praetor L. Postumius, to whom the province of Tarentum had fallen, avenged the great conspiracies of shepherds and prosecuted with care the remainders of the Bacchanalian investigations.

Here are some of the same elements as in the case of 331. First, a large number of people were involved; second, although no pestilence raged, these poisonings still had an impact on state security. At the same time as Naevius was investigating these poisoning cases, L. Postumius was prosecuting what was left of the Bacchanalian conspirators. The Bacchanalian conspiracy, begun a few years earlier, must have lent credence to rumors of the sort that brought about an investigation such as the poisoning cases Naevius investigated. If such large numbers were involved, these poisonings may have been considered another conspiracy, especially coming on the tail end of the Bacchanalian.[31] The senators therefore decided that the event was important enough to warrant an investigation.

Poisoning trials occurred again a few years later. In 180 the senate ordered an investigation into poisonings that were thought to have something to do with the contemporaneous pestilence, much like the case of 331. By the time *quaestiones* were established, the pestilence had lasted three years and during the previous year was serious enough to have limited the ability of the state to raise an army. When Livy first mentions the event, he writes of prodigies, national sacrifices, not enough people in the army, and too many funerals all over Italy. Then in 180 people are suspected to be the cause. It was in this year that a praetor and a consul "and many other illustrious men of all ranks" succumbed to the pestilence.

Praetor Ti. Minucius et haud ita multo post consul C. Calpurnius moritur, multique alii omnium ordinum illustres viri. Postremo prodigii loco ea clades haberi coepta est. C. Servilius pontifex maximus piacula irae deum conquirere iussus decemviri libros inspicere, consul Apollini Aesculapio Saluti dona vovere et dare signa inaurata quae vovit deditque. Decemviri supplicationem in biduum valetudinis causa in urbe et per omnia fora coniciliabulaque edixerunt; maiores duodecim annis omnes coronati et lauream in manu tenentes supplicaverunt. Fraudis quoque humanae insinuaverat suspicio animis; et veneficii quaestio ex senatus consulto, quod in urbe propiusve urbem decem milibus passuum esset commissum, C. Claudio praetori, qui in locum Ti. Minucii erat suffectus, ultra decimum lapidem per fora conciliabulaque C. Maenio, priusquam in Sardiniam provinciam traiceret, decreta. Suspecta consulis erat mors maxime. Necatus a Quarta Hostilia uxore dicebatur. Ut quidem filius eius Q. Fulvius Flaccus in locum vitrici consul est declaratus, aliquanto magis infamis mors Pisonis coepit esse; et testis exsistebant qui post declaratos consules Albinum et Pisonem, quibus comitiis Flaccus tulerat repulsam et exprobratum ei a matre dicerent quod iam ei tertium negatus consulatus petenti esset, et adiecisse, pararet se ad petendum: intra duos menses effecturam ut consul fieret. Inter multa alia testimonia ad causam pertinentia haec quoque vox, nimis vero eventu comprobata, valuit cur Hostilia damnaretur.[32]

The praetor Tiberius Minucius died and not much later the consul C. Calpurnius, and many other distinguished men of all ranks. Finally, the disaster came to be regarded as a portent. C. Servilius, the *pontifex maximus,* was directed to inquire into the manner of averting the wrath of the gods and the decemvirs to look into the Books; the consul was ordered to vow gifts and to give gilded statues to Apollo, Aesculapius, and Salus; these he vowed and gave. The decemvirs vowed a two-day period of prayer for health not only in the city but in all the rural settlements and communities; all people above the age of twelve, wearing garlands and carrying laurel branches in their hands, made the supplication. Moreover, the suspicion of human deceit insinuated itself into people's minds, and the investigation of the poisonings that had taken place in the city or nearer to it than ten miles was, by decree of the senate, entrusted to the praetor C. Claudius, who had been chosen to succeed Tiberius Minucius [who had died of the pestilence], and beyond the tenth milestone throughout the rural settlements and communities to C. Maenius before he departed for Sardinia. The death of the consul was especially suspicious. He was said to have been killed by his wife, Quarta Hostilia. When indeed her son Q. Fulvius Flaccus was proclaimed consul in place of his stepfather, the death of Piso began to cause many more ugly rumors; and witnesses came forth who said that after Albinus and Piso had been declared consuls at an election in which Flaccus had suffered defeat, Flaccus had been upbraided by his mother because this was now the third time that his candidacy for the consulship had been refused; let him, she added, prepare to apply again: within two months she would bring it to pass that he should become consul. Among much other testimony bearing on the case, this one speech, being all too well confirmed by the actual result, availed to bring about the conviction of Hostilia.

This poisoning case contributes to our understanding of the motivations for a public trial in an important way. We can see in it the same qualities of the earlier trials: the large numbers of victims and culprits and the senate's involvement after more important citizens were affected by the trial. Moreover, the way Livy reports this case demonstrates that the connection between public trials and citizens of high status is based in a true reflection of the way the public courts worked in the middle republic.

A year passed between Livy's first mention of the case in 181, when "the pestilence was so severe in the country and in the villages and in the city that Libitina [goddess of death, corpses, and funerals] could scarce take care of so many funerals,"[33] and the establishment of the *quaestio* in 180. During this year the senate carried on business as usual, seeing embassies from the Greek east and fighting various battles (despite the manpower shortage). Only when magistrates began to be afflicted did the actions of the senate turn toward a judicial investigation. The reason for this may be that no offense was reported to the senate before 180, but Livy's presentation of the event is instructive. He indicates specific ways the pestilence and poisoning disrupted the running of the state when he introduces the trial in this way: "In the beginning of this spring, while the levy was detaining the new consuls in Rome and then the death of one and the election to choose a new consul in his place had caused delay in all business of the state."[34] Thus, the government officials became involved not only because people they knew were involved, but also because the victims themselves were central to the running of the *res publica*. Their deaths had a significant impact on the governing of Rome.

Thus, the status of the people involved was a motivating factor for public trials. The senators were concerned about the administration and the safety of the *res publica* and they believed—not unjustly—that their own welfare was inextricably tied to the welfare of the state and vice versa. This belief was especially true when the victims of homicide were magistrates, for that would disturb the administration of the state. The discussion, by Livy, of the pestilence in the previous year recorded two separate incidents when generals had complained that the pestilence had caused a scarcity in the number of soldiers available to them, and still no investigation had been begun.[35] Admittedly, these investigations were customarily begun when misdeeds were reported to an official of the government, and this may not have happened earlier, yet it does seem striking that the Romans were not worried about humans committing offenses until members of the senatorial class were killed.

This status-oriented procedure is found not only in the discussion of the actual cases but also in general discussions of public law. Polybius reveals the importance of status in Roman penal law when he writes, "It is by the people then, in many cases, that offenses punishable by a fine are tried when the accused have held the highest office."[36] Here it is the procedure regarding fines that Polybius represents as being unequal, but he shows that the ideology of inequality existed in the legal mechanisms or at least in the customary practices. This same circumstance is reflected in the early empire in the trial of Piso, when Tiberius would allow the trial to take place in the senate because of the status of the victim.[37]

There is some indication that poisoning may have come to be tried more regularly in the middle of the second century, even before the creation of a *quaestio perpetua* for the trial of poisoners, and yet the motivation for a public trial seems to be the same: the status of the participants. The case of Publilia and Licinia, however, also illustrates that the government was not the only venue for homicide-related offenses, perhaps especially when these offenses had been committed by women:

> De veneficiis quaesitum. Publilia et Licinia, nobiles feminae, quae viros suos consulares necasse insimulabantur, cognita causa, cum praetori praedes vades dedissent, cognatorum decreto necatae sunt.[38]

> Investigation of poisoning. Publilia and Licinia, noble women, who were being accused of killing their ex-consul husbands, when the case was known, when they gave sureties to the Praetor, were put to death by the decision of their relatives.

Valerius Maximus also reports this case to us.

> Publicia autem, quae Postumium Albinum consulem, item Licinia, quae Claudium Asellem viros suos veneno necaverant, propinquorum decreto strangulatae sunt: non enim putaverunt severissimi viri in tam evidenti scelere longum publicae quaestionis tempus expectandum. Itaque quarum innocentium defensores fuissent, sontium mature vindices extiterunt.[39]

> Publicia [i.e., Publilia], however, who was married to the consul Postumius Albinus, and Licinia, who was married to Claudius Aselles, killed their husbands with poison, and by the decision of their relatives they were strangled. For the most severe men did not think they should wait for the long time of a public *quaestio* in the face of such evident wickedness. Because there were defenders of their innocence, people to offer surety were quickly found.

Before concluding the discussion of *veneficium*, and having examined the specific cases, attention needs to be given to the question of the importance of magic in these trials. While the word *veneficium* is properly translated as "poisoning," it (as does φαρμᾰκείᾱ) also includes the notion of magic potion or spell. What impact the magic aspect of *veneficium* had on the trials of the middle republic is difficult to assess. The problem derives both from our limited knowledge of the trials that occurred and from the development in the meaning of the words over the course of the republic.[40] Early in Roman history, poisoning may have been inseparable from magic. Later, however, the word *venenum* (whence the word *veneficium* is derived) could be used synonymously with *medicamentum* or "medication" in an apparently profane usage. When the trials to be discussed first took place, both of these meanings—poison and medicine—were possible. The trials that took place later in the permanent public courts *de veneficiis* seem to have had nothing to do with magic, even though the connection between *veneficium* and magic lasted well into the empire.

The relevance of magic to the institution of a public investigation was minimal at best. The trial of 180 came on the heels of many religious rites aimed at averting the danger of the pestilence, which might seem to indicate a more mystical quality to this case. But about the poisoning investigations themselves, Livy says that the suspicion of human fraud, not any mystical activity, came to people's minds. Furthermore, in the case of 331, it seems obvious that the women had no intention to poison. They were probably trying to cure people of the disease, not kill them. They were, or so they thought, creating medicine. Thus, when it was suggested that they drink the potion they had concocted, they barely hesitated.[41] In addition, in this case, too, it was *fraus* ("deceit"), not magic, that was to blame. This is not to say that the poisoning cases were entirely free from the concept of magic, for the term *veneficium* did have those supernatural connotations. Nevertheless, the magic aspect of *veneficium* did not cause these cases to be tried publicly. The particular aspects of these poisoning cases that caused a public trial were that they involved large numbers of people and, more importantly, that they involved people of high status.

PARRICIDE

Although both the *sicarii* and the poisoners found themselves tried in public courts before the creation of the *quaestiones perpetuae,* there existed no laws concerning them before the creation of these standing courts. In the entire period of three hundred years from the XII Tables until the creation of the *quaestiones perpetuae,* only one general law that regulated any form of homicide or homicide related offense was promulgated in Rome, so far as the evidence indicates. This law, perhaps promulgated around 200, instituted a particularly atrocious punishment for parricide.[42]

Poena parricidii . . . instituta est, ut parricida virgis sanguineis verbera-
tus deinde culleo insuatur cum cane, gallo gallinaceo et vipera et simia:
deinde in mare profundum culleus iactatur.[43]

A punishment was instituted for parricide: that a parricide is flogged,
with blood-colored rods, then sewn up in a sack (*culleus*) with a dog, a
dunghill cock, a viper, and a monkey; then the sack is thrown into the
depths of the sea.

Notice that this law did not define the offense, nor did it explain how the
offense should be prosecuted. The primary concern of the legislator was
not the legal aspect of trial, but the propitiation of the gods. Cloud noted
the following:

The *culleus* penalty has the hallmarks of a *procuratio prodigii:* its purpose
is not so much to deter the parricidally inclined but to avert the anger
of heaven against the community, once the unnatural crime has been
perpetrated.[44]

As Cloud argued, the promulgation of this law was more the result of the
attempt to make Rome safe by propitiating the gods than to define a crime
in a legal context.[45]

Because the only legislation promulgated about any type of homicide
concerned parricide, the community of Rome must have had a particular
interest in seeing that act punished. The law is but one type of evidence that
demonstrates the severity of this offense and the danger inherent in it. In
addition to the law, the sources record trials of parricide throughout Roman history. These trials, and the way parricide is discussed by the sources,
demonstrate that public judicial activity in parricide can be explained in
part by the horror the act evokes.

The evidence about parricide trials in the republic demonstrates the
atrocity that this offense was thought to be.

Non ita multis ante annis aiunt T. Caelium quendam Terracinensem,
hominem non obscurum, cum cenatus cubitum in idem conclave cum
duobus adulescentibus filiis isset, inventum esse mane iugulatum. Cum
neque servus quisquam reperiretur neque liber ad quem ea suspicio
pertineret, id aetatis autem duo filii propter cubantes ne sensisse quidem
se dicerent, nomina filiorum de parricidio delata sunt . . . Tamen, cum

planum iudicibus esset factum aperto ostio dormientis eos repertos esse, iudicio absoluti adulescentes et suspicione omni liberati sunt. Nemo enim putabat quemquam esse qui, cum omnia divina atque humana iura scelere nefario polluisset, somnum statim capere potuisset, propterea quod qui tantum facinus commiserunt non modo sine cura quiescere sed ne spirare quidem sine metu possunt.[46]

There is a story that not many years ago a certain Titus Caelius of Tarracina, a not obscure man, after he had dined and had gone to bed in the same room as his two grown-up sons, in the morning he was found dead with his throat cut. Because neither any slave nor any free man could be found on whom suspicion might have fallen, while the two grown-up sons who slept near their father declared that they had not noticed anything, they were indicted for parricide. . . . Because it was made clear to the judges, however, that the young men had been found asleep when the door was opened, they were acquitted and freed from all suspicion. For no one thought there would be anyone who, after he had violated all human and divine laws by an impious offense, would be able to go to sleep immediately, because those who have committed such a deed are not only unable to rest without anxiety, but they cannot even breathe without fear.

The judges were unable to believe that any children could sleep after killing their own father, and so they acquitted the sons. Such an attitude toward parricide helps to explain why it was an offense of which the public courts took cognizance.[47]

The atrocity of the idea of parricide is also evident in the rhetorical use of it. Suetonius reports that because of Julius Caesar's assassination, the senate voted to call the ides of March "the day of parricide."[48] By using the term *parricidium,* the political opponents of the assassins were able to evoke the sense of horror that the Roman audience would have felt at the act. Plutarch also reports the seriousness of the crime. He claims that Romulus did not write a law about patricide because it was inconceivable to him that such an offense would be committed.[49] Whether this was Romulus' motivation is not as important as the fact that it was later considered to be his motivation. Patricide was so terrible that it was incomprehensible.

The Roman belief in the atrocity of the act is unquestionable and provides substantive motivation for a public trial. I propose, however, an additional motivating factor of a public trial that is less obvious, namely, that a reason for public trials for parricide can be found in procedural and ideological considerations. The main alternative to public action was the practice of domestic jurisdiction (as seen in the case of Publilia and Licinia, above). When the victim of a parricide was a father, this familial jurisdiction was at least curtailed if not completely eliminated, and so some other mechanism was required. Furthermore, even if a different family member was killed, it may have indicated that the *pater familias* was not strong enough to carry out his duty. If a killing could occur within the family, perhaps the society had little trust that the *pater* would have had authority in punishing the killer. The position of the *pater* in the family was absolutely central to the family's functioning, and so his absence or weakness seems a likely reason for parricide trials to enter the public sphere.[50]

Furthermore, as demonstrated in Chapter Two, the stability of individual families was necessary for the stability of the *res publica*. If a father lost his capacity to control the behavior of his own family members, either because of his own death or because one family member killed another, then he could not have been a reliable building block for the *res publica* itself. Thus, if the act of parricide did not directly remove a *pater* from his position in the family, it indicated that he was unsuitable for a position in the *res publica*. If he could not act, then his role needed to be assumed by the community.

Valerius Maximus presents us with an example of how a family should have handled such matters before a parricide was ever committed. He tells of a certain Lucius Gellius who called a *consilium* together to hear charges laid against his son. The son was alleged to have committed adultery with his stepmother and to have attempted to kill his father.[51] It was the responsibility of the family, particularly of the father, to correct misbehavior. If Gellius' son had succeeded in committing parricide, then the family would have been shown to have been unable to deal with its own members and some other mechanism would have been necessary.

Versions of the legend of Horatius, who killed his sister,[52] also reveal that the act of parricide was of concern to the government. Different versions reveal different charges laid against Horatius. One is parricide; the other is *perduellio* ("treason"). Significant conclusions can be derived from the fact that the name by which the offense was called does not seem to have affected the story of the trial. The ancient authors who claim that the charge was parricide, an offense of an apparently more domestic nature than *perduellio*, do not change other aspects of the story. The implication is that parricide could be as disruptive to the community as *perduellio*. This is probably because both of these acts disrupted the fabric of society, and, furthermore, they did so in a way that simple murder did not.

Even the strange acts of Quintus Fabius Maximus make sense as an act of parricide when one considers one of the main offenses in the act to be the disruption of the family unit, a building block of the republic. As we saw in Chapter Two, with the help of two of his slaves whom he subsequently set free, Q. Fabius Maximus killed his own son.[53]

In later years, the act of parricide would be defined by lawcodes by listing the various possible familial relationships between the victim and the perpetrator, but during the second century, the act was not defined by the law. The specific family members listed in the later laws changed over time, but no version of the parricide laws themselves included sons among the possible victims.[54] The reason is that the Roman father had the ideological right to put his children to death. Fabius Maximus lost that right because of the manner by which he carried out the killing, and thus, he could be charged with and convicted of parricide.[55] That governing officials would react to any of these procedural failings on the part of the father suggests that they had a vested interest in individual families functioning according to contemporary norms and that the family's stability was essential for the stability of the *res publica*.

Parricide may also have been dangerous to the community for religious reasons; the punishment of the sack was instituted to expiate any potential pollution the culprit attracted. The punishment remained the standard punishment for parricide at least until the last few years of the republic, and it appeared again in the imperial period.[56] Furthermore, the status of the victims seems to have been an issue in the trials of parricide as in trials for other offenses. Horatius was a hero, Titus Caelius was a *homo non obscurus*. This does not mean that high status necessarily resulted in a public trial. Lucius Gellius had been a censor, but he was able to call upon his peers to conduct a private investigation of his son.[57] But the sources record no parricide cases tried in a public venue in Rome of lower-class Romans.[58] Parricide was also the most atrocious act imaginable, and for all these reasons, trial of parricide could occur in a public venue long before the creation of the *quaestiones perpetuae*.

Parricide and the other offenses that were actionable in a public venue before the advent of the relatively more regular judicial system starting in the mid second century should not be considered crimes in the sense of being a collection of acts that were illegal and punishment for which was defined by law. They only became actionable in specific instances because of the specific circumstances to which the government—through the senate, the people, and individual magistrates—was responding. As such, none of them were really crimes. The only near exception to this was the person who killed a relative because a law did exist that articulated a punishment for the offense. Even without the laws, however, there are certain offenses that do seem to have entered into the public venue in a more regular way over time. Murder was not one of these.

Even after the creation of the *quaestiones perpetuae,* murder was not a crime. By the time Sulla was about to enter his unconstitutional dictatorship in 81, though, committing parricide, wielding a weapon with the intent to commit theft or kill someone, and poisoning someone had become crimes. It is unfortunate that the circumstances for the creation of each *quaestio perpetua* (each with specific supervision over each of these offenses) is lost, because that means the specific motivation for each court is lost. Because it is clear from other cases that there always was a specific and often a personal motivation, this information would have been useful. Nonetheless, it seems likely that the same general motivations that created the temporary courts informed the decision to create the permanent ones.

In the case of one homicide-related offense, the motivation of the promulgator of the law that created the court is reported. This is the *quaestio ne de capite civium,* the so-called judicial murder court, created by Gaius Gracchus. In this court is illustrated the idea of the relationship between homicide and the officials and institutions of the *res publica,* and so it shall be discussed in the next chapter.

FIVE

CAPITAL JURISDICTION, 449–81 B.C.E.

The Romans are infamous in history for their many ingenious methods of killing and for the abundance of the killing that took place during their regime. Much of this killing, however, was not a product of the republic. Indeed, what is so striking about the republic in this regard is that, outside of war and the military, officials and institutions of republican government seldom killed anyone.[1] Even the gladiatorial games of the republic are striking in how few deaths took place compared with the number of deaths in such games during the empire.

Furthermore, capital punishment included not just the literal *caput* ("head") but also loss of citizenship, and so "capital punishment" did not even necessarily mean death. In addition, when a citizen was condemned to death in an assembly or by a *quaestio,* that citizen could (and apparently nearly always did) choose to leave Rome at any point during the judicial proceedings—up until the very last moment—and thus suffer exile rather than death.[2] From a modern perspective, then, the Romans were less barbaric than the United States is today with its continued employment of capital punishment, yet the reason for the rarity of death as a punishment was not so much a matter of humanity as a matter of the perceived role of the government, the extent of its power, and the nature of Roman politics.

As a general rule the Romans did not want their government to have control over the life of a citizen. The result of such thinking was that throughout the republic, the power to kill lay in the hands of the people privately; as individuals involved in a dispute beyond the purview of the government; or publicly, grouped together in an assembly. In Chapter Three I argued that the Romans originally limited the power to kill citizens to the Roman assemblies because the assemblies were the institutions that most closely resembled the community as a whole. This is not to say that the assembly was not also an institution of government, but only that it served as the most broad representation of the community. This practice continued over the course of the next two hundred and fifty years.[3] The *iudicia populi* ("courts of the people"), as the assemblies came to be known in the times they dealt with judicial matters, were almost the exclusive locations of capital trials, and yet there are almost no examples of executions resulting from condemnations in these assemblies. "In fact, since the death of M. Manlius Capitolinus, in 384, no example of the execution of a death sentence pronounced by the assembly is recorded in history."[4]

The early second century B.C.E., as an outgrowth of imperial expansion, saw the employment of ad hoc *quaestiones* ("investigations") in which magistrates or a small group of senators would be selected by the people and by the senate to respond to emergency situations. Magistrates or a special commission would be appointed to investigate (*quaerere*) a reported offense, and these men would sometimes then temporarily wield the people's power to condemn to death. This development was almost certainly a product of the growing number of Roman citizens.[5] Some of these resulted in judicial decisions that ended with capital punishment. In a few cases, the senate, without the authority of the people, assigned magistrates to conduct these *quaestiones,* and they may have become a relatively regular occurrence by the mid second century.

These temporary *quaestiones* established by the senate alone originally met with little resistance, but when the senate began, starting in 149 B.C.E., to establish regular standing courts (*quaestiones perpetuae*) for particular offenses, some with capital jurisdiction, there was a backlash. The creation and eventual permanent status of courts with capital jurisdiction created by the senate reveals an increased centralization of power, but the backlash reveals how attempts at increasing the government's responsibilities, even for practical reasons, met with ideological obstacles. Before turning to the courts that predated these *quaestiones,* however, it will be fruitful to examine the responsibilities of those officials whose role was connected explicitly to capital punishment: the *quaestores parricidii* and the *tresviri capitales.*

QUAESTORES PARRICIDII

The very existence of these officials has the potential to bring into doubt the claim in this chapter that the Romans did not want officials or institutions of the government (with the exception of the assemblies) to have the power to kill citizens. With titles like the "three men in charge of capital matters" and the "quaestors in charge of parricide" (possibly translatable as "investigators of homicide"), these officials suggest precisely an official interest in capital matters. A closer examination of their roles and responsibilities, however, reveals the hesitancy with which the government, particularly individual magistrates, punished citizens with death.

The *quaestores parricidii* likely date to the earliest periods of Roman history and ceased to function around the beginning of the third century B.C.E.[6] Unfortunately, the evidence about them is limited and contradictory, making it impossible to determine, with any certainty, their precise role. With regard to the question of the government and its ability to punish citizens with death, the contradictory nature of the evidence is regrettable. Nevertheless, in considering possible scenarios, it seems almost impossible that despite their title, these officials represent any regular interest or ability on the part of the government to decide upon and to execute capital punishment in the early centuries of the republic.

The ancient confusion about these officials is evident in the emperor Justinian's compilation of the *Digest,* in the fifth century C.E. The jurist Ulpian indicates that the *quaestores parricidii* were created during the monarchy.[7] Meanwhile, the jurist Pomponius, also quoted in the *Digest,* seems to contradict the claim of monarchic origins when he implies that the *quaestores* were a product of the republic and not of the monarchy. Pomponius furthermore suggests that the *quaestores parricidii* are uniquely suited to the republic because the Romans did not choose to grant the power to kill to regular Roman officials:

Et quia, ut diximus, de capite civis romani iniussu populi non erat lege permissum consulibus ius dicere, propterea quaestores constituebantur a populo, qui capitalibus rebus praeessent: hi appellabantur quaestores parricidii, quorum etiam meminit lex duodecim tabularum.[8]

And because, as we have said, it was not permitted to the consuls to give judgment concerning the *caput* of a Roman citizen without the judgment of the people, for that reason *quaestores* used to be constituted by the people; [these officials] would preside over capital matters: these used to be called *quaestores paricidii,* of whom even a law of the XII Tables speaks.

If Pomponius is right, the *quaestores paricidii* may have been chosen by the people to act as judges on a capital charge. If this was the case, these officials would have had to have been appointed in an ad hoc manner to deal with exigent circumstances; otherwise, there would have been no difference between selecting *quaestores parricidii* and allowing any other magistrate in Rome the power to kill Roman citizens without the authority of the people, which the Romans were remarkably loath to do (and which would contradict the implications of Pomponius' own statement). If Pomponius is right, in particular circumstances the people of Rome would have appointed a body of men — almost certainly senators — to investigate serious accusations and to determine a punishment for the offenders. Given their title, this punishment could have been capital. If the task of these officials as judges was ad hoc, they should be more properly associated with the *quaestiones extraordinariae* than with the *tresviri capitales,* with whom they are explicitly connected by Varro,[9] which means that other scenarios are possible.

Another report from some ancient sources is that the *quaestores parricidii* were the same officials as the regular quaestors who functioned as assistants, primarily with regard to finances, to the consuls. If this is so, they must have constituted a regular magistracy.[10] Livy's report about the legend of the prosecution of Spurius Cassius might then be taken as evidence for the role of the *quaestores parricidii.* If so, they did not themselves act as judges but rather brought cases before the assembly, in other words, before the citizens of Rome who ideally were supposed to have been the only venue for the trial of capital offenses. According to the legend, when his term of office expired, Spurius Cassius was condemned and put to death. Livy found different versions:

> Invenio apud quosdam, idque propius fidem est, a quaestoribus Caesone Fabio et L. Valerio diem dictam perduellionis, damnatumque populi iudicio, dirutas publice aedes.[11]

> I find among other authors, the more believable story, that on the day set for the trial by the *quaestores* Fabius Caeso and Lucius Valerius, he was condemned by a court of the people on the charge of *perduellio* ["treason"].

If this is an example of how the *quaestores parricidii* functioned, it suggests that they did not act independently of the people. It also suggests that the ancient authors who perceived them as the quaestors, largely treasurers and assistants of the consuls, may have been correct.

The very contradictions that fill the sources suggest that later Romans themselves could make little of these *quaestores.* An attempt to reconcile all the pieces creates a picture something like this: originally (either in the monarchy or in the republic), the *quaestores parricidii* (either temporary officials appointed in an ad hoc way or permanent officials whose other job was to function as assistants to the consuls and perhaps, earlier, to the kings) had jurisdiction over the act of parricide, presumably killing a citizen, unless the meaning of the term had already evolved before the creation of the *quaestores*.[12] Eventually they took on responsibility not only for homicide but for *maleficia* ("bad deeds") more generally, until finally they were replaced (or this particular aspect of their job was taken over) by the *tresviri capitales,* whose functions, as we shall see, do not seem to have been the same.

Modern scholars reject the majority of the interpretations of the ancient jurists and other ancient authors, and some of these scholars articulate a role for the *quaestores parricidii* that is based simply on their title. Their conclusions possess a certain appeal. The term *parricidii* is associated with the legislation of Numa on intentional and unintentional homicide (as seen in Chapter One). The *quaestores*' responsibility in the newly introduced differentiation between intentional and unintentional killing was to help decide whether any one particular act of homicide was unintentional or not and therefore what the consequences of such an act were to be. Thus, the *quaestores parricidii* assisted private individuals engaged in disputes to determine the appropriate kind of vengeance but probably not to exact it.[13]

This scenario is appealing and logical, and one would like to accept it despite the absence of evidence. Whatever the role of these *quaestores*, however, it seems supremely unlikely that the Romans had officials with regular jurisdiction from the monarchy or the beginning of the republic who possessed independent authority to investigate a culprit and then to punish him or her with death without the authority of the people. Such a capacity to act would not only contradict the implications of Pomponius' claim, that the office was created because the Romans did not want to grant such powers to superior magistrates, but it would also contradict Roman attitudes about granting such power to government officials.

TRESVIRI CAPITALES

The *quaestores parricidii* apparently ceased to exist sometime in the third century, possibly a little earlier, and perhaps were replaced by the *tresviri capitales* ("three men in charge of capital matters").[14] The *tresviri capitales* are better known than the former but still the subject of much scholarly debate, because, unfortunately, evidence for their creation appears only in the summary of Book Eleven of Livy's work;[15] the complete book is lost and so, too, is the reason for the creation of the *tresviri capitales* and the description of their responsibilities. The implications of their responsibilities require some consideration to understand the capacity of Roman government to punish with death.

The conclusions here are complicated by the nature of the evidence as well as by its many lacunae. Nonetheless, the conclusions will be as follows: Because the *tresviri* were not judges of citizens, the decision to put a citizen to death did not lay in their hands. Although they supervised executions, there is no evidence that they ordered the execution of any citizens on their own authority during the time period covered in this book. Finally, their creation does not represent a change in the general Roman desire to keep the power to kill as much as possible out of the hands of individual government officials and institutions.

Starting with a negative may seem to be an unusual way to begin a job description, but the excellent work of Wolfgang Kunkel (*Untersuchungen zur Entwicklung des römischen Kriminalverfahrens in vorsullanischer Zeit*) has influenced all subsequent discussions of the *tresviri capitales,* and Kunkel argued that the *tresviri* were judges of ordinary citizens who committed nonpolitical crimes. That the *tresviri capitales* were not judges of citizens, however, has been argued recently and persuasively by Cosimo Cascione in his thorough investigation of these officials: *Tresviri capitales: Storia di una magistratura minore.*[16] Cascione convincingly rejects Kunkel's theory that the *tresviri* had a regular capital judicial authority over Roman citizens.[17]

The absence of a capital criminal judicial jurisdiction for the *tresviri,* however, does not entirely resolve the issue at stake in this chapter. Although the *tresviri* did not preside over capital cases involving citizens, they do seem to have had the responsibility for supervising the executions of citizens condemned to death at the order of others.[18] In fact, it seems possible that their title came from the fact that they were in charge of supervising government executions.[19] Their activity in this sphere, however, may not have been as great as we are sometimes led to believe.

One reason in support of this claim is that the variety of jobs performed by these officials suggests that they could seldom have had enough time. Their original title was that of *tresviri nocturni,* and their job continued to include helping to ensure public safety in the city during the nighttime.[20] This included, and was probably primarily, prevention of the spread of fires, a constant threat to safety in the city in republican Rome.[21] They and their subordinates were also apparently supposed to keep their eyes open for threats of any other kind[22] and to supervise the prison.[23] They even served as police in the sense that misdeeds by the nonelite classes of Roman citizens, and especially by slaves and foreigners, could be brought to their attention by private individuals.[24] In addition they might have had some authority to take a more active role in patrolling the streets for wrongdoers,[25] including the apprehension of runaway slaves.[26] Thus, the *tresviri capitales* seem to have been catch-all officials for whom a general look-out for the well-being of the city was their primary role. Their role as executioners must have been seldom played.

In addition to their being otherwise occupied, there is not a single example of an execution of a citizen supervised by the *tresviri* during the entire period covered in this book.[27] If it were not for their provocative title and for their later supervision of executions, there would be no reason to assume that they had this task. The absence of evidence is not conclusive in this regard, but it is suggestive. Furthermore, scholars would do well to avoid anachronism in attempting to understand the impact and the responsibility of the *tresviri*. Tacitus, writing at the beginning of the second century C.E., uses the words *supplicium triumvirale* or "triumviral punishment" about the strangulation of Sejanus' children during the early empire. The use of this term suits Tacitus' usual brilliant eloquence in intensifying the horror of the scene he is describing. It seems perilous, however, to use the term to speak about triumviral activity under a different form of government around two hundred years earlier, because such a use implies that in the second and early first centuries B.C.E., the numbers of executions supervised by the *tresviri* were so great and important that the officials gave the executions their name.

Nonetheless, one of the tasks of the *tresviri capitales* was that of supervising executions,[28] and the implications of this must be considered despite the hyperbole of "*supplicium triumvirale.*" Claire Lovisi, in her fascinating book on the penalty of death, has seen the creation of the *tresviri capitales* as somewhat of a revolutionary change in the Roman government's employment of death as a penalty. She argues that with the creation of the *tresviri*, the Romans abandoned private executions based on vengeance and instead employed state executions.[29] This conclusion follows from her faith in her own conclusions about the role of the *quaestores parricidii* as arbitrators.[30] Because she sees the *quaestores parricidii* with a responsibility to help arbitrate private disputes, and the *tresviri* as employers of public punishments, she is able to see a dramatic shift between private vengeance and official punishment.

She associates the creation of the *tresviri* with what she sees as the employment of three new forms of execution imposed by the government on citizens over the course of that same century: the punishment of the sack for parricide,[31] the introduction of the Carthaginian practice of crucifixion, and the employment of strangulation.[32] The three forms of execution about which she writes, however, make problematic the conclusions about growing government responsibility for executing citizens.

One form of execution is crucifixion, but, as she acknowledges, crucifixion is used for punishing slaves; thus, it should not be seen as evidence of a growing state responsibility in the execution of citizens.[33] The only two republican examples of citizen crucifixions not only do not take place in Rome but are exceptional in other ways. One of them is the execution by the governor of Sicily, Verres, of a man accused of spying for Spartacus.[34] An aide of a rebellious slave must be deserving of servile punishments. In addition, Verres himself was no paragon of ethics, as is suggested by the source of this information: a speech against him on a charge of provincial extortion. Thus, his choice of punishments should not be seen as the norm. The other exceptional case was Scipio Africanus' punishment of deserters at the end of the Second Punic War.[35] If Lovisi is correct that crucifixion is a method of punishment the Romans learned from the Carthaginians,[36] this was a particularly suitable punishment after the great war between Rome and Carthage. Furthermore, "The war had immeasurably intensified the cruelty employed to maintain military discipline,"[37] and this particular punishment never became a norm in military situations after this one event.

Another form of execution that may have come into existence at the end of the century is the employment of the sack for parricides ("kin-killers"),[38] but here the circumstances have more to do with the government's responsibility for religious expiation than with the execution of citizens.[39] Lovisi, taking her cue from Tacitus,[40] refers to strangulation as the *supplicium triumvirale*[41] and assumes it exists this early because it is a triumviral punishment. She does not, however, cite the evidence for its introduction at this early of a date, and there are no examples before 63 B.C.E. Because crucifixion was for slaves, because the *culleus* ("sack") was a form of expiation, and because the phrase *supplicium triumvirale* is probably anachronistic, it seems unlikely that the authority to kill citizens was being directly asserted by the government in any significant way with the creation of the *tresviri capitales.*

IUDICIA POPULI

My suspicions about the activities of the *tresviri* rest in part on the belief that in the early third century, the right to kill did lie almost exclusively in the hands of the people as a whole. This was probably true to a large degree even later. Polybius, who lived in Rome in the second century,[42] wrote:

> κρίνει μὲν οὖν ὁ δῆμος καὶ διαφόρου πολλάκις, ὅταν ἀξιόχρεων ᾖ τὸ τίμημα τῆς ἀδικίας, καὶ μάλιστα τοὺς τὰς ἐπιφανεῖς ἐσχηκότας ἀρχάς. θανάτου δὲ κρίνει μόνος.

> It is by the people then, in many cases, that offenses punishable by a fine are tried when the accused have held the highest office; and they are the only court that may try on capital charges.[43]

Polybius himself knows of an exception to this rule, yet this is the way he chooses to state the degree of popular sovereignty at Rome. Polybius' slight inaccuracy suggests a couple of possibilities. One is that while Polybius lived in Rome the assemblies were still the most common form of trial in which the penalty of death was a probable consequence of conviction. The other possibility is that the Romans of the mid second century believed that punishing a citizen with death was the purview of the people and they did not think that this rule was in jeopardy from the institutions to be discussed below. If Polybius and his contemporaries believed this without cause, then the ideology of this limitation on republican government must have been just as strong as if the assemblies still were the main institutions for capital trials.

It does not seem to have mattered which magistrate presided over a *iudicium populi* (as the assemblies could be called when functioning as courts) or indeed in which assembly the people met; it only mattered that the people were present. Trials could take place in the *comitia centuriata* or in the *concilium plebis.*[44] The latter could try cases of appeal but also cases of first instance.[45] This flexibility suggests that the jurisdiction of the people in capital trials mattered more than the jurisdiction of any one particular magistrate.[46]

Despite the flexibility of the *iudicia populi,* the administration of Rome—over time—made the ideal of popular control of capital punishment a difficult one to maintain. While ideologically important, it became impractical for assemblies to deal with every case that arose. From Polybius' point of view, however, even when other methods of trial were used, the people still had a voice in decision-making. He writes,

τὰς δ᾽ ὁλοσχερεστάτας καὶ μεγίστας ζητήσεις καὶ διορθώσεις τῶν ἁμαρτανομένων κατὰ τῆς πολιτείας, οἷς θάνατος ἀκολουθεῖ τὸ πρόστιμον, οὐ δύναται συντελεῖν, ἂν μὴ συνεπικυρώσῃ τὸ προβεβουλευμένον ὁ δῆμος.

The senate cannot carry out inquiries into the most grave and important offenses against the state, punishable with death, and their correction unless the decree of the senate is confirmed by the people.[47]

The inquiries of which Polybius speaks are the *quaestiones* (known among modern scholars as *quaestiones extraordinariae*). Some instances confirm Polybius' claim. In 141 the consul Servilius was placed in charge of investigating Hostilius Tubulus for taking bribes while he presided over a *quaestio inter sicarios.* An investigation was first called for in the plebeian assembly, and subsequently the senate appointed the consuls to investigate.[48] The senate and the people (SPQR) shared the power of assigning the task to the consuls, and the consuls on the authority of the senate and the people had capital jurisdiction.

Evidence of this joint responsibility for setting up these *quaestiones* may go as far back as the fifth century. In 413 the consuls were ordered to investigate the killing of Postumius, a general who had been stoned to death by his army troops because he denied them the spoils that he had promised. The senate told the tribunes of the plebs to ask the plebeians in the assembly whom they would choose to place in charge of the investigation. The plebeians unanimously chose the consuls, who investigated the matter and punished the guilty.[49] A particular historical circumstance—namely, the tension between the patricians and the plebeians during the Struggle of the Orders that was being exacerbated by the actions and subsequent death of Postumius—may explain the specific reasons for a joint decision on the part of the plebeians and the senate. Still, the joint decision was the ideal method for beginning an investigation.

Of course, a substantial difference exists between claiming the sole right of capital jurisdiction and ceding that right to another entity, however temporarily. Furthermore, despite Polybius' claim, it appears that *quaestiones* that might result in a citizen's death could have been established by the senate alone. Presumably, expediency in emergency situations sometimes took precedence over ideological considerations. The introduction of investigations instigated by the senate alone was not a radical departure from senatorial responsibility generally, and it was probably not a conscious attempt to usurp the authority of the people. Senatorial responsibility for creating *quaestiones* evolved naturally, on the one hand, out of the regular sphere of responsibility (*provinciae*) that the magistrates of Rome possessed outside the city of Rome and the task the senate had of assigning those *provinciae*[50] and, on the other hand, out of emergency situations that arose in the city itself and demanded immediate action.

An early emergency situation to which the senate ultimately responded with what Livy labels a *quaestio* took place in 331 B.C.E., and it illustrates how these responses to extraordinary situations may have originated in rather random ways. In this incident, a slave reported to one of the curule aediles that she knew the reason for the pestilence, after which the aedile informed the consuls, who referred the matter to the senate, who authorized a promise of immunity to the slave, who then reported (presumably to the body of senators directly) that certain women were concocting poisons, and all the senators immediately rose and followed her to find these women. The senators found potions in some twenty houses and brought these into the forum, whither an apparitor summoned the women in whose houses the potions had been found. The women, pleading their innocence, drank the concoctions and died. Others were then accused and condemned. Though the procedure by which the latter happened is not clear from Livy's text, he does claim, "*Neque de veneficiis ante eam diem Romae quaesitum est.*"[51] ("Yet before that day there had never been a public investigation concerning poisonings in Rome.") Livy does not report whether, by what means, or by whom punishment was meted out.

Livy's comment about the uniqueness of the *quaestio de veneficiis* illustrates, as does the unusual procedure by which the conspiracy was investigated, the impact that expediency could have on judicial action. This case, and particularly the march of all the senators in a crowd to see what was happening, also reveals the degree to which, in the late fourth century, there were not regular judicial mechanisms available to try and punish wrongdoers. This, in turn, suggests that the Roman government did not generally concern itself with the punishing of citizens by means of senatorial *quaestiones* or indeed by any other means. This conclusion seems to hold not just for the fourth century but through the third and into the beginning of the second. For although the complete text of Livy for most of this period is lost, the summaries contain no references to *quaestiones* for this period. When Livy's text resumes in 218, no record of a *quaestio* appears until the infamous Bacchanalian conspiracy over thirty years later, which was considered *extra ordinem* ("beyond the ordinary").[52]

Although the details of the Bacchanalian conspiracy and of the poisoning case of 180 do not illustrate the same kind of random response as seen in 331 when the entire senate went out to see what was happening, they still reveal the *quaestiones* to be ad hoc and exceptional responses to emergency situations that threatened the safety of the *res publica*. They also reveal that the government, under these extraordinary circumstances, could claim the power to kill people, and there was no immediate objection to their doing just that.

> Qui tantum initiati erant et ex carmine sacro, praeeunte uerba sacerdote, precationes fecerant, [in] quibus nefanda coniuratio in omne facinus ac libidinem continebatur, nec earum rerum ullam, in quas iureiurando obligati erant, in se aut alios admiserant, eos in uinculis relinquebant: qui stupris aut caedibus uiolati erant, qui falsis testimoniis, signis adulterinis, subiectione testamentorum, fraudibus aliis contaminati, eos capitali poena adficiebant.[53]

> Those who had only been initiated and who, with the priest before them saying the words of the sacred songs, made prayers in which was contained an irreligious conspiracy in every bad deed and libidinous desire but they had not actually committed through themselves or others any of these things which they had been obligated by oath, these they left in chains. Those who had been defiled by debaucheries or slaughters, and those who had contaminated themselves by giving false evidence, forging seals and wills and by other fraudulent practices, these they subjected to capital punishment.

Not only could the government kill under these circumstances, but the senate could decide that an act for which there was no prescribed penalty deserved death. This is because the primary concern of the senators was the protection of the *res publica* and not the punishment of crime per se. The poisoning case in 180 is, as was the case in 331, explicitly connected to a plague. Given recent events, it seems likely that the tension from the Bacchanalian conspiracy was to blame for the senate acting quickly and without pausing to consult the people.[54]

TRANSITION TO STANDING COURTS

By the early second century, the senate's responses to emerging situations like the mass poisoning case of 331 seem to have grown slightly more controlled. The size of the government had increased enough to make the appointment of *quaestiones* more expeditious than moving the entire senate out of the *curia* to investigate. All the *quaestiones* within the city of Rome that are reported in the extant sources for the early part of the century were these ad hoc investigations arising out of emergency situations. Furthermore, there is no indication that the people objected to the senate's usurpation of their power to try, to condemn, and to execute citizens under extraordinary circumstances. This is probably because such cases endangered the *res publica;* presumably, the senate's immediate response was appreciated by the people as suited to its responsibility to act quickly to defend the *res publica.*

Yet by the middle of the second century, when Polybius was making his claims, the regular judicial authority of the urban praetor over *quaestiones* appears to have already been fairly well established, and the praetor seems to have been able to exercise capital jurisdiction through these *quaestiones.* Evidence of this is suggested not only by the creation of the *quaestiones perpetuae,* which will be discussed shortly, but even by *quaestiones* established before this time.

In 154 B.C.E., thirteen years after Polybius' arrival in Rome, the trial of two Roman matrons, Publilia and Licinia (discussed in Chapter Four), began. They were accused of poisoning their husbands. A trial was begun by the praetor but taken over by the women's kin. The initiation of a judicial proceeding makes it seem as though a *quaestio* could be a regular course for handling the misbehavior of Roman elite citizens. Although the women were ultimately turned over to a domestic jurisdiction before the case was heard, Valerius Maximus' report shows that the *quaestiones* might have been becoming frequent over the course of the second century, because the family seemed to know what to expect from a praetorian *quaestio.*[55]

The regularity of *quaestiones* evidenced in the case of Publilia and Licinia began to be codified five years later with the institution of the first *quaestio perpetua* or standing public court. These *quaestiones* existed only for individual offenses. The first one in 149 was a court for the accusation of provincial extortion.[56] Though this first court did not have capital jurisdiction, shortly thereafter courts were created that did. As seen in Chapter Four, a *quaestio inter sicarios* probably existed by 142[57] and a *quaestio de veneficiis* by at least the early 90s.[58] The exceptional *quaestiones* of the senate early in the century met with no resistance, and there does not even seem to have been much of a response to the growing regular jurisdiction of the praetor (though note how Publilia and Licinia's relatives did not want them to be tried by the government but wanted to do it themselves). Nevertheless, with the creation of permanent or standing criminal courts, the discomfort on the part of the Romans to the usurpation of their authority becomes evident.

USURPATION OF THE PEOPLE'S POWER

It does not, however, become evident in an uncomplicated way, for the instigator of great changes in the fledgling court system was none other than the rabble-rousing tribune Gaius Sempronius Gracchus (tribune of the plebs in 123), whose brother's followers had been put to death by an extraordinary *quaestio* after the assassination of his brother Tiberius himself. Like his brother's use of the tribunate, Gaius Gracchus' use became extraordinary. Nonetheless, all the legislation of Gaius to be discussed here will outlive him, which means that the legislation reflected the values of other Romans besides Gaius. This legislation includes his *ne de capite civium* (literally, "concerning the head of citizens") law that forbade the creation of *quaestiones* without the approval of the people, his law that made senators no longer eligible to serve as jurors in the *quaestiones perpetuae,* and his so-called judicial murder law. All these laws suggest that Gaius did not approve of senatorial usurpation of the people's power, ideally exclusive, to punish citizens with death, and the laws suggest that he mistrusted the magistrates who possessed the power to do just that.

For example, Gaius removed judicial power from the senators when he instigated a law that required the juries of the *quaestiones perpetuae* be made up of equestrians. The inclusion of equestrians had a great deal to do with the increase in the importance of that particular class in the management of the territorial empire and their vested interest in the outcome of the trials. It is nevertheless noteworthy that the jurors under the new law were not the political rulers of Rome, who, for their other responsibility, would advise magistrates and thereby influence the decisions of the government. That jurors were not senators might have been comforting to those who were anxious about the growing power exhibited by members of the senatorial class in the sphere of a citizen's life.

A further indication of the anxiety of the Romans about providing such power over the life of citizens to representatives of the government is Gaius' law against judicial murder, which instituted a standing court for presiding judges who took a bribe to ensure a capital condemnation resulting in the death of an innocent man. This law suggests that Gracchus suspected that the ability to wield such power, if uncontrolled, might lead to abuse of that power. This law reflects the Romans' long-held suspicion of excessive magisterial power.

Finally, the *lex Sempronia ne de capite civium iniussu populi iudicaretur* ("the Sempronian law that the *caput* ['head'] of citizens not be judged without the order of the people")[59] returns some of the power to decide about the life of a Roman citizen to the Roman people. Laws that required a citizen have recourse to the people were already in existence in the *provocatio* legislation of the early republic. *Provocatio,* however, was not available to someone condemned in the *quaestiones extra ordinem,* and it was with these court decisions that Gracchus was concerned.[60] He does not directly transfer such power to the people because it would not have been feasible for the assembly to function as a regular court. What the law did, however, was to ensure that capital courts could not be established on the authority of the senate.[61] A practical motivation for the *ne de capite civium* law is that Gaius, by promulgating it, was able to demonstrate to his own followers that they would be protected from prosecution by the senators, and if they stuck with him, then persecutions would not happen to them as they had to his brother's followers.[62] He may have also wanted to protect himself from the possibility of a senatorial investigation without recourse to the people, especially if he had in mind the other reforms he wanted to make, which he must have realized would put him at odds with many senators.[63] Thus, he promulgated the law to facilitate his own political agenda.

Although Gaius' peculiar circumstances contributed to the particular legislation that he chose to promulgate, his legislation remained in place long after his demise. So far as the evidence allows us to determine, his *ne de capite civium* law meant that never again in the republic were any *quaestiones extraordinariae* created by the senate alone.[64] The judicial murder law remained in place, however obsolete it may have become by then, until the drafting of the *Digest* of Justinian five hundred years later.[65] Finally, although the law regulating that senators not serve as jurors on the courts remained in effect only until the legislation of Sulla some fifty years later, a similar law was reinstated after the dictatorship of Sulla.

CAPITAL PUNISHMENT?

Gaius Gracchus' personal motivations for instituting his laws complicate the interpretation of those laws, but at the same time the role of the personal in Roman government helps to explain one of the most striking features of the Romans' relationship with capital punishment: that under normal circumstances, the government put no one to death. Despite all the discussion in this chapter about which institutions and which officials had a legal capacity to put citizens to death, the evidence suggests that seldom was a Roman citizen actually executed. No evidence exists for an execution of a citizen after a condemnation in an assembly since the legendary period of the early fourth century.[66] Indeed, Michael Alexander's collection of *Trials in the Late Roman Republic* reveals that, between 149 and the dictatorship of Sulla, despite the proliferation of capital courts, nobody was put to death as a result of a trial in any public venue whatsoever.

Some citizens were condemned, and no more word was heard; far more often, the result of a trial in which the accused would probably have been condemned was "voluntary" exile, for the accused could choose to leave the city at any time before the final pronouncement of the jury. A few Romans chose to kill themselves, but by doing so they took the responsibility for their own deaths onto themselves. The government may have exerted pressure, but it did not kill on a regular basis. Even the case of Publilia and Licinia can be read as showing that the change of venue was brought about in fear that a condemnation would not occur if the trial took place in a public *quaestio.*

One reason the Romans had for not killing citizens is to be found in their suspicion of government and governing officials, and their reluctance to grant such power to magistrates and institutions. The other reason has more to do with those governing than with those governed. Here the agenda of magistrates complemented the agenda of "the people." The personal nature of Roman politics meant that no abstract government was responsible for putting people to death; instead, individual magistrates would be seen as having that responsibility. The nature of Roman political structure was so intensely personal that should a Roman magistrate condemn—or preside over a court that condemned—a Roman citizen to death then that magistrate would be likely to face personal, political repercussions. Such a circumstance helps to explain the otherwise bizarre and inexplicable temporary magistracy of the *duumviri perduellionis* (the two men in charge of treason).

DUUMVIRI PERDUELLIONIS

The sole purpose of the *duumviri perduellionis*[67] seems to have been to take responsibility for condemning citizens that a presiding magistrate (or, perhaps, earlier a king) did not wish to take. The *duumviri* appear in the historical record three times, once in a legend of the monarchy, briefly during an incident in the middle republic, and once in a trial of the late republic. Each of these cases involves an act of homicide: the legend of the trial of Horatius for killing his sister; the trial of Manlius Capitolinus; and the trial of Gaius Rabirius centuries later for the killing of Saturninus. From these examples scholars have correctly concluded that the *duumviri* were *ad hoc* magistrates.[68] Disputes over the precise authority of the *duumviri*, however, have yet to be resolved because as judicial magistrates the *duumviri* were unique in Rome: they had no ability to make decisions.

According to the legend of Horatius, summarized in Chapter One, after being victorious in battle, Horatius returned home and killed his sister. Thus, his glory was marred by an act of parricide, and retribution had to follow. The difficulty, however, was in meting out retribution to the champion of the kingdom:

> Atrox visum id facinus patribus plebique, sed recens meritum facto obstabat. Tamen raptus in ius ad regem. Rex, ne ipse tam tristis ingratique ad volgus iudicii ac secundum iudicium supplicii auctor esset, concilio populi advocato "Duumviros," inquit, "qui Horatio perduellionem iudicent; secundum legem facio." Lex horrendi carminis erat: duumviri preduellionem iudicent; si a duumviris provocarit, provocatione certato; si vincent, caput obnubito; infelici arbori reste suspendito; verberato vel intra pomerium vel extra pomerium. Hac lege duumviri creati. Qui absolvere non rebantur ea lege ne innoxium quidem posse cum condemnassent, tum alter ex iis "Publi Horati, tibi perduellionem iudico," inquit; "i lictor colliga manus."[69]

> Horrid as this deed [Horatius killing Horatia] seemed to the *patres* and the plebeians, his recent service was an offset to it; nevertheless, he was seized and brought before the king for trial. The king, that he himself might not become the author of a judgment so sorrowful and disagreeable to the populace, and of the punishment which must follow the judgment, having called together a meeting of the people said, "I appoint *duumviri* who will judge Horatius for *perduellio* according to the law." The law was in this terrible formula: The *duumviri* should make a judg-

ment of *perduellio;* if he appeals from the *duumviri,* let the *provocatio* be called for; if they are victorious, cover his head, suspend him with a rope from a barren tree, or lash him either inside or outside the *pomerium.* By this law the *duumviri* were appointed. Who, according to that law, considered that they could not absolve him even if he were innocent and having given a verdict of guilty, one of them pronounced the words, "Publius Horatius, I judge you a traitor; go lictor, bind his hands."

Publius Horatius did appeal to the people for help and was tried before them and ultimately absolved. The *duumviri,* however, seem to have had no authority to acquit Horatius. According to Livy, the purpose of the *duumviri* was to allow the king to avoid making an unpopular decision. Evidence for later trials suggests that this was the regular function of the *duumviri.*

The trial of Manlius Capitolinus provides similar information. Livy mentions that the *duumviri* appear in an alternative version of the legend to the trial by the tribunes. In this case, as in the case of Horatius, condemnation would have been difficult to achieve because of all the glory Capitolinus had brought to Rome. In Livy's version of the tribunician trial, he even reports that the tribunes had to move the meeting place where the vote was to take place because they did not think they could achieve a condemnation in sight of the Capitol. This demonstrates that a condemnation of Capitolinus would have been as unpopular as a condemnation of Horatius would have been.

After this version of events, Livy goes on to say, "S*unt qui per duumviros, qui de perduellione anquirerent creatos, auctores sint damnatum*" ("There are those who say the authors of the condemnation were the *duumviri* who were appointed for prosecuting *perduellio*").[70] The word *anquirerent* implies a more prosecutorial action than *inquirerent. Inquirere* means simply "to investigate," while *anquirere* means "to investigate (in a prosecutorial sense)." If the *duumviri* were to prosecute and to judge the case at the same time, then condemnation was the only possible result, and indeed, according to the story, Capitolinus was convicted and executed.

In both instances the *duumviri* were appointed to convict the accused; the same circumstance holds true for the trial of Rabirius. Our evidence for his trial at the end of the republic shows this same limitation of the role of the *duumviri.* In the year 63 he was charged with *perduellio* for the killing, thirty-six years earlier, of Saturninus, a tribune of the plebs.[71] "The most convincing explanation of the Rabirius affair is that Labienus' original bill provided simply that the *duumviri* should charge and condemn Rabirius without giving him an opportunity to defend himself."[72] Thus, like their appearance in the trial of Horatius, the *duumviri* in the trial of Rabirius do not seem to have been allowed a choice.[73]

By virtue only of having passed sentence, without having made any decision, the *duumviri* must have accomplished something. Santalucia argues that they made a decision about whether the accused was caught in the act, but even that seems to give them more authority, certainly, than the first story would imply.[74] In the Horatius story and the Capitolinus story the compelled condemnation by the *duumviri* makes sense: they took away the responsibility for an unpopular decision from the king in the first case, and from republican magistrates in the second case, thus allowing them to avoid a politically precarious situation.[75] The case of Rabirius does not provide such an obvious motive, but the *duumviri* were appointed to convict. These cases show that in certain circumstances a case could arise that could potentially have overwhelming consequences for a presiding magistrate, but with the employment of the *duumviri perduellionis,* such an official could avoid taking direct responsibility for condemning (or even acquitting) a popular Roman citizen.

Thus, though the Roman government could put citizens to death under extraordinary circumstances that threatened the stability of the *res publica,* and though certain of its institutions claimed a regular capital jurisdiction, it did not practice capital punishment on a regular basis. Changes in the government brought about by the requirements of managing an empire did not change the essential desire of the Roman magistrates and of the Roman people more generally. The increasing judicial mechanisms of the government did not punish Roman citizens with death, just as those requirements had not changed the fact that the Romans did not possess a murder law. Nevertheless, the increasing pressures of the administration of the territorial empire did have an impact on the treatment of homicide in Rome, and the involvement of Roman officials in the extralegal act of intentional homicide, as we shall see in Chapter Six.

SIX

LICENSE TO KILL

In a book about the relationship between homicide and political power, the killings of Roman tribunes and their supporters, starting with the death of Tiberius Gracchus in 132, hold a particularly profound place. In 133 B.C.E., Publius Cornelius Scipio Nasica Serapio, nominally a private citizen but in fact a powerful man in Roman government, led a band of senators into the tribal assembly and participated in the killing of two hundred Roman citizens, including the tribune of the plebs—a Roman official by the name of Tiberius Sempronius Gracchus. The homicide of Tiberius Gracchus and its many consequences led to attempts to legitimize instances of homicide so that certain Roman officials could protect the *res publica* by killing those they considered dangerous to its safety. This attempt at legitimizing such killings was a decree of the senate known to modern scholars as a *senatus consultum ultimum* (*scu*).

But the Romans demonstrated great ambivalence about it,[1] neither completely accepting the concept of justifiable homicide for the protection of the *res publica* nor ever able actually to outlaw it. In this ambivalence is reflected Roman attempts to negotiate political power in the context of a rapidly expanding territorial empire. In particular, discourse surrounding the justification, or lack thereof, of the *scu* seems to reflect the notion of diffuse versus centralized power in Roman government. The attitude toward these homicides remained ambivalent throughout the republic.

To demonstrate that the attitude of the Romans toward justifiable homicide for the protection of the *res publica* was ambivalent, and to determine the reasons for this, I examine the incidents of such homicides, paying particular attention to four aspects: the repercussions for those magistrates who killed Roman citizens allegedly for this reason, the occasional hesitancy of magistrates to employ the decrees of the senate for killing, the laws written to forbid such acts and the extent of their effectiveness, and the wording of the decrees themselves. By examining the killing of Tiberius, the creation of the so-called *scu* for the elimination of Gaius Gracchus, and the subsequent use of this final decree of the senate, we will see that legalization of homicide by Roman officials was just as absent from the Roman world as making murder illegal.

TIBERIUS GRACCHUS

When Tiberius Gracchus, a tribune of the plebs, was becoming politically powerful in arguably unethical and certainly unprecedented ways in the Roman world, many Roman senators feared his ever-increasing power and believed he was behaving tyrannically.[2] Plutarch, describing the debate in the senate that preceded the death of Tiberius, states that someone reported to the senators that he saw Tiberius in the tribal assembly asking for a crown. Because monarchy was an anathema to the Romans, when Nasica heard this, he: ὁ δὲ Νασικᾶς ἠξίου τὸν ὕπατον τῇ πόλει βοηθεῖν καὶ καταλύειν τὸν τύραννον ("demanded that the consul should come to the rescue of the state and put down the tyrant").[3] The presiding consul, P. Mucius Scaevola, refused, saying that he would not use violence or put a citizen to death without a trial, and Nasica "thereupon sprang to his feet and said: 'Because the chief magistrate betrays the *res publica,* you who wish to save the laws, follow me.'" With a crowd of senators and others with him, he went to the tribal assembly, and a fight ensued in which hundreds of Romans died, including Tiberius, who was beaten to death with sticks by Publius Satyreius, one of his colleagues in the tribunate, and by Lucius Rufus.[4]

The moment before Tiberius' death he was allegedly seeking to dramatically alter the structure of republican government. Even though this is likely to have been slander against Tiberius, the attack on him was justified in some people's eyes by the possibility that he was making the claim to absolute power. Furthermore, his political machinations leading up to this meeting of the assembly threatened the balance of power created by the system of patronage by which Roman government functioned. They also threatened the relative power of the senate (over the tribunate and over the people) by asserting control over the monies from Pergamum. Control of the financial resources of the provinces was supposed to be the purview of the senate.[5] By deposing a colleague in the tribunician college, Tiberius also assumed a political power beyond any tribune before him. Furthermore, he discussed this arguably unconstitutional act in terms of the rights of the people. Tiberius' actual and assumed attempts to manipulate the political power that he possessed as tribune of the people are one illustration of the renegotiation of political power in the last half of the second century B.C.E.

The other part of the picture is the responses to the killing of Tiberius, which reveal a great ambivalence among the Romans about how much power members of the government had to kill Roman citizens. The killing of Tiberius was not a crime according to any Roman law.[6] Even those who participated in the fighting did it with rocks and sticks and broken furniture, not with any instrument that was exclusively a weapon.

The extent to which the act was considered a crime might be illustrated by the consequences for those who participated in it. Those men who actually beat him to death, Publius Satyreius and Lucius Rufus, seem to have survived the incident just fine, as is suggested by the absence of any evidence of a trial of either of them. Enough references are made to this incident and its consequences in enough different sources that the silence on the fate of these two killers is significant. If they had been brought to trial the sources would still contain some trace of those trials, especially because the sources do record that Rufus bragged about his role in the killing.[7] Satyreius was a tribune of the plebs himself and therefore immune to prosecution during his term of office, but if he had been tried at the completion of his term the sources would contain some reference to that trial.

Furthermore, Appian writes:

ἡ δὲ πόλις ἐπὶ τῷ Γράκχου φόνῳ διῄρητο ἐς λύπην καὶ ἡδονήν, οἱ μὲν οἰκτείροντες αὑτούς τε κἀκεῖνον καὶ τὰ παρόντα ὡς οὐκέτι πολιτείαν, ἀλλὰ χειροκρατίαν καὶ βίαν, οἱ δ᾽ ἐξειργάσθαι σφίσιν ἡγούμενοι πᾶν, ὅσον ἐβούλοντο.

On the subject of the homicide of Gracchus, the city was divided between sorrow and joy. Some mourned for themselves and for him, and deplored the present condition of things, believing that the commonwealth no longer existed but had been supplanted by force and violence. Others considered that their dearest wishes were accomplished.[8]

The ambivalence recorded by Appian about the homicide of Tiberius is evident throughout the entire affair. The ambivalence first appears in the meeting of the senate that preceded Tiberius' death. Nasica was an ex-consul and the Pontifex Maximus (chief priest) in Rome.[9] He was an oligarch in the strictest sense of the word, with no patience for the masses, and a personal enemy of the Gracchan faction.[10] Tiberius, for his part, had been using the tribunate, the traditional protectorate of the masses, to a far greater degree than anyone before him, and he had a great amount of popular support. For the conservative Nasica and other Roman senators, he represented a serious threat to political order and stability. When Scipio Nasica recommended an attack on a tribune of the plebs, no agreement existed in the senate that his action was acceptable.[11] The disagreement is reported by Plutarch:

> ἀποκριναμένου δὲ πράως ἐκείνου βίας μὲν οὐδεμιᾶς ὑπάρξειν οὐδὲ ἀναιρήσειν οὐδένα τῶν πολιτῶν ἄκριτον, εἰ μέντοι ψηφίσαιτό τι τῶν παρανόμων ὁ δῆμος ὑπὸ τοῦ Τιβερίου πεισθεὶς ἢ βιασθείς, τοῦτο κύριον μὴ φυλάξειν.

> All the senators were, of course, greatly disturbed, and Nasica demanded that the consul should come to the rescue of the state and put down the tyrant. The consul replied with mildness that he would resort to no violence and he would put no citizen to death without a trial; if, however, the people, under persuasion or compulsion from Tiberius, should vote anything that was unlawful, he would not regard this vote as binding.[12]

Scaevola, a Roman jurist, was uncomfortable with the notion of using violence generally, and with the notion of killing a citizen without a trial specifically. His decision not to take violent action in this matter was probably founded on a number of considerations. He had been part of the Tiberian faction (in so far as factions existed),[13] and so this might have played a role in his decision, but his subsequent actions show that his alliance to the Gracchan faction did not outweigh his own personal political survival. He must have recognized that to support the killing of Tiberius, even though the act may not literally have been illegal, might be political suicide. His own self-interest and perhaps his sense of justice also informed his decision.[14]

Whatever Scaevola's precise motivating factors were, the explanation for his decision is significant. He did not refuse to take action by arguing in the senate that Tiberius' actions were lawful or even acceptable. Rather, he said that he would not commit a wrong himself. Thus Scaevola implied that Nasica's intended violent response to Tiberius' unethical activity was wrong. Scaevola, for his part, agreed that he might take legal action against Tiberius: he said he would reject any laws unlawfully passed.

Once Tiberius was dead, however, even Scaevola himself supported Nasica's actions. Cicero refers to this event when he talks about his own considerations as he was contemplating some decades later what to do about his own personal enemy Clodius.

> Sed publicam causam contra vim armatam sine publico praesidio suscipere nolui, non quo mihi P. Scipionis, fortissimi viri, vis in Ti. Graccho, privati hominis, displiceret, sed Scipionis factum statim P. Mucius consul, qui in gerenda re [publica] putabatur fuisse segnior, gesta multis senatus consultis non modo defendit, sed etiam ornavit.[15]

> But I [Cicero] did not wish to take up the public cause against armed force without a public guard; not that the violence of that bravest of men, and a private citizen, P. Scipio [Nasica] against Ti. Gracchus displeases me. The consul, P. Mucius [Scaevola], however, who was thought to have been slow in taking action, when Scipio's deed was done immediately defended Scipio's action with many decrees of the senate, and even honored it.

With what senatorial decrees did Scaevola defend Nasica?[16] One senatorial decree of which we know is the order to the consuls to investigate Tiberius' allies, that is, to create a *quaestio extra ordinem*. If Cicero's comment that Scaevola defended Nasica's action with decrees of the senate is true, then this is probably one of the decrees Scaevola supported. Once the killing had occurred, the majority of the senators, with Scaevola as presiding consul, moved to support it. By demonstrating the guilt of those men who were associated with Tiberius, the accusers were able to demonstrate that Tiberius himself had also been guilty. The culpability of the followers was a reflection of the culpability of the leader. If Tiberius was wrong, then he was justly slain.[17]

But it is unlikely that Tiberius' followers were prosecuted only because the senators who supported the *senatus consultum* that instituted these emergency *quaestiones* wanted to prove that the killing of Tiberius was a justifiable act. They must have believed that he and his followers had committed a wrong. Beyond the political meaning of the condemnation of Tiberius' allies lay a real danger perceived from their actions. By stirring up the masses, they could be seen as fomenters of revolution. Although the danger to Rome was considered to be real, whether homicide was justifiable if it was for the protection of the *res publica* remained an unanswered question.[18]

The entire issue, however, was put to the test further because in the chaos of the situation following the death of Tiberius, many of his supporters were killed or exiled without a trial. Precisely who these people were or what they did is unknown. Others were actually brought to trial before they were put to death or fled into exile. Those who were condemned in a court include Diophanes, C. Blossius, Vettius Sabinus,[19] and hundreds more unnamed defendants.[20] What little is known of their trials demonstrates that the followers of Tiberius were being persecuted for treasonous activities.

One indication of the charge against Tiberius' followers is found in the record of Nasica's motivation for killing Tiberius himself. Nasica claimed that Tiberius was aiming at tyranny, a treasonous act.[21] If this was true, then his companions could have been suspected of treason as well. One trial demonstrates that this is precisely what did occur. Blossius, a rhetorician from Cumae and a friend of Tiberius, was brought before a *quaestio* specifically created to deal with the still-living followers of Tiberius. He claimed in court that he would do whatever Tiberius told him to do, including burn down the temple of Jupiter Optimus Maximus, because, he went on, Tiberius would never have told him to do something that would bring harm to the *res publica*. To his hearers, however, his statement that he would burn down a temple of the chief god demonstrated that he was, in fact, a danger to Rome. Blossius, perceiving that he was in imminent danger of condemnation, went into voluntary exile and later died in the company of an enemy of the Romans.[22]

Plutarch and Cicero both report the story of Blossius' trial, but they give different prosecutors: the former reports Nasica; the latter, Laelius. Most scholars accept Cicero's version.[23] If Nasica (or his friend Laelius) could prove that the followers of Tiberius were villains who deserved to be killed, then he could justify his own action in contributing to the death of their leader. This appears to be precisely what occurred. From the point of view of his accusers, and the jurors in the senatorial *quaestio*, Tiberius was a demagogue who was able to convince his followers that the destruction of a temple to Rome's chief god was beneficial to the *res publica*. Perhaps it was also felt that it was right to kill a man who could persuade his partisans to commit treason and even to attack the gods, even if he was a tribune of the plebeians, and it was necessary to lead a mob of senators into the assembly and beat him to death in a remarkable act of public violence.

The same belief that Nasica acted properly was still part of the Roman psyche nearly a century later. I refer again to Cicero's comment, quoted above, in which he speaks of Nasica's killing of Tiberius as an act to be emulated. Admittedly, Cicero had his own political agenda for this claim.[24] Nevertheless, his ability to make it at all indicates that the act was acceptable to at least some of his audience. In 63 Cicero defended one rabble-rousing tribune of the plebs by the name of Milo for killing another rabble-rousing tribune of the plebs, Clodius. Even though Cicero's primary argument was that his client had the right to defend himself against Clodius' violence, he nevertheless frequently mentioned that Milo's act was not only in his own defense but in the defense of the *res publica*. Therefore, Milo acted on behalf of the republic as Nasica had before him. According to Cicero, because Milo committed the same act as Nasica, for the same reason, Milo should be acquitted.[25]

The evidence suggests that attitudes toward this idea of killing for the protection of the *res publica* were divided, to some extent, across class lines. For example, in Rome a statue of Tiberius and one of his brother Gaius, whose story will be examined shortly, would eventually be set up in Rome, and the lower classes worshiped these men as heroes, leaving baskets of fruit and the like as offerings at the base of the statues.[26] This adoration by the ordinary Romans makes the Gracchi martyrs to the cause of the people and implies that their assassinations were unjustified in the eyes of the lower class.

Other than the worship at the statues, the activities of the lower class are barely represented in our sources. The same persons who have provided to posterity information about the Roman world are the elite, the ones who shaped the legal system of Rome. One important aspect of the absence of mention of the lower class in this chapter is the failure of any of our sources to think that the killing of hundreds of Romans was significant. The numbers of the unknown are recorded, but the culpability for their deaths is never brought up. When the Romans discuss the events in the assembly on that fateful day, it is Tiberius' death with which they are concerned. The deaths of the hundreds of unknown plebeians is seldom mentioned. This is more than a mere reflection of the attitudes of the authors, it is a reflection of the attitudes of the elite. Nevertheless, the masses do play some role in what would happen next.

Nasica, like the followers of Tiberius, was now to be prosecuted himself. Shortly after Tiberius' death and the special investigations of his followers, Nasica was to discover that killing a Roman official, even, allegedly, for the saving of the *res publica,* was not without repercussions. A challenge was being made against the idea that such an act of homicide was justifiable. According to Plutarch, Nasica was brought to trial to conciliate the people who were feeling the absence of Tiberius.[27]

Although class distinction is evident, it would be a mistake to think that Nasica was brought to trial only to conciliate the masses. He was charged by a friend of Tiberius Gracchus, in a senatorial *quaestio*, not before the people. Cicero, commenting once on Scipio Nasica's wit, wrote,

> Placet etiam mihi illud Scipionis illius qui Tib. Gracchum perculit: cum ei M. Flaccus multis probris obiectis P. Mucium iudicem tulisset, "Eiero," inquit, "iniquus est"; cum esset admururatum, "Ah," inquit, "P.C., non ego mihi illum iniquum eiero, verum omnibus."[28]

> Also pleasing to me is the statement of that Scipio who destroyed Tiberius Gracchus: when M. Flaccus had brought before him as juror P. Mucius [Scaevola], after many insults were put forth, "I object," he said, "[Scaevola] is prejudiced"; when a murmuring occurred he said, "Ah, I don't say that he is prejudiced against me, but against everyone."

This passage demonstrates a number of important points: Nasica did stand trial, or at least a trial was begun, and this trial was a *quaestio extra ordinem*.[29] Thus, he was accused in a trial established by the same means as the ones that had been used to try Tiberius' followers, and so he too was tried by senators. "Such a *quaestio*, however, would presumably have been in the charge of the consuls, who were hardly likely to befriend the Gracchan cause."[30] The venue of this trial is significant for this very reason. If it was not the Gracchan cause that was being defended, then it was Nasica's killing of Tiberius and violent acts in the forum that were being prosecuted.[31] Although it is impossible to say for certain whether the trial came about because of the fear of political repercussions, or because of a real belief in the wrongness of the killing, Nasica was nevertheless being prosecuted by senators for this homicide.

The passage from Cicero is significant for other reasons as well. It demonstrates, again, the ambivalent attitude of one individual Roman about the events surrounding the killing of Tiberius. Scaevola, remember, is said to have supported Nasica after the fact.[32] This anecdote, however, shows that relations between those two were not smooth. If Nasica objected to Scaevola as a juror, it was probably because he expected Scaevola to vote against him in this trial. Even while Scaevola is said to have supported Nasica, tension continued to exist between the two after Nasica led the attack on Tiberius.[33]

The senators, presumably with one of the senatorial decrees by which Scaevola was thought to have shown support of Nasica, sent Nasica on a *libera legatio* to Asia, even though a judicial procedure had already been initiated against him. The *libera legatio* was an official assignment of the senate by which the senator was sent out at public expense to take care of some business, theoretically for Rome. Thus in the guise of an honor, Nasica effectively fled Rome, without ignominy. His departure was as good as saying that if he had stayed, he would not have won the trial; self-imposed exile in the guise of a government position was superior to a condemnation in court. The senators sent him away because they were uncomfortable with a trial of Nasica. The tides of opinion were shifting, and the senators were doing a balancing act to stay afloat.

Thus not only was Tiberius Gracchus killed, but his followers were wiped out. To some extent, those who participated in the attack on him were not punished. No sign exists that the two men who actually killed him were tried. Indeed, one of them is said to have bragged about the deed. Nasica, after some success against Tiberius' followers, had to leave Rome, but he was able to do so under the guise of an honor. Nasica died abroad soon after he left Rome, and so we do not know what consequences his return to Rome might have brought. A proposal was made that he be honored as a tyrannicide, but it was the Gracchi who received statues and were honored.

Scaevola first disapproved of taking violent action against a Roman citizen, then he supported the action which had been taken, then he demonstrated disapproval of the person who led the mob into the assembly and contributed to the killing of a tribune. If one single man, and he holding the highest political office in the republic and an educated expert in the law, was unable to provide blanket approval or blanket disapproval of this conduct, how was the entire population, or even the ruling class of Rome supposed to decide? The tension within Scaevola himself concerning the killing of Tiberius Gracchus and the ambivalent fate of Nasica are microcosms of the great contest that would continue through the end of the republic concerning who had the authority to kill and for what reasons.

GAIUS GRACCHUS

Because homicide was a means of defining power, Nasica tried to justify fomenting the act, Scaevola tried to dance around its legitimacy, and Gaius Gracchus, the brother of Tiberius Gracchus, would try to turn the clock back and allow control over it only to the Roman people. The justifiability of the killing of Tiberius was never resolved. Because of his killing, however, his brother was killed twelve years later. Important information is to be gained from two aspects of Gaius Gracchus' story. First, the choices that he made in the promulgation of his legal reforms demonstrate another reason, beyond the tension in the expanded authority of Roman government, why the issue of justifiable homicide was never resolved. Second, Gaius Gracchus was killed with the support of the senate, that is, according to senatorial decree, and so his killing brings into even sharper focus the debate about justifiable homicide.

Gaius' legal reforms demonstrate how homicide was an issue of political power. A decade after the death of Tiberius Gracchus, Gaius, following in his brother's footsteps, became a tribune of the plebs, at which time he promulgated the *lex Sempronia ne de capite civium iniussu populi iudicaretur*[34] discussed in Chapter Five, which forbade the killing or exile of a Roman citizen without the approval of the people. His legislative activity was directed toward rectifying the behavior of the government, not of private citizens, despite the evidence that among the people who killed his brother, only one man was not a private citizen. Gaius' *ne de capite civium law* suggests that murder itself was not as problematic as the political power wielded by the person or institution that did the killing. This is especially the case because Gaius was working in the tradition of the tribunate as defender of the rights of the people, and he established this law in that tradition.[35]

The Roman senators, however, were not to be hindered by Gaius' new law concerning the limits of senatorial authority. When they believed that he, like his brother, was fomenting unrest and probably aiming at tyranny, they were willing to kill him to stop him. To this end, they took a further step on the road toward the legalization of homicide for the protection of the *res publica*. The step they took was the creation of the "final decree of the senate," the *senatus consultum ultimum* (*scu*), which instructed the consuls to act as necessary for the preservation of the *res publica*.[36] The act the consuls took was fomenting the death of Gaius and killing his supporters.

The circumstances surrounding Gaius' death differ from those surrounding his brother's. In 133 neither side had been prepared for armed conflict, the consuls had not been involved in the attack on the tribune, and the killing of Tiberius occurred without any official support from the senate. By contrast, in 121 the senate voted that the consul, Opimius, should take action to support the *res publica*. In contrast to Scaevola in 123, Opimius was eager to carry out the *scu*. Indeed, evidence suggests that he may have proposed it himself.[37] The passage of the decree meant that the majority of the senators sanctioned the attack. In addition, both the Gracchan faction and the consuls were armed and ready for what was essentially a small-scale civil war.[38] Gaius Gracchus and his partisans were killed, after all, without a decision of the people.

Gaius Gracchus was killed after he tried to extend Roman citizenship to the entire peninsula and thereby in a different way, alter the content, if not the structure, of Roman government. This attempt to extend citizenship led to the demise in popularity that may have contributed to his death and to Opimius' acquittal. Thus again, an attempted alteration of political power, this time the power possessed by the people, through dilution of their numbers, is connected with homicide.

Despite the action being taken by the consul and not a private citizen, and despite the declared approval of the majority of the senators, the creation and the execution of the *scu* did not in and of itself make killing for the protection of Rome a legal act because the senate was not a legislative body. Moreover, it did not make such killing an acceptable act, as is demonstrated by the consequences for those who carried out such homicides. The repercussions for those who first used the *scu* to kill Roman citizens reflect the indecisiveness of the Romans on this issue.

In 120 B.C.E., L. Opimius was brought to trial before the people under the *lex Sempronia ne de capite civium* for killing a Roman citizen without a trial.[39] Cicero lays out quite nicely the issues of this case.

Interfecit Opimius Gracchum. Quid facit causam? Quod rei publicae causa, cum ex senatus consulto ad arma vocasset. Hoc tolle, causa non erit. At id ipsum negat contra leges licuisse Decius. Veniet igitur in iudicium licueritne ex senatus consulto servandae rei publicae causa.[40]

Opimius killed Gracchus. What is the substance of the case? That he did this for the sake of the *res publica*, because he called to arms by order of a *senatus consultum*. Strike out this plea and there will be no case. Decius [Opimius' prosecutor], however, denies the legality of the decree itself, as being contrary to the laws (*leges*). Therefore, the issue will be whether the senate's decree and the salvation of the *res publica* justified the act.

Opimius was acquitted. This has been seen as a sanctioning of the *scu* and a recognition that acts made under its authority were not in contravention of Gaius' *ne de capite civium law.*[41] This interpretation of events is not completely inaccurate. No one else was brought to trial under this law, so far as our evidence indicates, with one bizarre exception sixty years later.[42] Nevertheless, this does not mean that such killing was sanctioned.

First, Opimius was not the only person called to account for the death of Gaius Gracchus and his partisans. In the year preceding Opimius' trial, P. Cornelius Lentulus, who participated in the assault on Gaius Gracchus and his supporters, sought from the senate and was given by it a *libera legatio*. He probably took this, much like Nasica had, to avoid a trial for his involvement in the killing of Gaius.[43] Because Lentulus did not have the support necessary to face a trial, he fled Rome. Those people who subsequently accused Opimius of the same offense perhaps thought that they could frighten him into leaving Rome or that they could convict him. Opimius, however, had far more popular support than Lentulus.[44] More than demonstrating the security of the use of the *scu*, the events after Gracchus' death demonstrate that when a consul used this action, he needed to be certain of his own support if he wanted to avoid being prosecuted for killing a Roman citizen without the authority of the people.

This holds true not just for senatorial support but for popular support as well. Earlier, the trial of Nasica, the senator who led the attack on Tiberius Gracchus, was to take place before a senatorial *quaestio,* and Nasica was compelled (or at least thought it was a good idea) to leave Rome. Now Opimius, the leader of the attack on Gaius Gracchus, was tried in a popular assembly and acquitted.[45] The juxtaposition of these two trials helps to demonstrate that the ambivalence about killing Roman citizens without a vote of the people did not fall clearly along class lines. The people, not only the senators, acquitted Opimius.

The second condition that demonstrates that Opimius' acquittal was not a blanket approval of the *scu* is that many of those who subsequently used it suffered repercussions. Even with the acquittal of Opimius, this final decree of the senate was never a legal action from the perspective of the Romans. The *scu* was passed several more times, and the consuls who carried it out were never immune to prosecution because of the so-called precedent of Opimius' trial. Therefore, the second condition that demonstrates that Opimius' acquittal was not a blanket approval of the *scu* is that the act of carrying out the *scu* often had detrimental repercussions, as can be seen by an examination of the next situation in which it was promulgated: the killing of Saturninus and Glaucia and their partisans in 100.

Even with the acquittal of Opimius, the final decree of the senate was never a legal action from the perspective of the Romans. But, although precedent was without legal force in Rome, the senate was willing to make this decree again, and later magistrates were willing to employ it.

One caveat ought to be made before proceeding with this discussion. The *scu* was not a declaration of a state of emergency; therefore, it did not require a particular formula to be valid. That the *scu* was an emergency measure is clear, but an emergency measure is not precisely the same as a declaration of a state of emergency. The latter implies a systematic handling of these matters, that a certain procedure would be followed as a result of such a declaration.[46] This was not the case in the Roman republic, when the decision for how to act was left to the magistrates who were advised by the senate to protect the *res publica*.[47] Furthermore, each time the decree was voted on by the senate, the wording was different, another indication of the ambivalence that surrounded its promulgation.

SATURNINUS

The unsettled state of affairs with regard to *senatus consulta ultima* can be seen in the events surrounding the deaths of Appuleius Saturninus, Glaucia, and their partisans. Saturninus, like the Gracchi before him, was a tribune of the plebs. He was, however, involved far more than they in political violence and in using gangs for electoral and legislative support. The violence that finally provoked the senate to pass the *scu* was the attack upon and killing in the *contio* of a candidate for the position of tribune of the plebs for which Glaucia was also running.[48]

The wording of this particular *scu* suggests that an attempt was made to forestall possible attacks on those who would carry it out.

> Fit senatus consultum ut C. Marius L Valerius consules adhiberent tribunos pl. et praetores, quos eis videretur, operamque darent ut imperium populi Romani maiestasque conservaretur. Adhibent omnis tribunos pl. praeter Saturninum, praetores praeter Glauciam; qui rem publicam salvam esse vellent, arma capere et se sequi iubent.[49]

There was a *senatus consultum* that Gaius Marius and Lucius Valerius, the consuls, should summon tribunes of the plebs and praetors who seemed good to them, and they should see to it that the power and majesty of the Roman people be preserved. They summoned all the tribunes of the plebs except Saturninus and all the praetors except Glaucia. They ordered whoever wanted the *res publica* to be saved to take up arms and follow them.

The inclusion of all the tribunes and praetors the consuls saw fit to call meant that a majority of the magistrates had the opportunity to participate in the execution of the *scu*. Cicero goes on to say that they all obeyed the consuls and took up arms. By including all the co-magistrates of those men against whom the decree was promulgated, the consuls probably hoped to ward off potential personal attacks on themselves after the decree was carried out. This seems to indicate that they did not believe they could rely on the decree alone to protect them from prosecution, should prosecutors choose to come forward.

The phrase *ut imperium populi Romani maiestasque conservaretur* ("in order that the power and majesty of the Roman people be preserved") serves several telling functions. First of all, the language of the decree was probably formulated in exactly these words in response to specific legislation that had been promulgated by Saturninus himself, and in this sense it should be viewed as defensive language.[50] Probably during his first tribunate in 104 but certainly by the time of his death, Saturninus had promulgated a *maiestas* law that forbade the "diminution of the majesty of the Roman people."[51] The wording of the *scu* suggests that its promulgators might have been concerned that they could be subject to judicial action in the *quaestio de maiestate,* and it suggests that they might have recognized that unless they said otherwise, their act might be perceived as being against the people as opposed to for them.

Just to complicate the issue of relative positions of power, when Saturninus promulgated his law and when the *scu* was passed in response to his other actions, members of the senatorial class were excluded from serving as jurors of the *quaestiones perpetuae.* Thus, if Marius and his colleagues had been charged under the provisions of the *maiestas* law, they would have found themselves not before a senatorial court but before equestrians. Finally, the provision that the power and majesty of the Roman people had to be preserved would have been a powerful propagandistic call for support from the people themselves in the face of an act that served exactly the opposite purpose from its claim, an act that took from the people the right to decide to put Roman citizens to death or not.

The senate passed the *scu* and the consul Marius carried it out by bringing armed force against Saturninus and Glaucia and their partisans. These men surrendered to Marius and were locked up in the *curia*. Marius, once he had captured all those against whom the senate had aimed the *scu*, intended to use established legal means to put an end to their activity, for he did not kill them. Instead, he gave them a pledge of security to allow them to stand trial in a court of law. Others had different plans, and the prisoners were lynched by a mob.[52] Marius' pledge of security had done them no good.

Admittedly, Marius' motivation for not employing the *scu* to its extreme involves a complex set of circumstances, including his relationship with the leaders of the captives, who had earlier been his political allies. His hesitancy to commit homicide, however, may have lain not only in his earlier political relationship but in his own sense of self-preservation. He must have known that taking such a step could lead to his own demise, especially given his already stormy career. For, though Opimius' career famously survived the killing of Gaius Gracchus, Publius Cornelius Lentulus died before ever returning to Rome after his participation in enforcing the *scu*.[53] Marius' political enemies might not have hesitated to bring accusations against him had he actually committed homicide. Nevertheless, the imprisonment of those against whom the *scu* was employed demonstrates an important characteristic of the *scu,* that it did not have to be used for killing,[54] though it had been used to that end to lead to the death of Gaius Gracchus and to kill his followers.

According to our sources, the betrayal of Marius' agreement not to kill those who surrendered gave rise to even more anger on the part of the masses. No charges, however, were brought against anyone at this time, probably because the action had enough support among the aristocrats who controlled the courts that no one had the power or inclination to bring charges. Nevertheless, thirty-seven years later, in 63, Gaius Rabirius was charged with and convicted of *perduellio* for his involvement in the death of Saturninus. This trial, coming as it did nearly four decades after the offense, was politically motivated. Nonetheless, that the accusation was brought on account of Rabirius' participation in the employment of an *scu* to kill Roman citizens demonstrates that the act was still considered illegal and unjustifiable by some.[55]

Furthermore, the trial of Rabirius for treason, as discussed in Chapter Five, emphasizes the relationship between homicide and power. At issue is the extent of power that could be executed by the government against individual citizens. It is remarkable what is not at issue: that these acts of homicide were assassinations. Indeed, the people killed nearly always included tribunes of the plebs, officials of the government whose bodies were supposed to be sacrosanct. Thus, it is quite remarkable that the perpetrators of these acts of senatorially sanctioned homicide were charged with killing citizens without a trial. It is also noteworthy that no one ever felt compelled to legislate against assassination. The cases were always articulated as the government's (or its representatives') right to kill citizens without the approval of the people.

SUBSEQUENT EMPLOYMENT OF THE *SCU*

That the debate would remain unresolved even well past the dictatorship of Sulla is illustrated first by the promulgation of the *scu* against Lepidus in 77.[56] Then, in 63, Cicero would seek and be granted an *scu* against Catiline,[57] but a few years later he would be exiled for killing Roman citizens without a trial and later recalled from exile. The next promulgation of the *scu* that would give Pompey authorization from the senate to do whatever was necessary to protect the *res publica* would not result in homicide without trials but instead would result in judicial action (made possible by the employment of Roman troops). Pompey would be, like Marius, well aware of the fickle nature of popular and senatorial support, and he would not choose to risk his own career by employing the *scu* to kill citizens against the strongly held Roman belief that it was not the right of magistrates to employ that power against citizens.[58] Ironically, in one of the last uses of the *scu*, it would be passed against Julius Caesar, who would ultimately defeat those who tried to use it against him.[59]

The legitimacy of the *scu* was never fully established nor ever entirely rejected, reflecting the tension that was a part of Roman government from the beginning when the Romans granted the power of *imperium* to magistrates and then limited that power by means of *provocatio*. Although the *scu* is part of the enduring discourse on political power throughout republican history, at the same time it also emerged during a particularly tense moment of the republic, when the impact of territorial expansion was creating a need for the Romans to reconsider the structure of political power. Evidence for the impact of expansion comes, in part, by the creation of standing criminal courts for the first time in Roman history.

That the discourse on political power was a discourse about homicide was a result of the close relationship between homicide and definitions of power in Rome. Particularly provocative is that the language surrounding the employment of the *scu* is about homicide and the power of the people and never about assassination, though all these acts were acts of political assassination. As the evidence in this chapter attests, the Romans of the republic would never entirely resolve the issues surrounding homicide and political power until they finally would destroy the republic itself, and yet, before they were finished, the discourse, if one can use so tame a word, would escalate even beyond what is seen in the *senatus consulta ultima*, with the incredible violence introduced in Rome at the time of, and frequently on account of, the activities and decisions of Lucius Cornelius Sulla, as we shall see.

SEVEN

CENTRALIZATION OF POWER
AND SULLAN AMBIGUITY

In a book about homicide and its relationship to political power, Lucius Cornelius Sulla takes center stage. As consul in 88 B.C.E. he marched his troops against the city of Rome and then created the *hostis* ("enemy of the state") declaration, which made certain citizens of Rome (and personal enemies of Sulla) into enemies of the *res publica* and therefore subject to death. While proconsul and general fighting on the eastern fringes of the empire, he was himself declared a *hostis*. Upon his return to Rome, he waged a civil war. He became dictator for restoring the laws, in 81, around which time he created the proscriptions, a list of people whom one could kill with impunity, and then he promulgated the *lex Cornelia de sicariis et veneficiis,* known in many English-language texts as Sulla's murder law. He resigned his position of absolute political power eighteen months after he assumed it.

In his promulgation of the *hostis* declaration, Sulla conflated himself with the *res publica*. Nearly a decade later, along with the assumption of the dictatorship, Sulla took for himself, as preserver of the *res publica,* the power to determine who could be justly slain on its behalf. His treatment of homicide reveals his relationship to political power, in particular, his impermanent assumption of absolute power that resulted in a temporary centralization of political power in the last century of the Roman republic.

Twice in his career, in two different ways, Sulla attempted to legitimize the killing of his enemies by making them enemies of the Romans and the *res publica*. With hindsight, connections can be seen between the two attempts, but it is preferable to explore them separately, because the Sulla of 88 almost certainly had no inkling of the kind of temporary political revolution that the Sulla of 81 would bring about.

THE *HOSTIS* DECLARATION

As consul in 88 B.C.E., Sulla was allotted the command against Mithridates IV of Pontus, which was on the coast of the Black Sea.[1] While he was in southern Italy with his troops, preparing to set sail for the east, his *inimici* ("personal enemies"), by use of political and in some cases fatal violence, got the plebeian assembly to revoke his command and bestow it upon Marius.[2] In reaction to this, Sulla took an unprecedented step in the annals of Roman history: he led troops against the city of Rome. The minor skirmishes in the city that happened with the Gracchi and Saturninus pale in comparison with this act of civil war. Sulla was successful in his attack on Rome. Once there, with the implicit and sometimes explicit threat of violence by his soldiers, who were still present in Rome, Sulla had the senate and the assembly declare Marius, Sulpicius, and others of his *inimici* to be *hostes*.[3]

Although this act is often conflated with the *senatus consulta ultima*, like the one created for use against Gaius Gracchus, the *hostis* declaration was a new method for a magistrate to obtain the power to kill Roman citizens allegedly for the protection of the state.[4] The *scu* simply told the magistrates to take action to save the *res publica;* it did not define how that should be done, nor did it indicate which people were threatening the security of the *res publica*. The manner in which a magistrate chose to employ the *scu* was, in theory, entirely up to him. Labeling a particular individual as a *hostis* was an entirely different matter.

The *hostis* declaration was not simply an extension of the *scu*,[5] nor was it geographically defined when it was first created.[6] The argument that the *hostis* declaration applied only to people outside the city of Rome is belied by the declaration against Lepidus in 77. Lepidus not only was outside the city of Rome at the time, he was in command of an army, someone who would more easily fall under the category of *hostis* than Marius and his cohort did, yet Lepidus was not declared a *hostis*.[7] This suggests that in the 70s, and therefore in the 80s, the geographical distinction was not made, although their absence from Rome may have made it easier for Sulla to claim that his *inimici* were not Roman citizens.[8]

The meaning of the hostis declaration was far more powerful than geography. The *hostis* declaration identified the wrong-doers, and it converted them from citizens of Rome into enemies of Rome. This conversion meant not simply that these men were no longer Roman citizens, and therefore not deserving of protection, it meant that they were active enemies of Rome: not only could they be killed, but they should be. Therefore, the *hostis* declaration implicitly advocated the act of homicide in a way that the *scu* did not. Furthermore, the declaration granted more authority to commit homicide because it labeled someone an enemy and because of the method of the promulgation. Unlike the *scu,* the *hostis* declaration was a law, and therefore was agreed to by the people, who had the right to condemn to death.

That Sulla was willing to sanction and participate in killing to protect the *res publica* and to achieve his own ends was not his innovation. Periodically, since the killing of Gaius Gracchus, Roman officials had been willing to go to such extremes for political motives. In this regard, Sulla's actions should be seen as part of an escalation of the violence that occurred during the last century of the republic. Sulla's innovation came in naming his own enemies as enemies of the *res publica.* That this was what he was doing was obvious to his contemporaries:

> Dispulsas prostratisque *inimicorum* partibus, Sulla occupata urbe senatum armatus coegerat ac summa cupiditate ferebatur ut C. Marius quam celerrime *hostis* iudicaretur. Cuius voluntati nullo obviam ire audente solus Scaevola de hac re interrogatus sententiam dicere noluit. Quin etiam truculentius sibi instanti Sullae "licet," inquit, "mihi agmina militum, quibus curiam circumsedisti, ostentes, licet mortem identidem miniteris, numquam tamen efficies ut propter exiguum senilemque sanguinem meum Marium, a quo urbs et Italia conservata est, hostem iudicem."[9]

> After the party of his *personal enemies* had been driven asunder and overthrown, Sulla, armed with an occupied city, gathered together the senate and with highest desire proposed that Gaius Marius, as quickly as possible, be judged a *public enemy.* Whose desire no one dared to go against except Scaevola alone, who, when asked about this matter, did not wish to give his opinion but even more aggressively said to Sulla, who was threatening him, "Although you show me the battle line of soldiers with which you have surrounded the senate house, although you threaten me repeatedly with death, still you will never cause me, on account of my feeble and aged blood, to judge Marius — through whose agency the city and Italy were saved — an enemy of the state."

Valerius, in his juxtaposition of *inimici* with *hostes* reflects something of which the senators in that meeting and the people of Rome in the assembly must have been entirely aware: Sulla was using the resources of Roman government to declare his own personal enemies to be enemies of Rome.

Ironically, Sulla's forcefully ensured declaration of *hostes*, which helped to destroy republican stability in the long run and which would foment greater violence in response, also created for a brief moment in time a certain unity of purpose. This is not to suggest that Romans agreed with Sulla's actions, and the tales of those who hid Marius show that Sulla was not entirely successful in his attempts to persuade the Romans that this particular newly declared *hostis* was an enemy of the *res publica*. Yet the *hostis* declaration, making the enemies of a single individual into enemies of the *res publica,* did provide an artificial moment of unity.

Although Scaevola's remarks (as reported by Valerius Maximus) indicate that the Romans were not deceived into thinking that Marius was their enemy as he was Sulla's, the senate did pass the resolution.[10] The impact of this passage became more forceful when Sulla brought the resolution before the people. Sulla did not settle for only the approval of the senate when declaring Marius, Sulpicius, and their cohort to be public enemies. Appian writes that when Sulla was hiding in Minturnae, the magistrates of that town were hesitant to kill him despite the κήρυγμα τοῦ δήμου,[11] ("decision of the people"), which suggests that the *hostis* declaration was introduced into an assembly of the people. This means the decree, unlike the *senatus consulta ultima,* was probably ratified by the senate and then made into law by the people.

Practical considerations influenced these different forms of promulgation. At no point during the republic does a magistrate ask the people to make law of a *senatus consultum ultimum,* but this is largely because this senatorial advice was often directed against someone who was popular with the people. It would therefore have been foolish to approach the people on this issue. Sulla, on the other hand, had two advantages. By the time of his march on Rome, the Romans had already grown angry at the violent acts that had been perpetrated by those who were Sulla's political opponents. Even more importantly, Sulla had the advantage of the support of his fully armed legions, who would ensure that whatever legislation he would propose would be approved in the senate and then passed by the people.

Sulla's choice to appeal to the senate and the people might also have been influenced by both personal and ideological considerations; for Sulla, as for many Roman aristocrats, the two seem to have been one and the same. Sulla's march on Rome had come in response to the activities of the tribune Sulpicius Rufus who had appealed directly to the plebeian assembly, explicitly against the wishes of the senate, to recall Sulla from his potentially lucrative command of the troops about to set out to fight against Mithridates. It had been the decision of the people, made under the threat of violence and without senatorial support, that—from Sulla's point of view—compelled him to march on Rome in the first place. Sulla's more traditional and conservative approach of appealing first to the senate and then to the people to ratify his definition of Marius and his cohort as *hostes* could thus be considered a response to Sulpicius' radical approach to politics.

Whether Sulla had any particular opinions about tribunes before this time is difficult to say, but from this point until he retired from the dictatorship nearly a decade later, he would work to diminish the power of the tribunate.[12] He would still see the people of Rome as essential to decision-making, but the people should be decision-makers only under the guidance of the chief magistrates, not under the guidance of rabble-rousing tribunes. The manner of Sulla's deference to the people, because it circumvented the tribunes, had the effect of centralizing political power against the potentially scattering effects of ambitious tribunes.

When the manner of his promulgation of the decree is combined with the nature of the decree itself, the potential centralizing effects become more dramatic. When Sulla promulgated the *hostis* declaration, he implied that what was good for Sulla was good for Rome.[13] There was some justification for his opinion, namely, the violent and unusual actions of Sulpicius Rufus and his companions. Nonetheless, because the senate and the people passed the declaration, they too stated that the enemies of the *senatus populusque Romanus* and the enemies of Sulla were one and the same. For a brief moment in time in 88, Rome and Sulla were conflated to such a degree that opposition to the latter was opposition to the former.

The method whereby Sulla was able to give Rome a temporary cohesiveness, quite literally a body to identify as the *res publica,* was through acts of homicide. This unity was created not only in the act of voting for the law but also in the act of carrying it out. The law did not require Sulla to assign troops to the task; rather, it required the people to participate in the capturing and killing of the *hostes* for the good of Rome.[14] Although this too was motivated in part by practical considerations—Sulla's best use of resources was to get the people of Rome and Italy to do the hunting down and killing for him—it did mean that the act of homicide in theory unified the Romans.

The unification lasted only as long as Sulla and his troops were in the city.[15] The link between Sulla and the *res publica* was an artificial one, literally forced into place by Sulla's employment of the legions to get what he wanted, and it was a temporary one, for Sulla had no desire to remain in Rome. As soon as he went off to wage war against Mithridates, his still-living *inimici* returned to Rome and, in their turn, had Sulla himself declared a *hostis*. Even before this occurred, rumblings of retaliation against Sulla were evident. After the decree was executed, Sulla, like Lucius Opimius and Popillius Laenas before him and Gaius Rabirius after him, was probably accused of killing and exiling Roman citizens without trial.[16] A tribune of the plebs, M. Vergilius, at the bidding of the consul elect, Cinna, charged Sulla before the people.[17] Sulla could not have been certain of acquittal had he gone to court. In fact, his activity as consul in 88 would have rendered him vulnerable, had he disbanded his army and permitted himself to be tried in court. He would have been vulnerable still after he returned from the war against Mithridates, had he not engaged in civil war and then had himself made dictator.

PROSCRIPTIONS

When Sulla left Rome, the city, and especially Sulla's friends, had to endure an escalation of violence to such a degree that when he returned to Italy in 83, both he and his opponents were prepared for open and armed conflict. From this first full-blown civil war in Rome, Sulla emerged the clear victor. At his own request, he was made dictator in Rome for an unspecified amount of time, *legibus faciendis et reipublicae constituendae* ("for making laws and restoring the *res publica*").[18] Because of this dictatorship, the nature of political power in Rome temporarily became the opposite of what it was intended to be. Before this time, the dictatorship had been an official Roman magistracy, but the individual who held the post had more powers of coercion and command than any other official in Rome. He also had more power to kill citizens, because his decisions were not subject to *provocatio.*

Due to this exceptional amount of power concentrated in the hands of a single individual, the Romans limited the term of office for a dictator to a period of only six months, while all other magistrates held office for a year. In addition, the position was available only intermittently and only when the Romans were faced with a serious external threat.[19] The last time the position had been filled in Rome was in the war against Rome's greatest enemy, Hannibal, over one hundred years before Sulla's rise to power. L. Cornelius Sulla was the first dictator in Rome not to have his term of office limited to a particular time period.[20] Thus Sulla was put in a position of absolute power.

Shortly before or after his assumption of the dictatorship, Sulla created and employed proscriptions, supposedly in response to a request that the indiscriminate killing provoked by the civil war be brought under control. Rather than putting a stop to the killing, Sulla decided to control it by writing up a list of those who could—and should—be killed with impunity, hanging it up in the forum for everyone to see.

μένοις, μετελεύσεσθαι κατὰ κράτος. ταῦτα δ᾽ εἰπὼν αὐτίκα βουλευτὰς ἐς τεσσαράκοντα καὶ τῶν καλουμένων ἱππέων ἀμφὶ χιλίους καὶ ἑξακοσίους ἐπὶ θανάτῳ προύγραφεν. οὗτος γὰρ δοκεῖ πρῶτος, οὓς ἐκόλασε θανάτῳ, προγράψαι καὶ γέρα τοῖς ἀναιροῦσι καὶ μήνυτρα τοῖς ἐλέγχουσι καὶ κολάσεις τοῖς κρύπτουσιν ἐπιγράψαι. μετ᾽ οὐ πολὺ δὲ βουλευτὰς ἄλλους αὐτοῖς προσετίθει.

Sulla proscribed about forty senators and 1,600 *equites*. He seems to have been the first to make such a formal list of those whom he condemned to death, to offer prizes to assassins and rewards to informers, and to threaten with punishment those who concealed the proscribed. Shortly afterwards, he added the names of other senators to the proscriptions. Some of these, taken unawares, were killed where they were caught, in their homes, in the streets, or in the temples. Others were hurled through midair and thrown at Sulla's feet.[21]

Representatives of the government (including Sulla himself) had been attempting to assert the power to kill Roman citizens for some time through the *scu* and the *hostis* declaration. With the proscriptions, however, Sulla blasted through the earlier limits on the power of political figures to kill, just as he would surpass previous limitations on political power with the extended dictatorship itself.

While the *hostis* declaration created a forced and temporary conflation between Sulla and Rome, the proscriptions represented an arbitrary power to kill that could be asserted only by someone who had centralized power under himself. As he had with the *hostis* declaration, Sulla enlisted the support of the people by having them ratify his proscriptions by law.[22] He also rewarded those who helped in the killing and punished those who protected the proscribed.[23] The proscriptions, however, differed from the *hostes* declarations in a way that reveals how these assertions of the right to kill are linked with the extent of political power possessed by the person who asserts them.

In 88 Sulla needed to justify the killings by making those subject to death into enemies of Rome before their killing could be accomplished.

First, they had to be converted from citizens to enemies; then, they could be killed. For the proscriptions, no such justification was necessary because Sulla's power was so much greater, and the path to that power already so much bloodier, than either had been earlier in the decade. Furthermore, Sulla was either about to assume the dictatorship or he already had, which would grant him a legal claim to absolute power that he had not possessed in 88. It was not necessary to use homicide to conflate himself with the republic as he had in 88 because by virtue of holding the dictatorship, that conflation was accomplished through administrative means. This does not mean (as it had not meant with the *hostis* declaration) that he had undivided popular support; it only meant that he had the mechanisms of force to insist on compliance and that he spoke from a position of authority in a newly centralized government. The power he possessed required no justification, and so the proscriptions could be arbitrary.[24]

The *hostis* declarations, the proscriptions, and the *lex Cornelia de sicariis et veneficiis* (the Cornelian law on dagger-wielders and poisonings) together reflect Sulla's peculiar relationship to political power. Sulla followed each of his two marches on Rome with a decisive and brutal assertion of the right to kill. Each time, Sulla took power swiftly, absolutely and without hesitation, and each time, this power manifested itself in his taking control over the right to kill Roman citizens. After the second march, in addition to the proscriptions, Sulla took up the dictatorship by means of which he held absolute power through a legitimate political institution. Then, after he completed the task for which he was granted the dictatorship—that of drafting the laws and preserving the *res publica*—he gave it all up and retired from politics. This surprising relationship to political power, that is, the assumption of absolute power and the retirement from it, is reflected in his *lex Cornelia de sicariis et veneficiis*. The link between this law and political power is not as obvious as the relationship between political power and the *hostis* declarations and proscriptions, yet it is significant.

The *lex Cornelia de sicariis et veneficiis* is not quite a murder law. Just as Sulla brings the Romans to the brink of monarchy and steps back, so too does he bring to them a law that is almost a murder law, but murder is not yet a crime in Rome. While Sulla demonstrated with his proscriptions his willingness to act swiftly and with great finality in the face of a threat to himself and to the *res publica,* this act was a temporary act much like his assumption of the dictatorship would turn out to be. He took the Romans to the brink of monarchy but then stepped back from the precipice. The ambiguity of swift, decisive, complete, and unambiguous actions on the one hand, and their temporary nature on the other hand, make Sulla a

difficult man to fathom. The teetering on the precipice of monarchy is reflected in the *lex Cornelia de sicariis et veneficiis,* which teeters on the brink
of becoming a murder law.

THE *LEX CORNELIA DE SICARIIS ET VENEFICIIS*

While Sulla's decisions about killing people seem fairly straightforward, if
perverse (all Romans should be engaged in killing my enemies so that the
res publica can be protected), his legislation concerning the culpability for
homicide-related offenses is less clear. The *lex Cornelia de sicariis et veneficiis,* curiously, has received little attention in books about Sulla, and Sulla
has received little attention in arguments about this law. This is because
the importance of homicide in understanding political power in Rome has
not received the attention it deserves. The most commonly posed question
about the *lex Cornelia de sicariis et veneficiis* is whether it should be considered a murder law. Conclusions are problematic. More might be accomplished toward understanding this moment in republican history from an
exploration of the ambiguity itself, rather than attempting to resolve it. I do
not intend to argue that Sulla's ambiguity on this issue is intentional, only
that the ambiguity of the legislation reflects the ambiguity both of Sulla's
own relationship to political power and of the position of Rome in the first
quarter of the first century B.C.E., stressed as it was by forces threatening
its stability and threatening the very definition of *res publica* by which the
Romans had lived for centuries.

As dictator Sulla pursued an active role in reforming the Roman "constitution" and legislating new laws. Among his laws was the *lex Cornelia de
sicariis et veneficiis,* often referred to as Sulla's murder law.[25] The purpose of
this law was not the repression of murder; rather, along with Sulla's other
legislative activity, it was a complex yet strong political statement about the
restoration of order and the authority of the dictator. The promulgation of
the law, coming as it did upon the bloody heels of the proscriptions, stated
the reestablishment of order, and it allowed Sulla to create a public persona as lawgiver. More importantly, however, it reflects that despite Sulla's
temporary centralization of political power, Rome was not yet a monarchy
and a murder law was not yet appropriate. This argument is based on the
following observations: (1) Sulla did not do much, if anything, to change
the existing laws about homicide-related offenses and (2) the law was not
only or even primarily concerned with homicide.

An excerpt from Marcian's *Institutes* begins the *Digest*'s information about the *lex Cornelia de sicariis et veneficiis*:

Marcianos libro quarto decimo institutionum. Lege Cornelia de sicariis et veneficis[26] tenetur, qui hominem occiderit: cuiusve dolo malo incendium factum erit: quive hominis occidendi furtive faciendi causa cum telo ambulaverit: quive, cum magistratus esset publicove iudicio praeesset, operam dedisset, quo quis falsum iudicium profiteretur, ut quis innocens conveniretur condemnaretur. Praeterea tenetur, qui hominis necandi causa venenum confecerit dederit: quive falsum testimonium dolo malo dixerit, quo quis publico iudicio rei capitalis damnaretur: quive magistratus iudexve quaestionis ob capitalem causam pecuniam acceperit ut publica lege reus fieret.[27]

Marcian *Inst.* 14: Under the *lex Cornelia de sicariis et veneficis*, someone is liable who kills a person, or by whose malicious intent a fire is made, or who walks around with a weapon for the sake of killing a person or committing a theft, or who, when holding a magistracy or presiding over a public court arranged for someone to give false evidence so that some innocent person might be improperly and unjustly convicted and condemned. Also liable under the law is anyone who will have made or will have given poison to kill a person; or who will have deceitfully given false testimony so that someone is condemned in a public court to capital punishment; or any magistrate or presiding judge of a standing court for a capital offense who will have received money so that the accused is found guilty by public law.

According to Marcian, therefore, the *lex Cornelia de sicariis et veneficiis* included acts of homicide, but it also included other acts of violence such as arson.[28] Justinian's jurists compiled the laws for the *Digest* half a millennium after Sulla's dictatorship, and although it provides good and often accurate evidence of republican laws, the possibility of changes in the law over a five-hundred-year period must be acknowledged. Fortunately, contemporary sources provide evidence for the offenses included when Sulla promulgated the law.

Writings roughly contemporary with Sulla demonstrate that when it was compiled, this law contained all the offenses that Marcian records, and more. Cicero informs us that this law covered the organization of the *quaestiones de sicariis* ("who kills a person, or who walks around with a weapon for the sake of killing a person or committing a theft"),[29] *de veneficis* ("who will have made or will have given poison in order to kill a person"),[30] and the *ne quis quo iudicio circumveniretur* court ("who will have deceitfully spoken false testimony so that someone is condemned in a public court to capital punishment; or any magistrate or presiding judge of a standing court for a capital offense who will have received money so that the accused is found guilty by public law").[31]

In addition to the above offenses, the law also included under its rubric the offenses of arson and parricide. That Sulla's law also had under its rubric *incendium* (see the above passage from Marcian, "by whose malicious intent a fire is made") is seen in a passage from Cicero's *Paradoxa*.[32] We also know from Cicero's *pro Roscio Amerino* that parricide was actionable in a court created by this *lex Cornelia*.[33] The absence of parricide in *Digest* 48.8 can be explained by a law of Pompey in 55 or 52, the *lex Pompeia parricidii*, which regulated the parricide court and took the place of the *lex Cornelia*; thus, parricide in the *Digest* falls under another chapter.[34]

The *lex Cornelia de sicariis et veneficiis* was not about legal reform in the area of homicide. Four elements confirm this. First, the law did not create new offenses. Second, it appears to have been entirely tralatician, that is, it seems to have taken the earlier laws that originally instituted the courts and repeated them verbatim. Third, this law did not create a single standing court for the trial of the individual offenses over which it took cognizance. Fourth, the offenses tried in these courts were subject to different punishments.

Scholars are in general agreement that Sulla's law did little more than join together under one rubric courts that already existed.[35] For example, the speech of Cicero on behalf of Roscius implies that the procedure of a parricide case being tried in the *quaestio de sicariis* was a normal continuation of procedures that predated Sulla.[36] The evidence that permanent courts existed for parricide, poisoning, and being a *sicarius* before Sulla has been discussed in Chapter Four. Some of the evidence demonstrating their existence also provides further information on the tralatician nature of the law.

Not only did the offenses remain the same, but even the language of the laws was apparently unchanged. The section of the Sullan statute on judicial corruption was an exact replica of a statute first promulgated fifty years earlier by Gaius Gracchus. Cicero reports that Sulla did not change the offenders who would be liable under Gracchus' *ne quis iudicio circumveniatur* law.[37] The law, that is, retained its jurisdiction only over senators. The retention of Gracchus' restriction makes sense within Sulla's legislative activity; Sulla, however, took away the right of anyone but senators to sit as jurors in the standing courts anyway, and so there would have been no need to change the law.[38] Nevertheless, Sulla took the Gracchan law verbatim and incorporated it into his own statute.[39]

The Cornelian law therefore included a variety of offenses, but all had been actionable in the standing jury courts before the time of Sulla. Furthermore, these offenses were included in Sulla's law in an apparently arbitrary way; no change occurred in the form of the laws. In addition, this law did not even create a single court for trial of these offenses,[40] and condemnation for offenses contained by this law did not receive identical punishments.[41] In Cicero's speech on behalf of Roscius, Cicero makes it clear that his client would have been subject to punishment by the sack if convicted in the *quaestio* established by the *lex Cornelia de sicariis et veneficiis*.[42] It was not until over a decade later, when Pompey promulgated the law on parricide, that the punishment of the sack was done away with.[43]

Unfortunately, of the (at least) six chapters of the *lex Cornelia de sicariis et veneficiis*, the details of about only three can be reasonably reconstructed.[44] The first chapter is the section *de sicariis*, the fifth is the chapter on poisoning, and the sixth is the chapter on judicial corruption. What was contained in Chapters Two, Three, and Four is unknown. Parricide and arson were probably covered in these, but as to the others, we remain ignorant. Nonetheless, the obvious tralatician character of the extant chapters of the law mean that the chapters of the law retained the same impact of the earlier laws. Thus, the *sicarius* section, as has been so amply demonstrated by Cloud, was about public violence: "It is therefore reasonable to argue that the *quaestio de sicariis*, before which this speech was delivered in the first case tried by it since the reconstitution of the court by Sulla, was a court aimed at repressing gangsterism and the public disorders consequent upon it."[45] Nevertheless, while it is correct to say that part of the statute is about gangsterism and public violence, it is not accurate to say that Sulla's promulgation of the law was aimed at gangsterism particularly. If Sulla's law had been a simple attempt to repress gangsterism, there would have been no need to include the other chapters in this statute.

The chapter on poisoning shows that crimes that were not inherently such direct threats to public safety also fell under the rubric of this law. Thus, scholars who want to argue that the law was about public violence cannot account for matters of poisoning, and scholars who want to argue that the law is about murder cannot account for the inclusion of arson in the statute.[46] Some scholars have rightly been more cautious in defining the purpose of the *lex Cornelia de sicariis et veneficiis*. Santalucia, for example, writes that Sulla instituted "a *lex Cornelia de sicariis et veneficiis*, which introduced (or, as is more probable, reorganized) a capital *quaestio* with the object of prosecuting different types of attacks on the life of another."[47] Ugo Brasiello wrote that the law seems to have been not about making murder a crime but about making someone liable for the act of putting into being conditions in which killing can occur.[48] These remarks capture the broad range of offenses covered by this law.

The lack of innovation in the law should not be taken as an indication that Sulla's legislation with regard to the courts was not innovative: although this particular law of Sulla's was not innovative, Sulla was quite capable of innovation in the judicial sphere.[49] He did change some laws that had already existed before his dictatorship. For example, his *maiestas* law altered Saturninus' earlier *maiestas* law.[50] He also established new courts by promulgating entirely new laws: the *quaestio de iniuria* or "court for personal injury" was not even considered public but rather tried private offenses in a public court.[51]

With the *lex Cornelia de sicariis et veneficiis* the dictator who became dictator by use of public violence and homicide was able to declare public violence and acts of malicious and intentional homicide ended. During the civil war and subsequently the proscriptions, he had sanctioned many acts of killing and violence. Among these he had even sanctioned acts of parricide to lay waste to entire families.[52] Now his assignment was to restore order to the republic. An important way to do this was to affirm that killing and violence were not acceptable.

Thus, his law was not a culmination of legal, philosophical thought resulting in a single cohesive court; it was a reaffirmation that order was reinstituted and that these offenses were once again unacceptable, illegal, and punishable. This does not mean that Sulla ever thought that the proscriptions were comparable to unjustifiable homicide; rather, they had been the destruction of his enemies and therefore of the enemies of the state.[53] Furthermore, those who participated in the proscriptions were not subject to trial.[54] Nevertheless, the reestablishment of order required the reaffirmation that killing and violence were unacceptable.[55] By joining these particular courts together under the rubric of one law, Sulla was able to make this reaffirmation.

Furthermore, by his promulgation of so many laws, Sulla could claim that order in its entirety was restored. For he not only promulgated seven laws regulating the standing courts, but he also promulgated laws regulating who should be the jurors of those courts. He also increased the number of senators to staff the new jury courts. With his legislation he regulated the tribunate, and legalized the previously customary *cursus honorum* ("ladder of offices"). He promulgated sumptuary laws and many others. Because of his legislation, Sulla could claim that the government was functioning as it should, and therefore the republic was restored.

There was another benefit to Sulla's massive legislation, which he would have been unlikely to overlook. Sulla was capable of appropriating for himself acts of self-display for the creation of his own *auctoritas* ("authority," "reputation"). For example, he put up an equestrian statue of himself in the middle of the forum and created hundreds of Roman citizens, giving them the name *Cornelii*. Keaveney captures how the promulgation of law was part of this creation of a public image:

> The old had ended in strife and confusion, but the gods, who foretold the new, had ensured it would be a golden era by ordaining that, coincident with its opening, there should come one of the great Roman lawgivers whose wisdom could devise laws to bless it with concord and harmony.[56]

This use of legislation as part of the creation of a public persona was already known in Rome. The best example was the legislative activity of Gaius Gracchus. Gracchus promulgated laws both because of his own personal agenda and because of his position as tribune and therefore defender of plebeian rights. Sulla, too, had a political message: just as the role of the tribune was to be defender of plebeian rights, so the role of the dictator was to be defender of Roman security.

Self aggrandizement was for his own personal benefit as well as for defining his place as dictator of Rome. He managed to connect his name to all the laws by which Rome was governed even when it was legally unnecessary to promulgate a law because it was already in existence (such as the law for provincial extortion or the *lex Cornelia de sicariis et veneficiis*). His glory could be assured if it was forever attached to the laws that defined the greatest civilization of the known world.

While these results served the immediate needs of Sulla and of the Romans, the implications of his law go beyond the place of self-aggrandizement and the reaffirmation of stability and security. Sulla's relationship to political power in Rome was one of control and centralization, yet his centralization of power within himself was apparently meant to be temporary. This troubling juxtaposition of absolute but temporary power, as revealed in Sulla's assumption of the dictatorship and his retirement from that office less than two years later, is not reconciled by this examination of the *lex Cornelia de sicariis et veneficiis*. Yet the examination reveals precisely the ambiguity of Sulla's relationship with political power. The Romans were not yet able to create a murder law because they did not yet have a sense of the government as a state, that is, as an entity that could somehow be harmed by the act of one citizen killing another. Yet the gradual changes that will occur after Sulla's death, in particular the gradual evolution of his law into a murder law through the creation of laws on public and private violence, illustrate that the Romans were already on the path that Augustus would compel them to take even before the outbreak of civil war in the 40s. The government would begin to care, and murder would become a crime.

EPILOGUE

Each decade after Sulla's dictatorship ended saw an increase in political violence until, within fifty years after Sulla's dictatorship, the Roman republic came to an end. The pervasiveness of homicide in this period is infamous, for Sulla's march on Rome, his proscriptions, and his employment of the *hostis* declaration would be copied by ambitious Romans who came after him, as would the use of the *senatus consultum ultimum*. The decisions to use these mechanisms came in response to ever-increasing political violence and homicide on the streets of Rome.

At the same time, some Roman magistrates also chose to combat increasing urban violence by creating judicial change: in particular, the various pieces of legislation on public and private violence.[1] These changes would help to alter the purpose of the *lex Cornelia de sicariis et veneficiis* by helping it evolve into a murder law.[2] Thus, during the last moments of the Roman republic when the government was on the brink of a transition to empire and the creation of a centralized political institution that would last for centuries, murder became a crime.

NOTES

INTRODUCTION

1. Henry Campbell Black, *Black's Law Dictionary,* 6th ed. (St. Paul: West Publishing, 1990) s.v. murder, crime.

2. The definitions of both of these powers are more complex than this, but see Chapters Two and Three for further discussions.

3. Killing itself, though, is not necessarily the final act because there are a variety of things that can happen to the body after death. See, e.g., Katarina Mustakallio, *Death and Disgrace: Capital Penalties with post mortem Sanctions in Early Roman Historiography.* Annales Academiae Scientarum Fennicae Dissertationes Humanarum Litterarum 72 (Helsinki: Suomalainen Tiedeakatemia, 1994); Donald G. Kyle, *Spectacles of Death in Ancient Rome* (New York: Routledge, 1998); Claire Lovisi, *Contribution à l'étude de la peine de mort sous la république romaine (509–149 av. J.-C.)* (Paris: de Boccard, 1999) 98 n. 265.

4. For the definition of public law, see below on terminology.

5. For further discussion of the language of homicide in the courts, see Chapters Four and Seven.

6. The *lex Cornelia de sicariis et veneficiis* included *"qui hominem occiderit"* ("whoever will have killed a person"; *D.* 48.8.1), but that was not the main force of the law, as we shall see below.

7. Argument has been made that the use of the word was not infrequent in the republic. Fabio Lanfranchi (*Il diritto nei retori romani contributo alla storia dello sviluppo del diritto romano* [Milan: Giuffrè, 1938] 469) argues that *homicidium* and *homicida* were more common in the late republic than Mommsen thought because of the frequency of their appearance in Quintilian and Seneca. For further sources and discussion of the term, see Antonius Stankiewicz, *De Homicidio in Iure Poenali romano* (Rome: Officium libri catholici, 1981) 1–14.

8. "Im klassischen Latein fehlt es für den Mord an einem einfachen Ausdruck; das jung und nicht glücklich gebildete Wort *homicidium,* der Menschenmord, ist erst spät dafür eingetreten. Aushülfsweise werden in der klassischen Rechtsprache zur Bezeichnung des Mörders die Benennung des Banditen (*sicarius*) und die des Giftmischers

(*veneficus*) combinirt" ("In Classical Latin there is not one simple expression for the word murder; the young and not fully developed word *homicidium*, the murder of a person, is first employed late. Temporarily in Classical legal language the terms Bandit (*sicarius*) and poisoner (*veneficus*) were combined to mean murderer"): Mommsen, *Strafr.*, 613.

9. See, esp., J. D. Cloud, "The Primary Purpose of the *lex Cornelia de sicariis,*" zss 86 (1969), and the discussion below in Chapter Seven.

10. The Latin word *crimen,* whence the English word *crime* derives, did not mean crime during the republic. It meant "charge" or "accusation."

11. Similarly, "Diritto penale: è quello comprendente i diversi mezzi e la forma coi quali lo stato adempe all'altissimo ed essenziale compito di mantenere integro l'ordine giuridico e ripistinarlo quando sia turbata da infrazioni più o meno gravi, che pongano in pericolo la esistenza e la sicurezza della società." ("*Diritto penale* is that which includes the diverse ways and the form with which the state fulfills the highest and essential task of maintaining the juridical order whole and restoring it whenever it is troubled by more or less serious infractions, which put in danger the existence and the security of society"; Angelo Menghi, *Dizionario di terminologia giuridica,* 2nd ed. [Florence: Barbera, 1950] 94). "Das Strafrecht ist ein Teil des öffentlichen Rechts." ("Penal law is a part of public law"; Gerhard Köbler, *Juristisches Wörterbuch für Studium und Ausbildung* [Munich: Franz Vahlen, 1995], s.v. Strafrecht). The German and Italian terms are not as inaccurate as the English because they mean penal law and thus relate more closely to the Roman public law, because offenses tried in the public courts are (for the most part, though not always) subject to punishment.

12. This is the so-called Classical period of Roman law when many jurists were hard at work codifying and explaining the Roman legal system.

13. Barry Nicholas, *Introduction to Roman Law* (Oxford: Clarendon, 1962) 4; cf. D. 1.1.2: *Publicum ius est quod ad statum rei Romanae spectat, privatum quod ad singulorum utilitatem: sunt enim quaedam publice utilia, quaedam privatim.* ("Public law is that which looks to the state of Roman affairs, private law is that which is useful to the individual: for indeed certain things are of public utility and certain are of private.") But the evidence from the beginning of Rome to the end of its republic demonstrates that matters between and among individuals were sometimes a concern to the community and that matters of concern to the community were often handled in a private setting. Public law was far from the only means for dealing with actions directly affecting the state.

14. The assemblies functioning as courts of law provide another example of how terminology affects our perception of Roman judicial activity. The assembly of the people constituted one of the oldest public venues in Rome for charges brought against an offender. This practice existed long before institutions of a purely judicial nature. The terms *iudicia populi* and *iudicia publica* later came to be applied to this practice of using the assemblies as venues for trial, but even these terms were not precise. The *iudicia populi* did not even always mean the assembly in its capacity as court; some-

times it referred to the judgment itself, and sometimes it even referred to nonjudicial decisions. See Chapter Three and Andrew W. Lintott, "Provocatio. From the Struggle of the Orders to the Principate," *ANRW* 1.2 (1972) 247. Later, the term *iudicia publica* was applied to the purely judicial institutions of the *quaestiones perpetuae*, or permanent public courts.

15. E.g., Table VIII of the XII Tables claims that a thief shall be legally killed by the owner of the stolen property if the theft takes place at night. Macrob. *S.* 1.4.19; cf. Aul. Gell. *NA* 8.1, 20.17.

16. Pace Wolfgang Kunkel, "Ein direktes Zeugnis für den privaten Mordprozess im altrömishen Recht," *ZSS* 84 (1967).

17. It seems unlikely that nonelite perpetrators had a different judicial experience than elite perpetrators because even during the empire such a difference did not exist. See, for example, Rolf Rilinger, *Humiliores-Honestiores: Zu einer sozialen Dichotomie im Strafrecht der römischen Kaiserzeit* (Munich: Oldenbourg, 1988).

18. By "ordinary" what is meant is nonpolitical acts committed by nonpolitically significant (read "elite") men.

19. See, e.g., the title of Chapter Seven in Santalucia's *Studi.*

20. Wilfried Nippel, in two excellent books, has demonstrated how the Romans dealt even with those acts that did have a direct bearing on the safety and stability of the *res publica: Aufruhr und "Polizei" in der römischen Republik* (Stuttgart: Klett-Cotta, 1988) and *Public Order in Ancient Rome* (Cambridge: Cambridge University, 1995).

21. For a discussion of the term *parricidium*, see Chapters Two and Four. Pomponius says of their responsibility, "*capitalibus rebus*" ("concerning capital matters"; *D.* 1.2.2.23).

22. See, most recently, Lovisi, *Contribution*, 81–83.

23. Literally, the "three capital men," meaning men with some unspecified responsibility in capital matters.

24. Pace Kunkel, *Untersuchungen*, 71–79. See most recently Lovisi, *Contribution*, 81–83, and Cosimo Cascione, *Tresviri capitales: Storia di una magistratura minore*, Pubblicazioni del Dipartimento di Diritto Romano e Storia della Scienza Romanistica dell'Università degli Studi di Napoli "Federico II" 13 (Naples: Editoriala Scientifica, 1999). Wilfried Nippel is more hesitant to draw conclusions, but he makes some cogent responses to Kunkel's assumptions about the need for government involvement in summary criminal jurisdiction: *Public Order*, 22–26.

25. Though the actual executioner was a public slave, the *carnifex.*

26. Note, e.g., the Catilinarian conspirators et al.

27. See, e.g., Plaut. *Aul.* 415–418. One *triumvir* seems to have gone to the home of a culprit, but this was allegedly to elicit a bribe by means of blackmail, and so it cannot be construed as the ordinary behavior of a *triumvir.* Cic. *pro Clu.* 38–39.

28. Their five assistants (*quinqueviri uls eis tiberim*), who make an appearance in our sources and descriptions at emergencies, seem to have merely looked out for fires; Livy 39.14.

CHAPTER ONE

Portions of this chapter appear as an article, Judy Gaughan, "Killing and the King: Numa's Murder Law and the Nature of Monarchic Authority," *Continuity and Change* 18.3 (2003). Reproduced here with the permission of the publishers.

1. On the general story of Numa's reign, see, e.g., Plut. *Numa*; Livy 1.17–21.

2. Festus, s.v. *parricidi quaestores* (p. 247, L.).

3. For bibliography on the term *paricidas,* see J. D. Cloud, "*Parricidium:* From the *lex Numae* to the *lex Pompeia de parricidiis,*" zss 88 (1971) 1–18, esp. nn. 4–5. Since then: Salvatore Tondo, *Leges regiae e paricidas* (Florence: Olschki, 1973) 87–214; Giuliano Bonfante, "Paricidas," *Labeo* 22 (1976); Antonius Stankiewicz, *De Homicidio in iure poenali romano* (Rome: Officium Libri Catholici, 1981) 4–14; André Magdelain, "*Paricidas,*" in *Du Châtiment dans la cité: supplices corporels et peine de mort dans le monde antique* (Rome: Palais Farnèse, 1984) 549–570.

4. Scrv. auct. *Ecl.* 4.43. Cf. Vincenzo Giuffrè, *La repressione criminale nell'esperienza romana* (Naples: Jovene, 1997) 21; Santalucia, *Studi,* 109 n. 6. The manuscript reads *et acnatis;* for discussion and bibliography on the *agnatis* emendation, see Salvatore Tondo, "L'Omicidio involontario in età arcaica," *Labeo* 18 (1972) 314–318. For the *contione* emendation, see Santalucia, *Studi,* 109 n. 5.

5. So, too, Bernardo Santalucia, "Omicidio," *Enciclopedia del diritto,* vol. 29 (Giuffrè, Milano, 1979) 885–886.

6. For further discussion of the ram, restitution and expiation, see Chapter Three.

7. Cloud, "*Parricidium,*" 3.

8. Cloud, "*Parricidium,*" 2–18, esp. 3.

9. Alan Watson, "Roman Private Law and the *Leges Regiae,*" jrs 82 (1972).

10. The unreliability of later Roman historians on archaic Roman events is these days taken for granted, but for a more precise argument see, e.g., Gary Miles, *Livy: Reconstructing Early Rome,* (Ithaca, NY: Cornell University, 1995); Emilio Gabba, *Dionysius and the History of Archaic Rome,* Sather Lectures 56 (Berkeley: University of California, 1991).

11. Aside from the Horatius legend, no trial remains in the extant record for early Rome. The supposed accusation against Hercules, *de caede* ("for killing") in Livy 1.7 that led to Evander building an altar to this demigod after getting one good look at him should not be taken as an evidence for a trial. For *caedis* as homicide, see J. D. Cloud, "The Primary Purpose of the *lex Cornelia de sicariis,*" zss 86 (1969) 270, and Stankiewicz, *De homicidio,* 13.

12. Livy 1.24–26; Dion. Hal. 3.18–22; Florus 1.1.3–6.

13. Livy 1.26.5; Dion. Hal. 3.22.3.

14. For the decision not to try the case, Livy 1.26.5 and Dion. Hal. 3.22.4–6; for the appointment of specific officials to do so, Livy 1.26.5; for directions to convict, Livy 1.26.6; for recommendation to appeal, Livy 1.26.8.

15. Kurt Latte, "The Origin of the Roman Quaestorship," tapa 67 (1936) 33. For

more on the *duumviri,* see R. A. Bauman, *The Duumviri in the Roman Criminal Law and in the Horatius Legend, Historia,* Einzelschriften 12 (1969).

16. That *quaestores* existed as early as monarchy: *D.* 1.13.1; Tac. *Ann.* 11.22; Alan Watson, "The Death of Horatia," CQ n.s. 49 (1979) 441 n. 29; but not Mommsen, *Strafr.,* 523.

17. Festus, s.v. *parricidi quaestores,* p. 247, L. Cf. Dio (Zonar. 7.13); *D.* 1.2.2.23; Varro *de Ling. Lat.* 5.81.3; Lydus *de Mag.* 1.26.

18. *D.* 1.2.2.23: *Et quia, ut diximus, de capite civis Romani iniussu populi non erat lege permissum consulibus ius dicere, propterea quaestores constituebantur a populo, qui capitalibus rebus praeessent: hi appellabantur quaestores parricidii, quorum etiam meminit lex duodecim tabularum.* ("And because, as we have said, concerning the life of a Roman citizen, it was not permitted for the consuls to give judgment without the judgment of the Roman people, therefore the quaestors who presided over capital matters were established by the people: these were called *quaestores parricidii,* of whom even the law of the XII Tables makes mention.")

19. *D.* 1.13.1: *Origo quaestoribus creandis antiquissima est et paene ante omnes magistratus. Gracchanus denique iunius libro septimo de potestatibus etiam ipsum Romulum et Numam Pompilium binos quaestores habuisse, quos ipsi non sua voce, sed populi suffragio crearent, refert. Sed sicuti dubium est, an Romulo et Numa regnantibus quaestor fuerit, ita Tullo Hostilio rege quaestores fuisse certum est: et sane crebrior apud veteres opinio est Tullum Hostilium primum in rem publicam induxisse quaestores.* ("The origin of the creation of the quaestors is very ancient and is almost before the creation of all other magistrates. Gracchanus Junius, at least, in his seventh book concerning powers, wrote that even Romulus himself and Numa Pompilius both had quaestors, who were created not by their own call, but by a vote of the people. But as much as it is doubtful whether there was a quaestor when Romulus and Numa were ruling, it is certain that when Tullus Hostilius was king quaestors existed, and truly a more common opinion among our elders is that it was Tullus Hostilius who first introduced quaestors into the *res publica.*") Cf. Tac. *Ann.* 11.22.

20. Latte, "Origin," followed by A. Heuss, "Zur Entwicklung des Imperiums des römischen Oberbeamten," ZSS 64 (1944), and Max Kaser, *Das altrömische Ius* (Göttingen: Vandenhoeck & Ruprecht, 1949) 53-54, following Kurt Latte, RE Suppl. 7.s.v, "Todesstrafe" col. 1611; Kunkel, *Untersuchungen,* 40-43; Giuffrè, *Repressione,* 18, 37-40; Antonio Ortega Carrillo de Alborno *De los delitos y las sanciones en la ley de las XII Tablas* (Malaga: Universidad de Malaga, 1988) 38-39; Santalucia, *Studi,* 19. See Cloud's reservations, "*Parricidium,*" 17-18. See Chapter Three for further discussion of these officials.

21. Latte, "Origin," 24-33, and RE Suppl. 7.s.v, "Todesstrafe" col. 1611.

22. For the *perduellio* charge, see Livy 1.26; for parricide, see Festus, s.v. *sororum tigillum;* Florus 1.1.6; Dion. Hal. 3.22 is unclear.

23. "Death of Horatia," 438-441. Watson's argument derives from Christoph Heinrich Brecht, "*Perduellio*": *Eine Studie zur ihrer begrifflichen Abgrenzung im römischen Strafrecht bis zum Ausgang der Republik,* Münchener Beiträge zur Papyrusforschung und antiken Rechtsgeschichte 29. (Munich: C. H. Beck, 1938).

24. R. M. Ogilvie, *Commentary on Livy, Books 1–5* (Oxford: Clarendon, 1905) 114–115.

25. Dion. Hal. 3.22.7. Cf. *Schol. Bob.* (Stangl) 113. *Constitutis igitur duabus aris Iano Curiatio et Iunoni Sororiae superque eas iniecto tigillo Horatius sub iugum traductus est.* ... ("Therefore, when the two altars, to Janus Curiatius and Juno Sororia, were built and above them the crossbeam was hung, Horatius was led under the yoke."); Livy 1.26.13 (*velut sub iugum misit iuuenem* ["he (the father) sent the young man as if under the yoke."])

26. On the directions "to convict," see also the trial of Rabirius (Cic. *pro Rab. perd.* 12) and the discussion in Chapter Five.

27. Dion. Hal. 3.21.7–10.

28. Dion. Hal. 3.22.4.

29. Livy 1.26.9.

30. Dion. Hal. 2.26.4.

31. Dion. Hal. 2.25.6.

32. Pomponius suggests this same development in *D.* 1.2.2.1–2.

33. But note that Plutarch reflects a tradition that credits Romulus with this regulation: Plut. *Rom.* 22.

34. Although some scholars also see the right of *provocatio* as a monarchic institution. Luis Rodríguez-Ennes ("La 'provocatio ad populum' como garantia fundamental del ciudad romano frente al poder coercitivo del magistrado en la epoca republicana," in *Studi in onore di Arnaldo Biscardi* IV [Milan: Cisalpino 1983]) says that *provocatio* was monarchic. So too, Robert Develin, "*Provocatio* and Plebiscites," *Mnemosyne* 31 (1978). Also, I use the standard translation here, but see Chapter Three for further discussion of *provocatio*.

35. *D.* 1.2.2.16.

36. See, e.g., Alan Watson, *The State, Law and Religion: Pagan Rome* (Athens, GA: University of Georgia, 1992) 14.

37. Dion. Hal. 3.22.7; cf. *de vir. ill.* 4.9.

38. See, e.g., Carlo Gioffredi, *I principi del diritto penale romano* (Turin: G. Giappichelli, 1970) 41–44; Bernardo Santalucia, "Alle origini del processo penale romano," *Iura* 35 (1984).

39. Plut. *Numa* 7–16; Livy 1.18–21; Dion. Hal. 2.63–73.

40. Giuffrè (*Repressione*, 9), looking at this question from a different angle, argues that as the *civitas* became an entity in the monarchy, the king became the keeper of the *pax deorum*. If he is right, in the Roman monarchy the threat to the *pax deorum* would have been a threat to the king's authority since he was responsible for maintaining that peace.

41. For issues surrounding Numa's own succession, see Plut. *Numa* 2, 5–6; Livy 1.17–18; Dion. Hal. 2.57–58, 60, 62.

42. Watson, "Roman Private Law," 103.

43. See Chapters Two and Three.

CHAPTER TWO

1. "Citizens united in a community, the body-politic," Lewis and Short, s.v. *civitas*.

2. Richard P. Saller, *Patriarchy, Property and Death in the Roman Family* (Cambridge: Cambridge University, 1994) 189, and earlier in "*Patria Potestas* and the Stereotype of the Roman Family," *Continuity and Change* 1 (1986). With specific regard to the later republic and following periods, see Suzanne Dixon, "The Sentimental Ideal of the Roman Family," in Beryl Rawson, ed., *Marriage, Divorce and Children* (Oxford: Clarendon, 1991). With specific regard to *vitae necisque potestas*, see Yan Thomas, "*Vitae necisque potestas:* le père, la cité, la mort," in *Du Châtiment dans la cité*, Collection de l'École française (Rome: Palais Farnese, 1984) 545.

3. This is true to such a degree that women estate holders are subsumed under the heading *pater familias* in legal texts. Richard P. Saller, "*Pater Familias, Mater Familias,* and the Gendered Semantics of the Roman Household," *Classical Philology* 94 (1999) 185, 187, 188.

4. "A kind of abstract definition of power," Thomas, "*Vitae,*" 500.

5. Purportedly, the words spoken by the Pontifex Maximus before the *comitia curiata*. Aul. Gell. NA 5.19.9. Cf. Cic. *de domo* 77.

6. See Gaius 1.55, quoted below, as well as sources cited throughout this chapter.

7. Gaius 1.55; cf. 1.189; Just. *Inst.* 1.9.pr.2.

8. Caes. BG 6.19.3. Gaius' reference to the Galatians makes Harris' belief that Caesar's use of the *vitae necisque* phrase is pleonastic (William V. Harris, "Roman Father's Power of Life and Death," in Roger S. Bagnall and William V. Harris, eds., *Studies in Roman Law in Memory of A. Arthur Schiller* [Leiden: Brill, 1986] esp. p. 93 with n. 57) unjustified.

9. Furthermore, loss of citizenship also results in loss of paternal power. Gaius 1.128. For further evidence, see *The Institutes of Gaius,* W. M. Gordon and O. F. Robinson, trans. (Ithaca, NY: Cornell University, 1988) 35 §128.

10. *D.* 50.16.195.2, where the father's *potestas* is more clearly articulated as describing his position in the family. The *Digest*, however, postdates Constantine's removal of much of paternal power and so the earlier connection with being a Roman citizen was perhaps lost.

11. The citizen could, of course, also be under someone else's power (his oldest direct male ascendant's), but eventually he would be a *pater* in his own right. Furthermore, demographic studies suggest that probably two-thirds of Romans lost their fathers by the age of twenty-five (Saller, *Patriarchy,* 189). Thus, an adult Roman male would, for most of his adult life, have been more likely to have possessed *potestas* than to have been subject to it.

12. R. Yaron, "Vitae necisque potestas," *Tijdschrift voor Rechtsgeschiedenis* 30 (1962) 244.

13. Yaron, "Vitae," esp. 245–248; Raymond Westbrook, "*Vitae necisque potestas,*"

Historia 48 (1999). See also Westbrook's cogent response (208–209) to Harris' connection of *vitae necisque potestas* with *filium tollere* and the accepting or exposing of infants ("Roman Father's Power of Life and Death," 93–95).

14. See Westbrook's "Vitae," 219–221 and n. 57 on 220; for further bibliography on Near Eastern elements in early Roman laws, see 217–218 n. 48.

15. I am aware that Westbrook finds a small example of this power being possessed by fathers, but it is far more likely that this legal formula entered Rome through the notion of monarchic authority, which, as stated above, was far more pervasive. As Westbrook himself (*"Vitae,"* 213, 217) also states.

16. *D.* 1.2.2.16.

17. Alan Watson, "Roman Private Law and the *Leges Regiae*," JRS 82 (1972); see also Suzanne Dixon, *The Roman Family* (Baltimore: Johns Hopkins, 1992) 40–41, where she argues that fathers in the republic have greater power to decide to expose or not to expose infant children than fathers earlier.

18. Indeed, it is a power that some Roman sources say the kings gave to the *patres*. *Collatio* 4.8.1; implied in Livy 1.26.9, see Chapter One; Dion. Hal. 2.26 attributes it to Romulus, but the so-called "constitution of Romulus" in 2.7–29 is notoriously fallacious: T. J. Cornell, *The Beginnings of Rome: Italy and Rome from the Bronze Age to the Punic Wars (c. 1000–264 BC)* (London: Routledge, 1995) 59 and 412, n. 31, with reference to Emilio Gabba, "Studi su Dionigi da Alicarnasso. I. La costituzione di Romolo," *Athenaeum* 38 (1960) 175–225.

19. "To kill one's own son is almost always sacrilege, except when a father embodies the state or when the state is badly represented by a son." Thomas, *"Vitae,"* 545.

20. Yale H. Ferguson and Richard W. Mansbach, *Polities: Authority, Identity and Change* (Columbia, SC: University of South Carolina, 1996) 34.

21. The polity of the *familia* itself does not always function as a unified whole: "Families contain individuals who are by definition competing with other family members for a host of goods, material, emotional and symbolic." Suzanne Dixon, "Conflict in the Roman Family," in Beryl Rawson and Paul Weaver, eds., *The Roman Family in Italy* (Oxford: Clarendon, 1997) 165. For more on the divergent forces at work within the family, see Dixon, "Conflict," 150–151, n. 4.

22. Ferguson and Mansbach, *Polities,* 23.

23. Saller, *Patriarchy.*

24. Livy 2.3–5.

25. Harris, "The Roman Father's Power of Life and Death," 90.

26. Val. Max. 5.8.3 (Loeb translation); cf. Livy 2.5.5: *conspectius eo quod poenae capiendae ministerium patri de liberis consulatus imposuit* ("the consular office imposed upon a father the duty of inflicting punishment on his own children"); Dion. Hal. 8.79.2.

27. Harris, "The Roman Father's Power of Life and Death," 89–90.

28. Harris, "The Roman Father's Power of Life and Death," 82; so, too, Thomas, "Vitae," 514–518. Dionysius of Halicarnassus and Valerius see this in the category of harshness of fathers.

29. This appellation can be found throughout Latin literature; see specifically Livy 2.1.10–11; Cic. *de rep.* 2.23.

30. Livy 2.42.10–12; Dion. Hal. 8.77–80.

31. Livy 2.41.12; Val. Max. 6.3.1b; Dion. Hal. 8.78.

32. A *consilium* is an informal gathering of friends and relatives to act as advisers when important decisions need to be made. See further discussion of this institution below. Livy 2.41.10 (also, R. M. Ogilvie, *Commentary on Livy, Books 1–5.* [Oxford: Clarendon, 1905] 339); Val. Max. 5.8.2. Dion. Hal. (8.79.1–2) has the father call him before the senate, the senate condemns, and the father executes. Cicero (*de rep.* 2.60) puts them together and has the father testifying against him in the trial before the people. Some scholars who discuss the different versions assume that Livy's version with the *quaestores* postdates the version with the *pater* (Friedrich Münzer, RE 3, s.v. Cassius [no. 91], cols. 1751–1752; A. W. Lintott, "The Tradition of Violence in the Annals of the Early Roman Republic," *Historia* 19 [1970] 18–22). There seems to be no real reason for doing so. Harris ("Roman Father's Power of Life and Death," 82–83) sees it as the most plausible but does not discount other possibilities.

33. See Chapter Three for further discussion of venue.

34. Livy 3.44–50; *D.* 1.2.2.24.

35. Tension between the government of the decemvirs and the private *pater* is illustrated, for example, by Appius' attempt to arrest Verginius (Livy 3.48).

36. Livy sees the institution of the decemvirs as a change in the form of government parallel to the founding of the republic in place of the monarchy. He apparently sees the later transition as less significant than the former, only because it was so short lived (3.33).

37. In fact, the magistracy itself may have been intended to be permanent. For discussion of the decemvirate, see Cornell, *Beginnings,* 273–274.

38. Even the story of the founding of the republic and the rape of Lucretia draws this parallel, though the issue of paternal power does not appear in any direct way (Livy 1.57–59).

39. On the contemporary importance of national legends, see also Harris, "Roman Father's Power of Life and Death," 88, n. 34.

40. The one exception is in the writings of the Christian apologist, Orosius (4.13.18), who wrote that Fabius [M. Fabius Buteo] Censorius killed his son for theft. Harris ("Roman Father's Power of Life and Death," 84) rightly argues that Orosius' claim that such a killing occurred at all is suspect because of his attitude toward pagans. See also Emiel Eyben, "Fathers and Sons," in Beryl Rawson, ed., *Marriage, Divorce and Children in Ancient Rome* (Oxford: Clarendon, 1991) 122, though Eyben inaccurately credits this characteristic only to the early republic.

41. Val. Max. 6.1.3. See Harris, "Roman Father's Power of Life and Death," 87, Case 12. Note also Harris' belief that these are private acts.

42. Val. Max. 6.1.6. See Harris, "Roman Father's Power of Life and Death," 87, Case 13. *Stuprum* is, loosely, "criminal sexual activity."

43. Plut. *Numa* 10.

44. Holt N. Parker, "Why Were the Vestals Virgins? Or the Chastity of Women and the Safety of the Roman State," *AJPh* 125 (2004) 592, on the general point of the threat of women's sexuality to state; for *matronae,* see esp. 589–592.

45. For more discussion, see Chapter Four.

46. Livy 39.18; cf. Val. Max. 6.3.7. *Manus* is the power possessed by husbands as opposed to that possessed by fathers (Gaius 1.108–118).

47. For further discussion of the relationship between law and women, see L. Peppe, *Posizione giuridica e ruolo sociale della donna romana in età repubblicana.* Pubblicazione dell'Istituto di diritto romano e dei diritti dell'oriente mediterraneo, Rome, LXIII (Milan: Giuffrè, 1984) and Eva Cantarella's review in *Iura* 35 (1984); Pedro Resina, *La Legitimación activa de la mujer en el processo criminal romano,* (Madrid: Ediciones Clasicas, 1996); Olivia F. Robinson, "Women and the Criminal Law," in *Scritti in memoria di Raffaele Moschella.* Annali della Facoltà di giurisprudenza di Perugia n.s. 8 (Perugia: Università degli studi di Perugia 1987).

48. Richard A. Bauman, *Crime and Punishment in Ancient Rome* (London: Routledge, 1996) 18.

49. Such interpretations, however, beg the question, Who is meant to benefit from this demonstration of modesty: the women, their families, or the community? The ability to answer this question would further our understanding about the relative power of the public and private spheres, but interpretations so far are unsatisfying. Peppe (*Posizione giuridica,* 123 and n. 121) follows Edoardo Volterra ("Il preteso tribunale domestico in diritto romano," *Rivista Italiana per le Scienze Giuridiche* 3.2 [1948] 127), who turns to an eighteenth-century historian, Matteo Aegyptius, *Senatusconsulti de Bacchanalibus explicatio* (Naples, 1729) 133, cited in Volterra, 127, n. 48: *"Intra domesticos parietes in mulieres, bacchanalibus sacris pollutas, animadversum est, quum ut consuleretur pudori, tum ne pluribus caedibus suppliciisque facies Urbis dehonestaretur, neve plebs flecteretur ad misericordiam."* ("Women polluted by Bacchanalian rites were punished within domestic walls, both because that was thought to be modest, and lest by many deaths and punishments the face of the city would be dishonored, and lest the plebs be moved to pity.") For the families (apparently), see Richard A. Bauman, "Family Law and Roman Politics," in Vincenzo Giuffrè, ed., *Sodalitas: Scritti in onore di Antonio Guarino* (Naples: Jovene, 1984) 1299–1300. It seems unlikely that the beneficiaries would have been meant to be the women themselves, whose behavior had already been so reprehensible as to result in their capital punishment.

50. Val. Max. 6.3.7; though note that, contra Livy, Valerius writes, *"In omnes cognati intra domos animadverterunt."* ("They were punished at home among all their cognates.")

51. Richard A. Bauman, *Women and Politics in Ancient Rome* (London: Routledge, 1992) 56–57.

52. Val. Max. 6.3.8; Livy *Per.* 48.

53. The wives *in manu* during the Bacchanalian conspiracy reported by Livy are unlikely to have been an exception to this circumstance. Livy's inclusion of many other kinds of relatives negates the importance of the role of *manus* in the ability to kill these

women. Furthermore, other sources suggest that husbands possessing *manus* did not have power at all comparable to fathers in capital cases. See Dionysius of Halicarnassus' discussion of Romulus' rules: 2.25.6. See also Suet. *Tib.* 35 and Tac. *Ann.* 13.32, which, though imperial, refer back to earlier practice. Olivia Robinson ("Women," 530) suggests that "the power of the husband was restricted by a convention that the wife's blood relations must be consulted before any severe penalty could be imposed."

54. That this is a choice on the part of the relatives and not an instruction from the magistrates as the previous case indicated is suggested both by the epitome of Livy, which says that the relatives provided surety (i.e., paid for the right) and by Valerius Maximus who says that the relatives did not want to wait for a long trial.

55. Val. Max. 6.3.8.

56. Livy *Per.* 48.

57. On the ambiguity of *cognita causa,* see Remo Martini, *Il Problema della causae cognitio pretoria* (Milan: Giuffrè, 1960) 3–11.

58. Val. Max. 6.3.8.

59. Livy says *cognati,* and Valerius Maximus says *propinqui.* So far, it seems that attempts at defining these relatives are inconclusive, pace Volterra, 127–129, and Bauman, "Family Law and Roman Politics," 1283–1300.

60. For groups of women representing "anti-societies," see Parker, "Why Were the Vestals Virgins?" 592. For young men, consider (e.g.) the report of the rebellion of young men at the founding of the republic, Livy 2.3.

61. I was first introduced to this idea by an abstract by Paul W. Ludwig for the 2004 American Philological Association conference (http://www.apaclassics.org/AnnualMeeting/04mtg/abstracts/Ludwig.html, visited June 2005). Ludwig sees in Livy's story of Torquatus an indication that the *pater* is supposed to look after the community as a whole while the son looks after his family.

62. Livy 7.4.

63. Livy 7.4.

64. Livy 8.7. Harris (84) is mistaken in saying, "No source suggests that he relied on his legal rights as a father." See Dion. Hal. 2.26.4.

65. The use of *patres* as a term of respect for senators reinforces the importance of *patres* generally. André Magdelain refers to them as "*patres* par excellance" in "De l' 'auctoritas patrum' à l' 'auctoritas senatus,'" in *Ius imperium auctoritas.* Études de droit romain. Collection de l'École française de Rome. 133 (Rome: Palais Farnèse, 1990) 388. The same article appears in *Iura* 33 (1982) 25–45.

66. For more on the *senatus consultum ultimum,* see Chapter Five.

67. Val. Max. 5.8.5; cf. Sall. *Cat.* 39.5.

68. A similar tone can be found in the speech Livy puts into the mouth of the consul Torquatus (7.4.14–22).

69. Consul in 165. For the adoption as well as the date of Torquatus' consulship, see Cic. *de fin.* 24.

70. Val. Max. 5.8.3; cf. Livy *Per.* 54.

71. Val. Max. 5.8.3.

72. More will be said about this suicide below.

73. Valerius Maximus (5.8.3) refers to him as having *egregia multa rarae dignitatis* ("many honors of rare worth").

74. This incident occurred shortly after 141 B.C.E., when the *quastio de repetundis* was already in place (see Chapter Three).

75. καὶ τὰ μὲν ἄλλα οἱ ὕπατοι διῴκουν, Αὖλον δὲ Φούλουιον ἄνδρα βουλευτὴν αὐτὸς ὁ πατὴρ ἀπέσφαξεν, οὔτι γε καὶ μόνος, ὥς γέ τισι δοκεῖ, τοῦτ' ἐν ἰδιωτείᾳ ποιήσας· συχνοὶ γὰρ δὴ καὶ ἄλλοι, οὐχ ὅτι ὕπατοι ἀλλὰ καὶ ἰδιῶται, παῖδάς σφων ἀπέκτειναν. ("The consuls conducted most of the investigations, but Aulus Fulvius, a senator, was slain by his own father"; Dio 37.36 [Loeb trans.]). Dio continues, "And the latter was not the only private individual, as some think, who ever acted thus. There were many others, that is to say, not only consuls, but private individuals as well, who slew their sons."

76. Sall. *Cat.* 43.2.

77. Volterra, 106.

78. Val. Max. 5.9.1.

79. Westbrook, "*Vitae*," 216, cf. 209–211; Yaron, "Vitae," 245–248. For the specific Near Eastern legal meaning of giving life, see especially Westbrook, "*Vitae*," 210–217. For *vitae* as the right to pardon a child, see Alfredo Mordechai Rabello, *Effetti personali della patria potestas I: Dalle origini al periodo degli Antonini* (Milan: Giuffrè, 1979) 32–33, n. 26.

80. See Yaron, "Vitae," 249.

81. Cic. *de rep.* 3.23.

82. Cic. *de domo* 84. The juxtaposition of father, citizen, and son in the passage also reflects the relationship between family and *res publica* discussed earlier in this chapter, though such juxtaposition might also be explained by the context for the quote: Cicero is telling us that the censor passed over Clodius' father (thus the accusative case in the Latin) in a meeting of the senate.

83. For the accuracy of Quintilian in recognizing this Fabius Maximus as Eburnus, see Harris, "Roman Father's Power of Life and Death," 84, Case 6.

84. Orosius 5.16.8. J. D. Cloud, "*Parricidium:* From the *lex Numae* to the *lex Pompeia de Parricidiis*," ZSS 88 (1971) 40.

85. Harris, 84, case no. 6. See, also, Hadrian's oft-cited later ruling in *D.* 48.9.5, when the father was condemned *quod latronis magis quam patris iure eum interfecit* ("because he killed him in the manner of a bandit rather than of a father").

86. Cic. *pro Balbo* 28. Cf. Quint. *Decl. Mai.* 3.17; Val. Max. 6.1.5.

87. Sen. *de Clem.* 1.15.1. Augustus with his newly created role as father of the state had his own interest in acknowledging the father's authority.

88. Pace Wolfgang Kunkel ("Das Konsilium im Hausgericht," ZSS 83 [1966]); Yan Thomas, "*Parricidium,*" in *Melanges d'archeologie et d'histoire de l'École Française de Rome* 93 (1981) 663 n. 61; also in Yan Thomas, "Se Venger au forum: Solidarité familiale et proces criminel a Rome," in Raymond Verdier and Jean-Pierre Poly, eds., *La Vengeance: Vengeance, pouvoirs et idéologies dans quelques civilisations de l'antiquite*, La

Vengeance: Études d'ethnologie, d'histoire et de philosophie, 3 (Paris: Éditions Cujas, 1984) 499–548, and Rabello, *Effetti personali,* 149 n. 44 and citations therein. Valerius Maximus' report of the Lucius Gellius incident implies that Gellius chose to use a *consilium,* not that he had to. See also the case of Torquatus and Silanus above (Val. Max. 5.8.3), in which the former acts without a *consilium.*

89. So too, Volterra, 138, but his rejection of this as an example of a domestic court because of the constituents of the *consilium* is unreasonable.

90. E.g., see Emiel Eyben, "Fathers and Sons," 115: "The more humane society became, the more the paternal power was eroded, particularly as public opinion developed a distaste for undue strictness. From the days of the Empire onwards the legislators adapted themselves gradually to the altered mentality and took as their rule of thumb the maxim we find in the writing of the third-century jurist Marcianus: 'paternal authority must be based on affection, not on cruelty.'"

91. Ferguson and Mansbach, *Polities,* 44.

92. Thus, Carlo Venturini, *Processo penale e società politica nella Roma repubblicana* (Pisa: Pacini, 1996) esp. 8.

93. Harris, "Roman Father's Power of Life and Death," Case 8. Val. Max. 5.8.3; Livy *Per.* 54; *Oxyr. Per.* 54; Cic. *de fin.* 1.24. Gruen, RPCC, 32–33; Sachers 1086. See above for more on this case.

94. Harris, "Roman Father's Power of Life and Death," 91.

95. Harris, "Roman Father's Power of Life and Death," 86.

96. Harris, "Roman Father's Power of Life and Death," 86.

97. See above. One of the consequences of adoption is that the adopted person leaves the *potestas* of the biological father and goes under the *potestas* of the adopting father.

98. Val. Max. 5.8.4; cf. Harris, "Roman Father's Power of Life and Death," 85–86, Case 9.

99. *Genus* is clan, family in its broad sense.

100. See above.

101. Gruen, RPCC, 172–173.

102. For this claim, see the quote from Gaius' *Institutes* at the beginning of this chapter. For Fulvius' acts, see above; for Sulla's law, see Chapter Seven; for late republican attitudes, see Cicero's reference to Clodius' father, above. Pompey's law, *D.* 48.9.

CHAPTER THREE

1. The similarity of the meaning of *parricida* here and the meaning of *paricidas* in the *lex Numae* suggests a gradual change in attitudes about homicide between monarchy and republic and can be further explained: RS II 563: "It seems to us conceivable that Numa or some other king should have occupied himself with such matters as the Vestal Virgins, the religious aspects of homicide, the sprinkling of wine on a funeral pyre, and so on, and that elements of such rules should have flowed into the XII Tables."

2. Festus p. 318 lines 60–65. For an overview of the scholarship on *homo sacer*, see the first chapter of Roberto Fiori's work: *"Homo sacer": Dinamica politico-costituzionale di una sanzione giuridico-religiosa*. Pubblicazioni dell'Istituto di diritto romano e dei diritti dell'Oriente mediterraneo, 72 (Naples: Jovene, 1996) 7–24.

3. Harold Bennett, "Sacer Esto," *TAPA* 61 (1930) esp. 6.

4. Santalucia, *Studi*, 147–148.

5. The Festus text as it is transmitted to us shows that a single source can be used for a series of alphabetically ordered definitions. For more on this practice, see Louise Adams Holland, "Septimontium or Saeptimontium?" *TAPA* 84 (1953) 17, n. 3.

6. Cic. *de rep.* 2.53.

7. Livy 2.8, 3.20; Cic. *de rep.* 2.53–55; Dion. Hal. 5.19.4; Plut. *Poplic.* 11; Val. Max. 4.1.1,2; *D.* 1.2.2.16. Dionysius mistakenly includes a severe fine under the list of punishments from which appeal is permitted. Cicero (*de rep.* 2.53–55) claims that the pontifical record shows the right of appeal in existence even during the monarchy, but he still emphasizes Publicola's role in the limitation of magisterial power, both with the law and with his additional actions.

8. The term *imperium* is as problematic as any other term applied to the institutions of the early republic. Some modern scholars see the term as "from the first the sole basis of criminal jurisdiction" (James L. Strachan-Davidson, *Problems of the Roman Criminal Law*, vol. 1 [Oxford: Clarendon, 1912] 103). The Roman sources—all later than the period under discussion in this chapter—are divided about whether the right of summary execution belongs to the magistrates' *imperium* or their *iuris dictio* (Adolf B. Berger, *Encyclopedic Dictionary of Roman Law*, *TAPA* n.s. 43.2 [1953] s.v. *imperium*). I suspect that the Roman magistrates practiced summary execution because it needed to be practiced, not because it was based on either *iuris dictio* or *imperium*. Further evidence suggests that the proper approach to studying magisterial authority is not to consider these terms and limits of authority to be absolute. Magistrates could act in a manner that appeared to be exceeding the supposed limits of their authority. For example, the quaestors were able to call an assembly even though they technically did not have the *ius agendi cum populo* ("right to call a meeting of the people"). Also, the word *imperium* has been used in discussing the authority of magistrates who supposedly possessed no *imperium* (Richard A. Bauman, "Criminal Prosecutions by the Aediles," *Latomus* 33:2 [1974] 251). On the variations of *imperium* inside and outside the city of Rome, see Adalberto Giovannini, *Consulare Imperium* (Basel: Friedrich Reinhardt, 1983).

9. See, e.g., Andrew Lintott, "Provocatio. From the Struggle of the Orders to the Principate," *ANRW* 1.2 (1972) 227 with nn. 3–6. For later scholarly debate on this issue, see Flach, *Gesetze*, 61–62; Elster, *Gesetze*, 102–103; also Luigi Garofalo, "In tema di 'provocatio ad populum' (a proposito di un recente saggio)," *SDHI* 53 (1987); Andrew R. Dyck, "On the Interpretation of Cicero, *de Republica*," *CQ* n.s. 48.2 (1998) 566–567.

10. A *lex Valeria Horatia* of 449 removed the decemvirs from office and reinstated the right of *provocatio*, which had been in abeyance during their rule (Livy 3.55; Cic. *de rep.* 2.54, *de domo* 17.43, *pro Sest.* 30.65; cf. Dion. Hal. 11.45; 5.70.2; Festus s.v. *optima lex*

p. 198 M). At the same time, a *lex Duilia* extended the right of *provocatio* by providing that it also should lead to a trial before the *concilium plebis* and before the *comitia centuriata* (Livy 3.55.14). Another *lex Valeria* allegedly promulgated in 300 B.C.E. differed little from the previous laws (Livy 10.9). This final law is the one that some scholars consider to be real (see citations in previous note).

11. Robert Develin, "*Provocatio* and Plebiscites," *Mnemosyne* 31.1 (1978). So, too T. J. Cornell, *The Beginnings of Rome: Italy and Rome from the Bronze Age to the Punic Wars c. 1000-263 BC.* (London: Routledge, 1995) 226, with nn. 37 and 38, and 276-278 with additional citations at n. 18; Santalucia, *Studi,* 159-160.

12. These arguments would hold true even if the *provocatio* law had existed during the monarchy, as Cicero (*de rep.* 2.53-54) reports, though Dyck ("On the Interpretation of Cicero," 566-567) justly criticized Cicero's claim as an anti-*popularis* view of Publicola; Dyck also rejects the attribution to 509, on different grounds. E. S. Stavely ("Provocatio during the Fifth and Fourth Centuries BC," *Historia* 3 [1955], 413-414) also rejects the attribution to 509. In contrast, see Luis Rodríguez-Ennes, "La 'provocatio ad populum' como garantia fundamental del ciudad romano frente al poder coercitivo del magistrado en la epoca republicana," in *Studi in onore di Arnaldo Biscardi* IV (Milan: Cisalpino, 1983) 75-81.

13. The average Roman citizen may have had even less recourse to *provocatio* than the elite Roman, a condition that was true later in the republic (Kunkel, *Untersuchungen,* 24-37).

14. This very circumstance is envisioned in the legend of the decemvir Appius Claudius who, according to the story, tried to appeal from the accusation of Valerius that he tried to make a freewoman into a slave. Livy 3.56.

15. Livy 2.8, 3.20; Dion. Hal. 5.19.4; Plut. *Poplic.* 11. Even the symbolic lowering of the *fasces* (Cic. *de rep.* 2.53-54; Val. Max. 4.1.1) could have been done with a view toward leveling the power among the elite more than out of a concern about the feelings of the ordinary Roman.

16. Thus, to associate it exclusively with the plebeian struggle for power is wrong.

17. On the changing interpretation of *provocatio,* see Mommsen, *Strafr.,* 473; *Staatsr.,* 2.351; contra Mommsen, see Kunkel, *Untersuchungen,* 21-33; Santalucia, *Studi,* 157-161, 172 (esp. 161 n. 54); for an entirely different approach, see Lintott, "Provocatio," 228-238.

18. Although the law of the early republic is famously irreligious, the ritualistic nature of early republican law with the *in actio* procedure suggests that a ritual practice of appeal could have existed.

19. So, too, Kurt Latte, "The Origin of the Roman Quaestorship," TAPA 67 (1936) 24.

20. See the related example of the much later comment of Cicero that self-defense was understood to be permissible even though no statute regulated it (*pro Mil.* 10).

21. "Ancient codes give regulations only in those matters where the law is doubtful, or where a reform is at once needed and practicable." David Daube, "*Nocere* and *noxa,*" *Cambridge Law Journal* 7 (1939) 32 = *Collected Studies in Roman Law* (Frankfurt am

Main: Klosterman, 1991) 80. So, too, Cornell, *Beginnings*, 279–280. Additional discussion and bibliography in *RS* II.561 and (with an entirely different perspective on the origins) Raymond Westbrook, "Nature and Origins of the XII Tables" *ZSS* 105 (1988) 76.

22. E.g., J. D. Cloud, "*Parricidium*: From the *lex Numae* to the *lex Pompeia de parricidiis*," *ZSS* 88 (1971) 17; Kurt Latte, *RE* Suppl. 7, s.v. Todesstrafe, cols. 1599–1619; Kunkel, *Untersuchungen*, 40–43; Giuffrè, *Repressione*, 18; Santalucia, *Studi*, 109–110.

23. On the survival of the XII Tables generally, see, e.g., Alan Watson, *The State, Law and Religion: Pagan Rome*, 16–18; *RS* II, 556–557, 569–571.

24. Cic. *pro Tull*. 22; cf. August. *de lib. arbit.* 1.4.9.25.

25. Further references to this phrase appear in Cic. *de or.* 3.158, and August. *de lib. arbit.* 1.4.

26. Cic. *Top.* 64.

27. Lewis and Short, s.v. *aries*. http://www.perseus.tufts.edu/cgi-bin/ptext?doc= Perseus%3Atext%3A1999.04.0059%3Aentry%3D%233622 stable URL visited March 4, 2007. This translation is also in the far from literal Loeb translation by H. M. Hubbell: "This distinction supplies the beam which you use to prop up a weak case in your pleadings: Perchance he did not throw the weapon, but it slipped from his hand."

28. Salvatore Tondo ("L'Omicidio involontario in età arcaica," *Labeo* 18 [1972] 326, and reference in n. 100) suggests that Cicero is employing a double entendre, which is plausible, but such a reading is unnecessary.

29. Serv. auct. *Ecl.* 4.43. The Festus passage (470 L.) offers little help in this particular discussion since *aries* is supplied to it based on the passages from Cicero and Servius.

30. Tobias Reinhardt, *Marcus Tullius Cicero, Topica* (Oxford: Oxford University, 2003) 333.

31. Reinhardt, *Marcus Tullius Cicero*, 334.

32. Cic. *Top.* 81, cf. 80 and 82, and 86.

33. Cic. *Top.* 97.

34. Cic. *Top.* 1; also Cic. *ad fam.* 7.19.

35. Cic. *ad fam.* 7.10–13, 17–19, 21–22; *Top.* 65–66.

36. Cic. *Top.* 45.

37. For additional explicit contrasts of "your" with oratory see 32, 65; not in specific contrast to oratory, see 56, 72. His letters to Trebatius indicate the same use of the second person plural possessive pronoun. See, e.g., "*ius civile vestrum*" in Cic. *ad fam.* 7.19, which was written, presumably, immediately after the completion of the *Topica*. Citations for the pronoun discovered using *PHI CD ROM #5.3: Latin Texts and Bible Versions*, Packard Humanities Institute.

38. The other passages mentioned above and Festus, s.v. *subici*, 470.19 L. (where *aries* is supplied from *ar . . .*) and s.v. *subigere arietem*, 476.18 L. provide no help here because the context is not mentioned.

39. *XII Tables* 8.2 *FIRA* = *RS* II, *Table* 1.18. For further discussion, see below. See also, Cato *Orig.* 48.8, as quoted by Priscian (vi p710, Putsch): "*Si quis membrum rupit aut os fregit, talione proximus cognatus ulciscatur.*" ("If anyone breaks a limb or shatters a bone, let the closest cognate [of the victim] seek vengeance using *talio*.") See also, Gaius

3.223. Other acts whose punishment seems to be connected with the notion of *talio* (though not in as direct a manner as the limb breaking) include a patron who defrauds a client and is then declared *sacer* (*XII Table* 8.21 FIRA = RS II, *Table* 8.12.), presumably denied the protections that he himself should have been offering to his client. A person who intentionally burns buildings or crops can himself be burnt (*XII Table* 8.10 FIRA = RS II 8.6).

40. *XII Table* 8.12 FIRA = RS II.609–613, *Table* 1.17.

41. *XII Table* 8.24b FIRA = RS II.692–695, *Table* 8.13. The Elder Pliny even says, "*Frugem . . . furtim . . . pavisse . . . XII tabulis capital erat . . . gravius quam in homicidio.*" ("To eat fruit by stealth was a capital offense in the XII Tables—more serious than homicide.") See also RS II.688–689, *Table* 8.9.

42. *XII Table* 8.13 FIRA = RS II.609–613, *Table* 1.18.

43. *XII Table* 8.10 FIRA = RS II.685, *Table* 8.6.

44. *XII Table* 8.23 FIRA = RS II.692, *Table* 8.12: "*ex XII tabulis . . . si nunc quoque . . . qui falsum testimonium dixisse convictus esset, e saxo Tarpeio deiceretur. . . .*" ("In the XII Tables, if now also, let he who has spoken false testimony be convicted and cast down from the Tarpeian rock.")

45. *XII Table* 8.21 FIRA = RS II.691, *Table* 8.12.

46. *Table* 8.1 FIRA = RS II, Table 8.12. For the death penalty for this act, see RS II.679 and esp. Cic. *de rep.* 4, 12 (= RS II, *Table* 8.1c).

47. RS II.693, *Table* 8.13. For scholarly opinions on the significance of the ram, see Artur Völkl, *Die Verfolgung der Körperverletzung im frühen römischen Recht: Studien zum Verhältnis von Tötungsverbrechen und Iniuriendelikt* (Vienna: Bohlau, 1984) 97–117. More recently the overlapping meanings have been elucidated by Antonello Calore, "La 'pena' e la 'storia,'" in Eva Cantarella (ed.), *Scritti in ricordo di Barbara Bonfiglio* (Milan, Giuffrè, 2004). Tondo, "L'omicidio involontario," 331. See also Chapter One, note 4, p. 146.

48. Serv. auct. *Ecl.* 4.43. See also Chapter One.

49. Festus, 476 L (s.v. *subigere arietem*).

50. "We suggest that the phrase *reum agere* was in the mind of the author '. . . which can be "accused" instead of him, (and in fact) killed.'" RS II.693.

51. See Chapter Four for a discussion of the possible role of the *quaestores parricidii*.

52. For the vendetta, see Carlo Gioffredi, *I Principi del diritto penale romano* (Turin: G. Giappichelli, 1970) 41–44; Bernardo Santalucia, "Alle origini del processo penale romano," *Iura* 35 (1984); Calore, "La 'pena' e la 'storia,'" 87 and sources at n. 52.

53. Festus 363.6; cf. Aul. Gell. NA 20.1.

54. In particular, see *Tables* 1–3.

55. Though it should be acknowledged that the XII Tables also would try to articulate the authority of the father by saying how he can kill a deformed son. *Table* 5.1: *Cito necatus tamquam ex XII tabulis insignis ad deformitatem puer.* ("As is noted in the XII Tables, a deformed boy must be killed swiftly.")

56. Pliny *Nat. Hist.* 18.3.12: *Frugem quidem aratro quaesitam fortim noctu pavisse*

ac secuisse puberi XII tabulis capital erat, suspensumque Cereri necari iubebant, gravius quam in homicidio convictum; impubem praetoris arbitratu verberari noxiamve duplionemve decerni. ("Indeed, for an adult to eat and to cut ploughed fruit sought furtively at night, was a capital offense in the XII Tables, and the culprit would be sacrificed to Ceres, a conviction more serious than homicide; if he was a youth, at the will of the praetor he would be lashed or compelled to pay a double fine.")

57. See Chapter One, and Tondo, "L'omicidio involontario," esp. 327–332. Also, Calore, "La 'pena' e la 'storia,'" 85–97.

58. Aul. Gell. NA 20.1.53; *Table 8.23 FIRA = RS* II.692, *Table 8.12*.

59. Aul. Gell. NA 20.1.7; *Table 9.3 FIRA* and RS II.701.

60. See commentary and references in RS.692 II, *Table 8.12. Table 8.13 FIRA = RS* II.613–615, *Table 1.19*.

61. See commentary in RS II.703, *Table 9.5*, where the authors suggest that the *Digest* is in error.

62. *Table 9.6: Interfici . . . indemnatum quemcunque hominem etiam xii tabularum decreta vetuerunt* ("Even decrees of the XII Tables forbade killing any uncondemned man." = Salv. *de gubern. dei* 8.5.24).

63. This attitude toward magistrates and homicide further indicates that the concept of *provocatio* would not have been alien to the archaic Romans.

64. *Table 9.1: De capite civis nisi per maximum comitiatum . . . ne ferunto* ("Let them not pass a law concerning the *caput* of a citizen except through the greatest assembly"; Cic. *de leg.* 3.11); cf. *Table 9.2: Leges praeclarissimae de XII tabulis tralatae duae, quarum altera privilegia tollit, altera de capite civis rogari nisi maximo comitiatu vetat* ("There are two most illustrious laws of the XII Tables handed down to us, of which one bears a privilege, the other forbids a vote of capital punishment except by the greatest assembly." Cic. *de leg.* 3.44). For the meaning of comitiatus maximus, see Emilio Gabba, "Maximus Comitiatus," *Athenaeum* 65 (1987) 203–205; Kunkel, *Untersuchungen*, 31.

65. D. 1.2.2.6. "The connection between religion and law in the archaic period is indisputable," Santalucia, *Studi*, 145 and n. 1; cf. 146, 107. See also, Giuffrè, *Repressione*, 19. For the abundant bibliography on this subject, see Luigi Garofalo, *Appunti sul diritto criminale nella roma monarchica e repubblicana*, 2nd ed. (Padua: Cleup, 1993) 14 n. 11.

66. If Numa's law had remained in force, then parricide in the republic would have also meant murder and would not have taken on the more limited meaning of kin-killing. So, too, Enzo Nardi, *L'otre dei parricidi e le bestie incluse* (Milan: Giuffrè, 1980) 55.

CHAPTER FOUR

1. On the pervasiveness of arbitration generally, see Derek Roebuck and Bruno de Loynes de Fimuchon, *Roman Arbitration*. (Oxford: Holo Books, Arbitration Press, 2004). While the emphasis of their discussion is on private—what they call civil (see e.g., 12, 68)—law, there seems to be no reason to believe that acts of homicide would

be excluded from mediation or arbitration. They say, "In Rome, too, concern for the interests of the state fixed the limits of arbitrability . . . of what disputes could be settled privately."

2. Henry Campbell Black, *Black's Law Dictionary*, 6th ed. (St. Paul, West Publishing, 1990), s.v. murder, crime.

3. Ascon. *in Mil.* 32; Ps. Ascon. p. 141.

4. Probably already in existence by 142; see below.

5. After Sulla, *quaestiones perpetuae* were created both for public violence and for private violence, but at the time of Cassius Longinus, standing courts were something of a novelty. See further discussion of the *quaestio de sicariis* below. For the *lex Cornelia*, see Chapter Seven.

6. For the institution of permanent courts, see above. For this as a temporary *quaestio* and the subsequent attempts to define its jurisdiction and title, see Mommsen, *Staatsr.*, 2.583 n.2; *Strafr.*, 647 n. 3; Kunkel, *Untersuchungen*, 50; Santalucia, *Studi*, 117.

7. Cic. *Brut.* 85.

8. The precise dates are not important; for a tentative chronology, see Charles H. Buck Jr., *A Chronology of the Plays of Plautus* (Baltimore: Johns Hopkins, 1940).

9. Plaut. *Aul.* 415–418. See also Chapter Five regarding the role of the *tresviri*.

10. Chapter Five.

11. If Cic. *de fin.* 2.16 refers to a permanent court, as seems likely, then the *sicarius* court was in place as early as 142 B.C.E. On the permanency of this court, see, in favor of the temporary court, A. W. Zumpt, *Das Criminalrecht der Römischen Republik* II (Berlin: F. Dümmler, 1869) 54–55; A. H. M. Jones, *The Criminal Courts of the Roman Republic and Principate* (Oxford: Basil Blackwell, 1972) 55; Gruen, RPCC, 29, n. 261. The objection is based on the mistaken belief that the *quaestio inter sicarios* was a murder court. Santalucia finds the evidence inconclusive (*Studi*, 117). In favor of the permanency of the court, see Mommsen, *Strafr.*, 203, with n. 2; Kunkel, *Untersuchungen*, 64; Josef Lengle, *Untersuchungen über die Sullanische Verfassung* (Freiburg im Breisgau: Charitas Druckerei, 1899) 36–40; A. H. J. Greenidge, *The Legal Procedure of Cicero's Time* (Oxford: Clarendon, 1901) 420. Richard A. Bauman makes the clearest argument in support of the permanent court, and part of his argument, at least, is persuasive (*Lawyers in Roman Republican Politics*, Münchener Beiträge zur Papyrusforschung und Antiken Rechtsgeschicht, 75 [Munich: C. H. Beck, 1983] 272–275). Even if the court of 142 was not permanent, a standing court was established well before Sulla, (Cic. *de inv.* 2.59, quoted and discussed below).

12. J. D. Cloud, "The Primary Purpose of the *lex Cornelia de Sicariis*," ZSS 86 (1969). Cloud's argument is about a later incarnation of the court, after Sulla's law, but his argument about the meaning of the term is still applicable. The idea that this was a court primarily about public violence originated with Kunkel (*Untersuchungen*, 64–68).

13. Cloud, "Primary Purpose," 273.

14. Cic. *de inv.* 2.59.

15. *Recuperatores* (literally, "recoverers") are a panel of judges, often for trials concerning property.

16. *In iure* (literally, "in court") is a stage in the judicial procedure; for further discussion, see below.

17. Cic. *de inv.* 2.60; cf. Cloud, "Primary Purpose," 41.

18. *D.* 48.8.1. On arson, see below.

19. Indeed, a change in word order is not uncommon in the compilers of the *Digest* (Jean-Louis Ferrary, "Lex Cornelia de sicariis et veneficis," *Athenaeum* 79 [1991] 3).

20. Cic. *pro Mil.* 11. Kunkel (*Untersuchungen,* 65) uses this to prove his point but Cloud ("Primary Purpose," 260–262) is right in saying it fits Cicero's agenda too well to be an argument that stands on its own.

21. This is not dissimilar to the distinction in modern American law between lying in wait and acting in the heat of passion.

22. *Collatio* 1.3.1.

23. For further discussion of Ulpian's greater reliability, see Kunkel, *Untersuchungen,* 65, and esp. Cloud, "Primary Purpose," 264.

24. The Romans were always cautious about the bearing of weapons inside the walls. That is why the *comitia centuriata* met outside the walls, the army was mustered outside the walls, and the generals had to disarm and release their troops before re-entering the city after fighting Rome's wars. There also seems to have been a general rule about wielding knives within the walls of the city.

25. *Table* 8.25: *Qui venenum dicit, adicere debet, utrum malum an bonum; nam et medicamenta venena sunt* ("He who says *venenum* ought to add whether it is bad or good for *venena* are also remedies"; *D.* 50.16.236pr.).

26. Livy 8.18. The earlier portion of this text is quoted in Chapter Three.

27. We are never told whether or how they were punished.

28. See, e.g., the Roman response to the so-called Bacchanalian conspiracy. For this feeling of "vulnerability to conspiracies," see Wilfred Nippel, *Public Order in Ancient Rome.* Key Themes in Ancient History (Cambridge, Cambridge University, 1995) 27–30. Livy (8.18) and Valerius Maximus (2.5.3) both report 170 women condemned; Orosius (3.10.1) inflates the number to 370.

29. Livy 8.18.1.

30. Livy 39.41.

31. See, e.g., Clodine Herrmann, *Le rôle judicaire et politique des femmes sous la République romaine* (Brussels: Latomus, 1964) 78–79. For general scholarship on the Bacchanalian conspiracy, see references in Carlo Venturini, *Processo penale e società politica nella Roma repubblicana* (Pisa: Pacini, 1996) 126–127 n. 116.

32. Livy 40.37.

33. Livy 40.19.4.

34. Livy 40.37.8.

35. Livy 40.19.7–8, 40.26.

36. Polybius 6.14.5–7.

37. Tac. *Ann.* 3.13.

38. Livy *Per.* 49.

39. Val. Max. 6.3.8.

40. Robert Schilling (*La réligion romaine de Venus depuis les origines jusqu'au temps d'Auguste* [Paris: de Boccard, 1954] 43) for the early connection with magic. But see L. Monaco, "'Veneficia Matronarum' Magia, medicina e repressione," in *Sodalitas: Scritti in onore di Antonio Guarino* 4 (Naples: Jovene, 1984) 2016–2017, who sees a development in Plautus' use from complete connection with bad drugs and magic and a growing connection with medicine. Jean Gage, *Matronalia: Essai sur les devotions et les organisations cultuelles des femmes dans l'anciènne Rome* (Collection Latomus 60, Brussels: 1963).

41. So, too, Gage, *Matronalia,* 262.

42. For the date of promulgation and the first parricide case, see J. D. Cloud, "*Parricidium:* From the *lex Numae* to the *lex Pompeia de parricidiis,*" zss 88 (1971) 26–38; cf. Enzo Nardi, *L'otre dei parricidi e le bestie incluse* (Milan: Giuffrè, 1980) 68 and Santalucia, *Studi,* 116 n.30.

43. *D.* 48.9.9pr.

44. Cloud, "*Parricidium,*" 26–36. See, too, this same proposal put forth a century earlier by Gustav Landgraf, *Kommentar zu Ciceros Rede pro Sex. Roscio Amerino* (Leipzig: Teubner, 1914). For a discussion of the primary sources on the *culleus* as *procuratio prodigii* and *poena,* see Nardi, *L'otre dei parricidii,* 117–121.

45. Seneca the Younger during the early empire even wrote that parricide was *quam diu sine lege crimen fuit* ("for a long time a crime without a law"; Sen. *de Clem.* 1.23.1).

46. Cic. *pro Rosc. Am.* 64–65.

47. That this was a public trial is evident in the *nominis delatio,* the phase of a public trial in which the accuser makes an accusation to the magistrate.

48. Suet. *Iul.* 88.

49. Plut. *Rom.* 22.

50. Gaius 1.9.2. For further discussion of father's authority, see, e.g., Barry Nicholas, *Introduction to Roman Law* (Oxford: Clarendon, 1962) 65–69, 79–80; John Anthony Crook, "*Patria Potestas,*" cq 17 (1967); Walter Kirkpatrick Lacey, "*Patria Potestas,*" in Beryl Rawson, ed., *The Family in Ancient Rome* (Ithaca, NY: Cornell University); Richard Saller, "*Patria Potestas* and the Stereotype of the Roman Family," *Continuity and Change* 1 (1986); Alan Watson, *Society and Legal Change* (Edinburgh: Scottish Academic Press, 1977) 23–30.

51. Val. Max. 5.9.1. The text is quoted in its entirety in Chapter Three.

52. See Chapter Two.

53. Orosius 5.16.8. For the full quote, see Chapter Two. Cf. Val. Max. 6.1.5. This Fabius should perhaps be identified with Eburnus, who was consul in 116.

54. The much later Theodosian code will include them (*C. Th.* 9.15.1). For discussion of this imperial development, see Nardi, *L'otre dei parricidi,* 71 n. 6.

55. Yan Thomas, "Parricidium," in *Melanges d'archeologie et d'histoire de l'École Française de Rome* 93 (1981) 663 n. 61; Cloud, "*Parricidium,*" 38–41; William Harris, "Roman Father's Power of Life and Death," in Roger S. Bagnall and William V. Harris, eds., *Studies in Roman Law in Memory of A. Arthur Schiller* (Leiden: Brill, 1986) 85.

56. Pompey's law would make the punishment for parricide the same as the punish-

ment for other offenses of the *lex Cornelia;* see Chapter Seven. For the imperial period, Hadrian's constitution provided that if the sea was not close at hand a parricide could be thrown to the beasts, thus implying the sack was still in use. *D.* 48.9.9pr.

57. See Chapter Three.

58. For further discussion of the *tresviri,* see the Introduction.

CHAPTER FIVE

1. The specific exceptions to this in the assassinations of the second and first centuries are the subject of Chapter Six.

2. See, e.g., Bernardo Santalucia, *Diritto e processo penale nell' antica Roma,* 2nd ed. (Milan, Giuffrè, 1989) 88. See also George Willis Botsford, who wrote (in *The Roman Assemblies from their Origin to the End of the Republic* [New York: MacMillan, 1909] 250 with n. 8), "In fact, since the death of M. Manlius Capitolinus, in 384, no example of the execution of a death sentence pronounced by the assembly is recorded in history, with the possible exception of a certain plebeian named C. Veturius, date unknown." Also, Gordon P. Kelly, *A History of Exile in the Roman Republic* (Cambridge: Cambridge University, 2006) esp. 1.

3. The assemblies with such jurisdiction, however, changed over time and came to include, most notably, the plebeian assembly (*concilium plebis*).

4. Botsford, *Roman Assemblies,* paraphrasing Ludwig Lange (*Römische Alterthümer.* Vol. 2 [Berlin: Weidmannsche, 1879] 557). Each (Botsford in n. 8) also mentions the possible exception of C. Veturius whose dates are unknown. See Plut. *C. Gr.* 3.

5. For how complicated and time consuming the procedure before the *comitia* was, see, e.g., Santalucia, *Diritto e processo penale,* 84–88.

6. The last record of them is in 366. Varro *de Ling. Lat.* 5.19.

7. *D.* 1.13. For similar views on monarchic origins, see Festus, s.v. *Parici* and *Quaestores* and Tac. *Ann.* 9.22; for conflation with other quaestors, see Tac. *Ann.* 9.22 and Zonar. vii.13.

8. *D.* 1.2.2.23. On the rejection of the attribution of the *quaestores parricidii* to the XII Tables, see RS II 702.

9. Varro *de Ling. Lat.* 5.81. More on this below.

10. For conflation with other quaestors, see Tac. *Ann.* 9.22; Zonar. vii.13, *D.* 1.13. This was rejected by Kurt Latte, *Kleine Schriften zu Religion, Recht, Literatur und Sprache der Griechen und Romer* (Munich: C. H. Beck, 1968). Cloud, "Parricidium," 25, rejects the role of the quaestors as authorities in a murder trial, but not R. M. Ogilvie, *Commentary on Livy, Books 1–5* (Oxford: Clarendon, 1905) 416; Livy 3.11–13.

11. Livy 2.41.10–12. See also Dion. Hal. 8.77. Cf. Livy 3.24, in which the quaestors again bring a capital matter before the assembly.

12. *D.* 1.2.2.23 says they were in charge of *capitalibus rebus,* quoted above.

13. See, e.g., Claire Lovisi, *Contribution à l'étude de la peine de mort sous la république romaine (509–149 av. J.-C.)* (Paris: de Boccard, 1999) 81–83. The title *quaestores*

parricidii probably derived from the early use of the term parricide, by which a person having been determined deserving of death would be "treated as a parricide," as in Festus p. 318 lines 60–65. See Chapter Three.

14. *Quaestores a quaerendo, qui conquirerent publicas pecunias et maleficia, quae triumviri capitales nunc conquirunt.* ("The *quaestores* [who get their name] from *quaerendo* [investigating], [are] those who make a search for public monies and bad deeds, for which now the *triumviri capitales* make a search.") Varro *de Ling. Lat.* 5.81. J. D. Cloud, "The Constitution and Public Criminal Law," *CAH* 9, 2nd ed., 500, has taken this association with the *quaestores parricidii* as evidence that the *tresviri capitales* possessed "complete criminal jurisdiction over citizens," but see Cosimo Cascione, *Tresviri capitales: Storia di una magistratura minore* (Naples: Editoriale Scientifica, 1999) 85–86, for historiography on the question of the connection with the *duumviri capitales*.

15. Livy *Per.* 11. For modern discussion of chronology, see Cascione, *Tresviri capitales,* 6–24, esp. 9 n. 17.

16. Although the *tresviri* did not have judicial jurisdiction over citizens, the judicial (or at least decision-making) authority they seem to have possessed over slaves and foreigners is another matter. Wilfried Nippel may be correct that certain conclusions regarding the judicial role of the *tresviri* must remain unanswered, but his rejection of Kunkel's proposal of the *tresviri* as regular judicial magistrates is cogent and persuasive (*Public Order in Ancient Rome* [Cambridge: Cambridge University, 1995] 23–25). On the contentious issue of the extent of their judicial powers, see (since Nippel): Cascione, *Tresviri capitales,* 85–117; and Lovisi, *Contribution,* 102–105. Note also how the creation of the *tresviri capitales* seems to come on the heels of the creation of the praetor peregrinus, thus at a time when the Romans were trying to decide how to manage the influx of foreigners into the city; *D.* 1.2.2.28.

17. Cascione, *Tresviri capitales,* 85–169 (and for scholarship on the question, see his thorough notes). Note also the similar conclusions of Lovisi, *Contribution,* 98–101, as opposed to Kunkel, *Untersuchungen,* 71–79.

18. Though in a more chaotic time, even the executions were not carried out as a result of a judicial investigation. Note, e.g., their supervision of the executions of the Catilinarian conspirators.

19. *D.* 1.2.2.30: *Constituti sunt eodem tempore et quattuorviri qui curam viarum agerent, et triumviri monetales aeris argenti auri flatores, et triumviri capitales qui carceris custodiam haberent, ut cum animadverti oporteret, interventu eorum fieret* ("At the same time were constituted the Four Men in charge of the roads; the Three Men of the Mint, casters of bronze, silver, and gold; and the Three Men in Charge of Capital Matters [Tresviri Capitales] who were in charge of guarding the prison, so that when punishment was necessary, it was carried out by these men"), and yet 1.2.2.28 says the praetor peregrinus was established; section 29 says ten men for presiding over disputed cases ("hasta"), and section 31 says five men above the Tiber, five men below.

20. For creation of the *tresviri nocturni,* Livy 9.46.3; for the magistracies being one and the same, see Cascione, *Tresviri capitales,* 9–10, n. 18; Lovisi, *Contribution,* 98 with n. 262.

21. One triumvir was even accused before the people for neglecting his duty to diligently prevent fires. Val. Max. 8.1.*damn*.6.

22. E.g., the rise of the popularity of foreign cults during the Hannibalic war: Livy 25.1.6; see also Wilfried Nippel, "Policing Rome," *JRS* 74 (1984) 20–21. Some *tresviri* are censured for not preventing the growth of foreign cults (ca. 213, see Rüpke, Jörg, "You Shall Not Kill: Hierarchies and Norms in Ancient Rome," *Numen* 39 (1992).

23. Livy 32.36; Cic. *de leg.* 3.6.

24. Plaut. *Aul.* 415–418. Perhaps even the misbehavior of other classes was their concern as well: Cic. *pro Clu.* 38–39. Lovisi, 109–110.

25. Plaut. *Amphit.* 153–162. That the *tresviri* did not go after slaves and wrongdoers is the tentative suggestion of Nippel, *Public Order*, 22–26.

26. Though see Nippel's tentative rejection: *Public Order*, 22–26.

27. Livy's discussion (38.59) of the threat to L. Scipio Asiaticus is both hyperbole and at least as likely to be based on the later activities of the *tresviri* as on their activities in the second or early first century. In the end, although Asiaticus went to prison for a while, he was released by a tribune of the plebs. Also, Livy does not, in fact, mention the *tresviri* here.

28. The actual executioner was a state slave known as the *carnifex*. It seems unlikely that the lictors, subordinates of other magistrates, would have played this role under the supervision of the *tresviri* during the republic. They almost certainly supervised the *carnifex*. Some have suggested that the lictors also served as executioners, but it seems unlikely that the *tresviri* would supervise lictors who were not their own subordinates but must necessarily have been someone else's subordinates. Furthermore, there is no ancient evidence that the lictors performed this role under the *tresviri*.

29. State executions can also be seen as vengeance on behalf of the *res publica*. Lovisi, *Contribution*, 98: "l'abandon de l'exécution privée" ("the abandonment of private execution").

30. Lovisi, *Contribution*, 98: "Les *quaestores* surveillaient le *parricidium*, c'est-à-dire à notre sens l'exécution privée administrée par un vengeur." ("The quaestores look after parricide, that is to say in our meaning the 'execution privately administered by a person seeking revenge.") Cf. 81.

31. See Chapter Four.

32. Lovisi, *Contribution*, 98–100.

33. Lovisi, 99 with n. 267, for the date of the introduction. Martin Hengel (*Crucifixion in the Ancient World and the Folly of the Message of the Cross,* London: Fortress Press, 1977) provides examples of citizen crucifixions. The impact of the growing slave population on the creation of the *tresviri* specifically and on Roman criminal law deserves further exploration. Olivia Robinson, "Slaves and the Criminal Law," *ZSS* 98(1981) 213–254 is a good start, but there is much to be explored here.

34. Cic. *in Verr.* 2.5.158.

35. Livy 30.43.13; Val. Max. 2.7.12.

36. Although see Hengel's (*Crucifixion*, 39–44) conflation of crucifixion with

being hung from the *arbor infelix* (literally, "the unfortunate tree"), an old Roman punishment.

37. Hengel, *Crucifixion*, 40 n. 2.

38. Lovisi, *Contribution*, 99 with n. 268.

39. For more on religious expiation and parricide in general, see Chapter Four.

40. Tac. *Ann.* 59.

41. Lovisi, *Contribution*, 98 with n. 265. See also Rüpke, "You Shall Not Kill," 63 with n. 18 on p. 75.

42. Polybius lived in the city of Rome from 167 until 150, left in 149–146 and returned sometime after 146, departing again sometime before his death in 118. He worked with the most famous Romans of his day. He even probably witnessed Scipio's killing of citizens with crucifixion.

43. Polybius 6.12 (Loeb translation); Andrew W. Lintott's emendation to Polybius' statement seems unnecessary because Italy does not have to include Rome, and indeed Polybius seems specifically not to include Rome: in 6.13, Polybius seems to be treating Italy as distinct from Rome (*The Constitution of the Roman Republic* [Oxford: Clarendon, 1999] 151 with n. 12, 21 with n. 18).

44. Of course, the *concilum plebis* and the *comitia centuriata* were not constituted of exactly the same people, though by the mid second century they were probably close to the same. Furthermore, when it comes to the right of a citizen not to be killed, the discussion does not include the language of plebeian, only of *populus*.

45. It used to be believed that assemblies only functioned as courts of appeal, that is, they would only be called to act as courts when a Roman citizen, sentenced to capital punishment by a magistrate, called for his right of *provocatio* (Mommsen, *Staatsr.*, 1.149–150, 2.109–110, 3.351–354; *Strafr.*, 163–171, 473–478; see also A. H. M. Jones, *The Criminal Courts of the Roman Republic and Principate* [Oxford: Basil Blackwell, 1972] 1–39). Now it is generally and correctly agreed that assemblies also functioned as courts of first instance. This idea was proposed most thoroughly by Kunkel, *Untersuchungen*, 9–17. For bibliography, see Richard A. Bauman, *Crime and Punishment in Ancient Rome* (London: Routledge, 1996) 165–166 n. 5 and his text on 10–11. Furthermore, this authority of the assemblies is at least as old as the republic itself: Santalucia, *Studi*, 152 and n. 22.

46. For capital jurisdiction of magistrates, see, for tribunes: e.g., *D.* 1.2.2; Varro *de Ling. Lat.* 5.81; Dion. Hal. 6.89; Val. Max. 2.2.7; Plut. *Quaest.* 81; for aediles: Dion. Hal. 6.90.2–3 and Richard A. Bauman, "Criminal Prosecutions by the Aediles," *Latomus* 33 (1974) 245 n. 1, for the general scholarly consensus on the general judicial authority of the aediles. For a discussion on whether or not the aediles had jurisdiction in capital trials in addition to those in which the condemnation was simply a fine, see Santalucia, *Studi*, 65–76. In contrast, see Cicero's claims during the trial of Verres (Cic. *Verr.* 2.1.12–14, esp. 12, 5.151, 163, 173) and Clodius' actions against Milo: Cic. *ad Quint. Frat.* 2.3.2. cf. *in Vat.* 40; *pro Sest.* 95; Aul. Gell. NA 4.14.2, 10.6. Santalucia, *Studi*, and Dignös discuss mostly trials concerning fines. Georg Dignös, "Die Stellung der Aedilen im römischen

Strafrecht" (Munich: Doctoral Thesis, Universität München, 1962); Luigi Garofalo, *Il processo edilizio: Contributo allo studio dei "iudicia populi"* (Padua: CEDAM, 1989) 1–7; Andrew Lintott, *Violence in Republican Rome* (Oxford, Clarendon 1968) 92–101. On the date of the first aediles, see Joseph Wilhelm Kubitschek, RE 1, s.v. Aedilis, cols. 448–464. For quaestors: Livy 3.24, 6.20. Though the *comitia* as a court of first instance is thought by some to have been the purview only of the quaestors, tribunes, and aediles (Santalucia, *Studi*, 172). For consuls: Varro *de Ling. Lat.* 6.90–92. For consuls and praetors: Because the consuls and praetors had the authority to preside over assembly meetings for legislative or electoral purposes, it is difficult to believe that they could not have presided when the assembly functioned as a public court, especially if they wanted to do so. The reason for the absence of evidence may be that their provinces generally took them outside the confines of the city of Rome and not because they would not have had the capacity for convening a court had they been present and interested.

47. Polybius 6.14 (Loeb translation).

48. Cic. *de fin.* 2.54.

49. Florus 1.17.1–2; Livy 4.51.2–4, although Livy says the guilty are generally believed to have committed suicide. Cf. Zonar. 7.20.

50. E.g., Livy 39.41 (quoted in Chapter Four). The poisoning investigations of 184, within and beyond the city of Rome, were intended to be a quick job one of the praetors could manage on his way to his province in Sardinia. At the same time, one of his colleagues was rooting out the remainder of the Bacchanalian conspirators in Tarentum; thus, these investigations were presumably also sponsored by the senate (Livy 40.37; cf. Val. Max. 2.5.3), as were the investigations of the killings in the Sila forest in 138: Cic. *Brut.* 85.

51. 8.18. The passage following this has already been quoted in Chapter Four. Livy finds this story somewhat suspicious but is willing to believe it is true.

52. Livy 39.14. The scholarship on the Bacchanalian conspiracy is abundant; see Carlo Venturini, *Processo Penale e società politica nella Roma repubblicana* (Pisa: Pacini, 1996) 126–127 n. 116 for references. See also Val. Max. 6.3.7; Livy 39.8–19.

53. Livy 39.18.

54. Livy 40.43.

55. *Non enim putaverunt severissimi viri in tam evidenti scelere longum publicae quaestionis tempus expectandum.* ("For the most severe men did not think they should wait for the long time of a public *quaestio* in the face of such evident wickedness.") Val. Max. 6.3.8; cf. Livy *Per.* 49 and Chapter Four.

56. This court shows that the claims to power assumed by the senate were a consequence of the growth of the government in response to territorial expansion.

57. Cic. *de fin.* 2.54. That the court was permanent and not temporary, see Mommsen, *Strafr.*, 203, esp. n. 2; Kunkel, *Untersuchungen,* 64; Richard A. Bauman, *Lawyers in Roman Republican Politics* (Munich: C. H. Beck, 1983) 236. Contra A. W. Zumpt, *Das Criminalrecht der Römischen Republik* II (Berlin: F. Dümmler, 1869) 54–55; Jones, *Criminal Courts,* 55; Gruen, RPCC, 29, 261. That the evidence is inconclusive: Santalucia, *Studi,* 117.

58. Andrew Riggsby, *Crime and Community in Ciceronian Rome* (Austin: University of Texas, 1999) 50 with 200 n. 3, and *CIL* 6.1283.

59. Plut. *C. Gr.* 4.5.

60. Andrew W. Lintott (Provocatio. From the Struggle of the Orders to the Principate" *ANRW* 1.2 [1972] 253–255) has argued that this was not a legal restriction, but regardless of that, no record exists of *provocatio* being sought after a decision of a *quaestio.*

61. *Pro Clu.* 151, 154.

62. According also to Jürgen Baron Ungern-Sternberg von Pürkel, *Untersuchungen zum spätrepublikanischen Notstandsrecht, senatusconsultum ultimum und hostis-Erklärung* (Munich: C. H. Beck, 1970) 55.

63. Among these was the removal of the senators from the juries of the permanent courts and their replacement with equestrians, about which, more in the following chapter. No doubt, Gaius' continuation of his brother's agrarian reform and his law providing grain at a fixed rate to citizens might have been perceived by the other senators as steps toward his becoming a demagogue much like his brother before him. For sources on Gaius' legislation, see Broughton, *MRR*, vol. 1, 513–514, 517–518. See also Gruen, *RPCC*, 79–81, esp. 80 n. 3.

64. Gruen, *RPCC*, 82.

65. *D.* 48.8.1: *quive cum magistratus esset publicove iudicio praeesset, operam dedisset, quo quis falsum indicium profiteretur, ut quis innocens conveniretur condemnaretur.* ("Or whoever, when he was a magistrate or he presided over a public court, had tried to convict an innocent person, in a way that he would profit from a false indictment, let him be condemned.")

66. Botsford, *Roman Assemblies,* 557.

67. For the complexity about *perduellio* in general, see Venturini, *Processo Penale,* 116–122, and 117 n. 94 for bibliography.

68. For the scholarly consensus on this much, at least, see Richard A. Bauman, *The Duumviri in the Roman Criminal Law and in the Horatius Legend, Historia,* Einzelschriften 12 (Wiesbaden: Steiner, 1969) 5 n. 30; cf. Greenidge, 310; Mommsen, *Staatsr.,* 2.615.

69. Livy 1.26.5–8. For the entire legend, see Livy 1.24–26; cf. Dion. Hal. 3.22.

70. 6.20.4.

71. Cic. *pro Rab. perd.* The historians Suetonius and Dio both record this event, but their records of it are problematic because they represent a different reaction on the side of the crowd. Suetonius, the biographer of the Caesars, tells us that Julius Caesar "bribed a man to bring a charge of high treason against Gaius Rabirius who, some years previously, had earned the Senate's gratitude by checking the seditious activities of L. Saturninus, a tribune. Caesar, chosen by lot to try Rabirius, pronounced the sentence with such satisfaction that, when Rabirius appealed to the people, the greatest argument in his favor was the judge's obvious prejudice" (Suet. *Iul.* 12, Penquin translation). Dio (37.27) tells us, καὶ ἦν γὰρ αὐτὸς ἐκεῖνος καὶ μετὰ τοῦ Καίσαρος τοῦ Λουκίου δικάζων (οὐ γὰρ ἁπλῶς, ἀλλὰ τὸ δὴ λεγόμενον περδουελλίωνος ὁ Ῥαβίριος ἐκρίθη),

κατεψηφίσαντο αὐτοῦ, καίτοι μὴ πρὸς τοῦ δήμου κατὰ τὰ πάτρια, ἀλλὰ πρὸς αὐτοῦ τοῦ στρατηγοῦ οὐκ ἐξὸν αἱρεθέντες. ("Julius Caesar himself was judge together with Lucius Caesar, for the charge against Rabirius was no ordinary one, but that of *perduellio,* as it was called; and they condemned him, although they had not been chosen according to precedent set by the people, but by the praetor himself, which was not lawful" [Loeb translation].)

72. Lintott, "Provocatio," 261; cf. J. L. Strachan-Davidson, *Problems of the Roman Criminal Law* (Oxford: Clarendon, 1912) vol. 1, 188–190; Matthias Gelzer, RE 7, s.v. M. Tullius Cicero (no. 29), cols. 827–1091; Jochen Bleicken, *Lex Publica: Gesetz und Recht in der römischen Republik* (Berlin: de Gruyter, 1975) 388; contra Mommsen, *Staatsr.,* 3.357; *Strafr.,* 155 n. 1.

73. Cic. *pro Rab. perd.* 12.

74. Bernardo Santalucia, "Osservazioni sul *duumviri perduellionis* e sul procedimento duumvirale," in Yan Thomas, ed., *Du Châtiment dans la cité: Supplices corporels et peine de mort dans le monde antique,* École française de Rome (Rome: Palais Farnèse, 1984 = Santalucia, *Studi,* 35–48). This is the same argument made by some about the authority of the *quaestores parricidii* (see Chapter Two). Santalucia also argues that no appeal was allowed from the decision of the *duumviri.* He bases this argument, however, on the idea that the two cases for which we have the most evidence are the exceptions to the rule; this seems to me a dangerous proposition.

75. This has been recognized by others, Bauman, "*Duumviri,*" 5; cf. the review of this monograph by Wolfgang Waldstein, ZSS 88 (1971) 417–421.

CHAPTER SIX

1. That the employment of the *scu* was never completely acceptable has already been acknowledged. See, most recently, Wilfried Nippel, *Public Order in Ancient Rome.* Key Themes in Ancient History (Cambridge: Cambridge University, 1995) 60–69.

2. What the precise motivations were of those who took part in the attack on Tiberius, or what the straw was that broke the camel's back is not of concern here. Many other scholars have addressed this issue. See the review of the scholarship in Ernst Badian, "Tiberius Gracchus and the Roman Revolution," ANRW 1.1 (1978).

3. By using the word "tyrant," taken from the Greek with all its philosophical and political baggage that tyranny is evil and killing tyrants is expected, Scipio foretells his action in the forum. See below.

4. Plut. *Ti. Gr.* 19 (Loeb translation).

5. Polybius 6.13.

6. For homicide-related laws that were in existence, see Chapter Five.

7. Plut. *Ti. Gr.* 19.6.

8. App. BC 1.2.17 (Loeb translation, with emendations).

9. The status of Nasica as chief priest and the possible implications of the need for a religious leader to authorize a killing against an official who was sacrosanct and

untouchable are intriguing but not central to this study. The killing of Tiberius may have been a religious act.

10. See, e.g., Gruen, RPCC, 58–59.

11. Baron Jürgen Ungern-Sternberg von Pürkel, *Untersuchungen zum spätrepublikanischen Notstandsrecht, senatusconsultus ultimum und Hostis-Erklärung* (Munich: C. H. Beck, 1970) 7–25, esp. 7–8, 16–19, and ancient sources quoted therein. See also Richard A. Bauman, *Lawyers in Roman Republican Politics* (Munich: C. H. Beck, 1983) 272–275 and n. 312 for scholarship; Nippel, *Public Order,* 60–61.

12. Plut. *Ti. Gr.* 19.3.

13. Plut. *Ti. Gr.* 9.1; Gruen, RPCC, 51–53, 56–57; Bauman, *Lawyers,* 275; Friedrich Münzer, RE 16, s.v. P. Mucius Scaevola (no. 17), cols. 425–428.

14. For more on the character of Scaevola and how it may have influenced his decision making, see Bauman, *Lawyers,* 272–290.

15. Cic. *de domo* 91; cf. *pro Mil.* 72, where Cicero uses the glory of the killers of Tiberius to justify Milo's killing of Clodius: "Yes, [Milo] might cry, it is I who have slain . . . not a Spurius Maelius, not a Tiberius Gracchus, who unconstitutionally deposed a colleague from his office, and whose slayers filled the whole world with the glory of their name, but a rotten man like Clodius."

16. The idea that the senate would have passed several decrees has been rejected by at least one scholar. Bauman (*Lawyers,* 274) writes, "It is not at all clear why the senate should have become addicted to the habit of praising Nasica." Cicero's report does not require us to believe that Nasica was honored many times, but that the senate passed decrees in support of the act. Even so, evidence suggests that further debate did occur in the senate even after Nasica's death a short time later. Cicero reports that Laelius proposed that a memorial be built to Nasica as a tyrannicide (Cic. *de rep.* 3.8).

17. Nippel (*Public Order,* 62–63), too, recognized these trials more as a justification for the senators than a judgment on the defendants. Santalucia, *Studi,* 182 n. 117; Ernst Badian, "The Death of Saturninus," *Chiron* (1984) 118. For the persecution of Tiberius' followers in 132, see Cic. *de amic.* 37; Sall. *Iug.* 31.7; Vell. Pat. 2.7.3; Val. Max. 4.7.1; Plut. *Ti. Gr.* 20.3. Cf. Ungern-Sternberg, *Untersuchungen,* 38–43.

18. This sort of thorough follow-through when members of the senate believed Rome was in danger was not without precedent. The Bacchanalian conspiracy and the poisoning trials discussed in Chapters Three and Four are two indications of this.

19. Alexander, *Trials,* nos. 12–14 for references.

20. Plut. *Ti. Gr.* 20.3. Cf. Alexander, *Trials,* no. 15; Cic. *de amic.* 37; Val. Max. 4.7.1. C. Villius is listed among the dead by Plutarch, but he must have been convicted of parricide around the same time as the persecution of the Gracchan supporters. He became associated with Tiberius only for chronological reasons. So Gruen, RPCC, 61–62.

21. Cf. Diod. Sic. 34/35.33.6–7. See, e.g., J. R. Dunkle, "The Greek Tyrant and Roman Political Invective of the Late Republic," TAPA 98 (1967).

22. He killed himself when he was with Aristonicus in Asia. This story is recorded in Cicero's *de Amicitia,* through which it came to Valerius Maximus. Cic. *de amic.* 37, Val. Max. 4.7.1; cf. Plut. *Ti. Gr.* 8. 17. 20; Orosius 5.9.3.

23. Cic. *de amic.* 37; Val. Max. 4.7.1. Gaius Laelius, not Nasica, questioned Blossius, according to Ernst Badian, "Tiberius Gracchus," 708 and n. 120. So, too, Bauman, *Lawyers,* 289 n. 427. The questioning took place at a formal *quaestio,* according to Alvin Bernstein, *Tiberius Sempronius Gracchus: Tradition and Apostasy* (Ithaca, NY: Cornell University, 1978) 46; David Stockton, *The Gracchi* (Oxford: Oxford University, 1979) 71 n. 35; but not Gruen, RPCC, 61.

24. Cicero also killed Roman citizens to protect the *res publica;* see below.

25. Cic. *pro Mil.,* e.g., 8, 12, 14, 30, 72.

26. Nor would Clodius himself be much less popular sixty years later. The reaction to the plebs at the killing of Clodius resulted in burning the senate house to the ground (Dio 40.49.2-3). On this incident, see Nippel, *Public Order,* 77 and references there.

27. This was part of the conciliation of the people, and the senate became so alarmed for his safety that they passed a resolution to send him to Asia, although they had nothing for him to do there, Plut. *Ti. Gr.* 21.

28. Cic. *de or.* 2.285.

29. The phrase *iudicem ferre* ("to bring a juror/judge") is legal terminology for assigning a juror to a court. Cf. Gruen, RPCC, 63; Cic. *de or.* 2.263, *pro Rosc. Am.* 45. Although there was a *quaestio perpetua de sicariis* by this time, it is unlikely that Nasica was tried in it because he did not use a weapon. Gruen, RPCC, 63, suggests a temporary court.

30. Gruen, RPCC, 63. The prosecutor was M. Fulvius Flaccus: Alexander, *Trials,* 11 no. 18, and references there.

31. The sources do not preserve the *senatus consultum* that established this *quaestio,* and so we do not know precisely what the accusations were against Nasica. Because this was probably a trial in a temporary *quaestio,* the charges did not even require particularly clear definition (see Chapter Four). Evidence for this trial comes from Cic. *de or.* 2.285; Plut. *Ti. Gr.* 21.2; cf. Val. Max. 5.3.2e; D. Magie, *Roman Rule in Asia Minor to the End of the Third Century after Christ* (Princeton: Princeton University 1950) 2.1033 n. 1.

32. See above.

33. This passage is particularly telling because Cicero would have been happier if he could have shown his hero Scaevola to be willing to commit violence on behalf of the state, a step Cicero himself took.

34. Plut. *C. Gr.* 4.

35. For the tribunate as traditional defense of the people, see Polybius 6.16.5; Badian, "Tiberius Gracchus," 709-710.

36. The term *senatus consultum ultimum,* used by modern scholars, appears only in Caes. BC 1.5.3 and Livy 3.4.9. Cf. Bernd Rödl, *Das senatus consultum ultimum und der Tod der Gracchen* (Bonn: Habelt, 1969) 7.

37. Cic. *Phil.* 8. 14.

38. See references in Broughton, MRR, 520-521; Ungern-Sternberg, *Untersuchungen,* 56-57, esp. references in n. 9; Rödl, *Das senatus consultum ultimum,* 63-65.

39. Cic. *pro Sest.* 140; *de or.* 2.106, 132, 165, 169, 170; *Part. or.* 106; *Brut.* 128; Livy *Per.* 61. Cf. Mommsen *Strafr.,* 2.111 n. 2.

40. Cic. *de or.* 2.132.

41. See, e.g., Rödl, *Das senatus consultum ultimum,* 92; Richard A. Bauman, *Crime and Punishment in Ancient Rome* (London: Routledge, 1996), 42 (but cf. 45, where he appears to contradict himself). Andrew W. Lintott's view ("Provocatio: From the Struggle of the Orders to the Principate," *ANRW* 1.2 [1972] 261) that Opimius' acquittal "lent strength to subsequent decrees of this kind" is more accurate.

42. See the case of Rabirius, below.

43. Val. Max. 5.3.2f. For Decius, see Cic. *de or.* 2.135; *Part. or.* 104; Friedrich Münzer, *RE* 4, s.v. P. Cornelius Lentulus (no. 202), cols. 1374–1375; and Gruen, *RPCC,* 106.

44. Gruen, *RPCC,* 106, 107.

45. Livy *Per.* 61; Cic. *de or.* 30; Rödl, *Das senatus consultum ultimum,* 90 and n. 1.

46. Pace Giorgio Agamben (*State of Exception.* trans. Kevin Attell [Chicago; University of Chicago, 2005] 41–51), who claims that the *scu* was accompanied by a *iustitium,* which does not seem to have been the case.

47. This is why it seems fruitless to try to determine which of the reports of this advice to the magistrates was the actual wording of the *scu.* To try to determine the precise wording is to imply that the *scu* was formulated in technical language for use against Gaius Gracchus, and then it retained that technical form each time it was employed, but it is far more likely that the *scu* did not require precise wording. (For attempts to determine the precise wording, see Enrico Antonini, "*Il 'senatus consultum ultimum'*": *Note differenziali e punti di contatto col moderno stato d'assedio* (Turin: Regia Università, 1914) 44; Gerhard Plaumann, "Das sogennante senatus consultum ultimum die Quasidiktatur der späteren römischen Republik," *Klio* 13 (1913) 322; Rödl, *Das senatus consultum ultimum,* 59–62, esp. 60. Its basic meaning was that the state needed to be preserved by extreme means. Cicero records, among other references to the *scu* employed against Gaius: *uti L. Opimius consul rem publicam defenderet* ("that the consul L. Opimius defend the *res publica*"; Cic. *Phil.* 8.14); also, *uti L. Opimius videret, ne res publica detrimenti caperet* ("that L. Opimius see to it that the *res publica* does not suffer"; Cic. *Cat.* 1.4); cf. *de domo* 102; Plut. *C. Gr.* 14.2 and 3; Livy *Per.* 61; Val. Max. 4.7.1, 6.8.3, 9.4.3.

48. The *contio* was a public meeting, preliminary to an electoral or legislative assembly. See the following note for sources for this event, though see Badian ("Death of Saturninus," 116–117), who is skeptical of many of the reports of violence attributed to Saturninus and who believes that the killing of Nunnius took place in the Campus Martius but not at a meeting.

49. Cic. *pro Rab. perd.* 20; cf. Ungern-Sternberg, *Untersuchungen,* 71–74, esp. references 72 n. 88.

50. The wording of the consuls' orders to the other officials seems to be the same as the language used by Nasica, but the *scu* itself uses different language.

51. *Maiestatem minutam.* Cicero (*de or.* 2.107) is clear on this point, though most of the provisions of the law are unknown. See, e.g., Andreas Pesch, *De Perduellione, crimine maiestatis et memoria damnata* (Aachen: Shaker, 1995) 193 with n. 168. Cf. Olivia F. Robinson, *The Criminal Law of Ancient Rome* (Baltimore: Johns Hopkins,

1995), 75; J. D. Cloud, "The Constitution and Public Criminal Law," *CAH* 9, 2nd ed. (1994) 518–519.

52. App. *BC* 1.32–33; Cic. *pro Rab. perd.* 20; Val Max. 3.2.18; Dio 37.26; Orosius 5.17.8–9. See Gruen, *RPCC*, 182–183, for a discussion of Marius' role in this event; Nippel, *Public Order,* 63. For thorough discussion of events leading up to the *hostis* declaration, see Badian, "Death of Saturninus," 101–119.

53. Unlike Nasica, however, Lentulus appears to have had time to realize that he would never return to the good graces of the people that he had been in before his share in employing the *scu*. Val. Max. 5.3.2.

54. For Marius' relationship with the executed, see Badian, "Death of Saturninus," 119–124. Cloud is mistaken when he says the *scu* instructed the consuls to kill ("Constitution," 495).

55. E. G. Hardy, *Some Problems in Roman History* (Oxford: Clarendon, 1924) 27–35, 99–125, and W. B. Tyrrell, *A Legal and Historical Commentary to Cicero's Oratio pro c. Rabirio Perduellionis Reo* (Amsterdam: Hakkert, 1978). Also see discussion below for the events of 63–62. A discussion exists among modern scholars that the *scu* had been brought to an end by the surrender of the Appuleians, and thus this killing did not take place under the *scu*. The absence of any mention of the ending of the *scu* in the primary sources makes this highly suspect. Bauman, *Lawyers,* 336; Richard A. Bauman, "The *Hostis* Declaration of 88 and 87 B.C.E.," *Athenaeum* 61 (1973) 227 and n. 41; Ungern-Sternberg, *Untersuchungen,* 66 and references in n. 53.

56. Sall. *Hist.* 2.22; cf. Nippel, *Public Order,* 66. Pace Ungern-Sternberg (*Untersuchungen,* 78–81), there was no *hostis* declaration against Lepidus; the *scu* was passed against him for conspiring with enemies, but he was not himself declared one.

57. Sall. *Cat.* 29; Cic. *Cat.* 1–4.

58. Dio 48.49; Appian *BC* 2.24.

59. Appian *BC* 1.5. Cf. Cic. *ad Att.* 10.8.8, *ad fam.* 16.11.2, *Deiot.* 11; Livy *Per.* 109; Dio 41.33.3. The great irony is that the senate in the empire did obtain the authority to kill Roman citizens without the approval of the people. See, e.g., Wolfgang Kunkel, *Über die Entstehung des Senatgerichts* (Munich: Verlag der Bayerischen Akademie der Wissenschaften; Beck in Kommission, 1969) = *Kleine Schriften* (Weimar, 1974) 267–323.

CHAPTER SEVEN

1. For Sulla's early career, see, e.g., Pierre F. Cagniart, *The Life and Career of Lucius Cornelius Sulla through His Consulship in 88 B.C.E.: A Study in Character and Politics* (Austin: University of Texas, 1986).

2. See Richard A. Bauman, *Lawyers in Roman Republican Politics.* Münchener Beiträge zur Papyrusforschung und Antiken Rechtsgeschicht 75 (Munich: C. H. Beck, 1983) 337 n. 258, for scholarship on these machinations.

3. Cf. B. R. Katz, "The First Fruits of Sulla's March on Rome," *AC* 44 (1975); Richard A. Bauman, "The *Hostis* Declaration of 88 and 87 BC," *Athenaum* 51 (1973);

Arthur Keaveney, *Sulla, The Last Republican* (London: Croom Helm, 1982) 67–68; Baron Jürgen Ungern-Sternberg von Pürkel, *Untersuchungen zum spätrepublikanischen Notstandsrecht, senatusconsultum ultimum und hostis-Erklärung.* Beiträge zur alten Geschichte, Band 11. Munich: C. H. Beck, 1970) 74–78. Among the charges were that they stirred up sedition, they bore arms against the consuls, and they incited slaves to insurrection. For these charges, see Appian *BC* 60. For the story, see Plut. *Sulla* 6.10; 7.1–10.2, *Marius* 34.1–35.4; Appian *BC* 1.55–63, *Mith.* 22,30.

4. For the agreement among scholars that this was an innovation of Sulla, see Bauman, "*Hostis* Declaration," 276 n. 1.

5. Pace Ungern-Sternberg (*Untersuchungen*, 111–122, 117), who sees a systematic connection between the two, and A. Dupla Ansuategui ("El senatus consultum ultimum: ¿Medidà de salvación pública o práctica de depuración politica?" *Latomus* 49 [1990] 78), who believes the *hostis* declaration is implicit in the *scu*.

6. Ungern-Sternberg, *Untersuchungen*, 130–131.

7. Sall. *Hist.* 2.22; cf. Nippel, *Public Order*, 66. Ungern-Sternberg (*Untersuchungen*, 78–81) is mistaken when he says that a *hostis* declaration was made against Lepidus; the *scu* was passed against him for conspiring with enemies, but he was not himself declared one. For further sources on Lepidus' revolt, see Elimar Klebs, *RE* 1, s.v. Aemilius (no. 72), cols. 554–556. For Lepidus' career, see Gruen, *LGRR*, 12–18 and references therein.

8. So Bauman, "*Hostis* Declaration," 277–284, esp. 283.

9. Val. Max. 3.8.5. The italics in the English translation are mine. It does not seem necessary to equate Scaevola's objection with his activities as a jurist pace Bauman (*Lawyers,* 339), who credits Scaevola's disapproval to his interpretation of Roman legal technicalities.

10. Val. Max. 3.8.5, cf. 1.5.5. Cic. *Brut.* 168; Florus 2.9.8; Livy *Per.* 77; Plut. *Sulla* 10.1.

11. Appian *BC* 1.61. So, too, Plut, *Marius* 43 and Vell. Pat. 2.19.1.

12. Livy *Per.* 89; Cic. *de leg.* 3.22, *pro Tull.* 38–39; Caes. *BC* 1.5.7; Appian, *BC* 2.29.

13. He seems to have been of this opinion himself, anyway. Keaveney, *Sulla.*

14. So, too, Ungern-Sternberg, *Untersuchungen*, 75. This characteristic is also a difference from the *scu*, which required the magistrates to act (and over time more and more magistrates are called to act), but not the people.

15. See Ungern-Sternberg, *Untersuchungen*, 76–78, for references and discussion.

16. Despite there being a *lex* by the people authorizing the killing; Bauman, "*Hostis* Declaration," 271–275.

17. Livy *Per.* 77; Appian *BC* 1.60; Cic. *Brut.* 168; Plut. *Sulla* 10; Val. Max. 3.8.5; Florus 2.8, plus *MRR* 2.40. "The charge against Sulla forms a close parallel to that brought against Popillius Laenas in 123" (Gruen, *RPCC*, 230).

18. Appian *BC* 1.98–99; Cic. *de leg. agr.* 3.5; cf. *pro Rosc. Am.* 125; *ad Att.* 9.15.2; *Schol. Gronov.* p. 435, Orelli; Plut. *Sulla* 33.1; Livy *Per.* 89. See Hurlet, *La Dictature,* 102–105, for discussion of his title.

19. Appian *BC* 1.99. Or they could be appointed for a day for a religious ceremony.

20. E. A. Marino, *Aspetti della politica interna di Silla* (Palermo: Presso l'Accademia, 1974) 58–67.

21. Appian *BC* 1.11.95 (Loeb translation, with emendations); see also Vell. Pat. 2.28; Frederic Hurlet, *La dictature de Sylla: Monarchie ou magistrature republicaine?* (Brussels: Institut historique belge de Rome, 1993) 29–50. That this might have been proposed by one of Sulla's centurions, P. Fursidius (Orosius 5.21.3, 4). But see Keaveney, *Sulla*, 165 n. 3, for skepticism about this story.

22. Cic. *de leg.* 1.42 = *Iam vero illud stultissimum, existimare omnia iusta esse quae scita sint in populorum institutis aut legibus. Etiamne si quae leges sint tyrannorum? Si triginta illi Athenis leges inponere voluissent, et si omnes Athenienses delectarentur tyrannicis legibus, num idcirco eae leges iustae haberentur? Nihilo credo magis illa quam interrex noster tulit, ut dictator quem vellet civium <nominatim> aut indicta causa inpune posset occidere.* ("For it would be most foolish to believe that all things are just that are in the institutes or laws of peoples. Even if those laws are from tyrants? If those Thirty in Athens wanted to impose laws and if all the Athenians were delighted by the tyrannical laws, would those laws therefore have been just? I think no better of that law that our interrex proposed that the dictator could kill with impunity any citizen he wished whether or not an official accusation was brought.") Appian *BC* 1.98; Cic. *pro Rosc. Am.* 43; *Schol. Gronov.* p. 435, Orelli.

23. Cic. *Verr.* 1; Ps. Ascon. 193; Suet. *Iul.* 2.

24. This does not mean that he was free of the responsibility of justifying his killing. When he killed Ofella, he had to justify it. Appian *BC* 1.101.

25. This is a view taken by general historians of Rome, e.g., Michael Grant, *Cicero Murder Trials* (London: Penguin, 1975) 7–22. But see also the acceptance by, e.g., Dieter Nörr, *Causa Mortis: Auf den Spuren einer Redewendung.* Münchener Beiträge zur Papyrusforschung und antiken Rechtsgeschichte 80 (Munich: C. H. Beck, 1986) 88–89; Robinson, *Criminal Law,* 40–46; Giuffrè, *Il diritto penale,* 65–66. Richard A. Bauman ("Leges Iudiciorum Publicorum," *ANRW* 2.13 [1980] 120–122) considers the matter unresolved.

26. Some manuscripts have *veneficiis.* See the commentary for line 35 on p. 818 in Theodor Mommsen, Paul Krueger, and Alan Watson. *The Digest of Justinian,* vol. 4 (Philadelphia: University of Pennsylvania, 1985).

27. D. 48.8.1.pr. 1; cf. *Collatio* 1.3; Paul. *Sent.* 5.23.

28. In the *Digest,* under the chapter heading of this law (48.8), are also included some imperial decrees that later fell under its rubric. These, like the law itself, contain homicide and nonhomicide acts such as castration and abortion.

29. Cic. *pro Rab. perd.* 19; *pro Mil.* 11; *Para. Stoic.* 31; *Phil.* 2.22.

30. Cic. *pro Clu.* 148; *pro Cael.* 51.

31. Cic. *pro Clu.* 144–157. In listing other offenses actionable under the law, Cicero adds, *Qui incendium fecerit* ("who will have made a fire"; *Para. Stoic.* 31).

32. 31; cf. *Collatio* 12.5.1; *Codex Iust.* 9.1.11.

33. Cic. *pro Rosc. Am.* 11.

34. D. 48.9.

35. Opinions reflecting this agreement can be tentative or certain: J. D. Cloud ("The Primary Purpose of the *lex Cornelia de Sicariis*," zss 86 [1969] 272 n. 13) writes, "Sulla may have done no more than amalgamate the two pre-existing *quaestiones* into a single *quaestio* and transfer to it offences previously governed by a *lex sempronia ne quis iudicio circumveniatur* (for the more certain conclusions, cf. Ursula Ewins, "Ne quis iudicio *circumveniatur*," JRS 50 [1960] and the literature cited therein). Jean-Louis Ferrary ("Lex Cornelia de sicariis et veneficis," *Athenaeum* 79 [1991]) believes Sulla was without a doubt the first to unify *sicarius* and *veneficium* into one law. See also Andrew W. Lintott ("*Quaestiones de sicariis et veneficiis* and the Latin *lex Bantina*," *Hermes* 106 [1978] 127 n. 12) who says separate *quaestiones de sicariis* and *veneficiis* existed both before and after Sulla. But see also Andrew Riggsby ("Criminal defense and the conceptualization of Crime in Cicero's Orations," Doctoral dissertation, University of California, Berkeley [1993] 84 n. 2), who allows the possibility, at least, that the *veneficus* and *sicarius* might have been joined together in a law even before Sulla.

36. Cic. *pro Rosc. Am.* 11.

37. Cic. *pro Clu.* 151.

38. When the standing courts were first established, their juries consisted of only senators. Gaius Gracchus promulgated a law adding equestrians to the album of jurors. Sulla took away this equestrian privilege. For this *lex Cornelia iudiciaria,* see Vell. Pat. 2.32.3; Appian BC 1.100; Giovanni Rotondi, *Leges publicae populi romani: Elenco cronologico con una introduzione sull'attivita legislativa dei comizi romani* (Hildesheim: G. Olms, 1962) 351. *Lex Plautia iudiciaria* of 89 and other post-Sullan laws came up so that eventually equestrians and tribunes were included on the album of jurors. Asconius p. 79 Clark; Cic. *pro Corn.* 1 fr. 53; cf. Ps. Sall. *in Cic.* 2; Aul. Gell. NA 13.5.3. See Bauman, "Leges iudiciorum."

39. See, too, Ewins, "Ne quis iudicio," 94, and Lintott ("*Quaestiones de sicariis,*" 127), who also provides examples for other Sullan statutes; cf. CIL I.197 lines 7–13; Cic. *Verr.* 2.1.155.

40. A *iudex quaestionis* for poisoning functioned simultaneously as a different *iudex quaestionis de sicariis*: Cic. *pro Clu.* 126. There is also evidence that two *iudices quaestionis* presided over two separate courts for trial of a sicarius (Cic. *pro Clu.* 147). James L. Strachan-Davidson (*Problems of the Roman Criminal Law,* vol. 2 [Oxford: Clarendon, 1912] 149) thought that there were two courts even after Sulla's law. Kunkel, *Untersuchungen,* 70 and n. 264, and Wolfgang Kunkel, RE 24, s.v. *quaestio.*

41. Pace Vincenzo Giuffrè, *Il diritto penale nell'esperienza romana: Profili,* 4th ed. (Naples: Jovene, 1989) 65.

42. Cic. *pro Rosc. Am.* 30, 72.

43. D. 48.9.1. This, too, is a matter of some debate; see, e.g., Lucia Fanizza ("Il parricidio nel sistema della 'Lex Pompeia'" *Labeo* 25 [1979] 284), who sees no change in punishment between Sulla's law and Pompey's.

44. As has been done by Ferrary, "Lex Cornelia de sicariis et veneficis," and more recently and briefly in RS II, 749–753. See, too, the texts of primary sources quoted in these two works.

45. Cloud, "Primary Purpose," 275–276. See also Santalucia, *Studi*, 122–123, regarding arson. Primary material about this chapter of the law can be found in *Collatio* 1.3 (attributed to the jurist Ulpian) and 1.2 (attributed to the jurist Paulus); Marcianus, *D.* 48.8.1 pr. (quoted above); *D.* 48.19.16.8. Even Nörr (*Causa Mortis*, 88–89), who disagrees with the conclusions of Cloud and Kunkel, acknowledges that the word order of the text places attempt first.

46. Santalucia has pointed out (*Studi*, 123) that poisoning seems also to have been greatly concerned not just with homicide by poisoning but with the aspects surrounding homicide. Its preparation, and buying and selling, is as punishable as its employment.

47. Bernardo Santalucia, *Diritto e processo penale nell' antica Roma*. 2nd ed. (Milan: Giuffrè, 1989) 72: "Una lex Cornelia de sicariis et veneficiis, che introdusse (o, come è più probabile, riorganizzò) una quaestio capitale avente per oggetto la persecuzione di diverse forme di attentato all'altrui vita." But he goes on to list the activities punishable under law.

48. "Non coloro che hanno ucciso, ma coloro che pongono in essere i presupposti per cui si arriva alla morte" ("not those who have killed, but those who have put into being the preconditions by which one arrives at death"). Ugo Brasiello, "Sulla ricostruzione dei crimini in diritto romano. Cenni sulla evoluzione dell'Omicidio," SDHI 42 (1976) 253. Expansion on this concept is to be found in Nörr, *Causa Mortis*, 86–115. See also Sarah Currie, "The Killer within: Christianity and the Invention of Murder in the Roman World," *Differences: A Journal of Feminist Cultural Studies* 8(1996) 156.

49. Yet the purpose of Sulla's legislation in regard to the standing courts has been so uncertain that scholars have been able to make diametrically opposing claims about Sulla's plan. This was pointed out by Josef Lengle (*Untersuchungen über die Sullanische Verfassung* [Freiburg im Breisgau: Charitas-Druckerei, 1899] 17), who commented that some scholars have said that Sulla created courts for common crimes while they already existed for crimes done by officials (Zumpt) and others have said precisely the opposite (Mommsen), that courts for common crimes predated Sulla. In addition, Sulla's legislation has been characterized as being more concerned with procedural than with substantive law. Kunkel (*Untersuchungen*, 70) speaking of the *lex Cornelia* writes, "Die von Sulla gewollte und durchgeführte Neuerung scheint also in der Hauptsache darin bestanden zu haben, daß die bis dahin vor verschiedenen, ständigen oder nichtständigen Quästionen verfolgbaren Straftaten nunmehr als Zuständigkeitsbereich einer und derselben quaestio perpetua zusammengefaßt wurden. Der Zweck des Gesetzes war demnach im wesentlichen eine Reform der Gerichtsverfassung und nicht materiellen Rechts." ("The improvements desired and carried out by Sulla appear thus to have been primarily concerned with combining the various standing or not standing courts, each responsible for the prosecution of different crimes, into one all-encompassing *quaestio perpetua*. The purpose of the law was essentially to reform legal procedure and not to make a change in substantive law.")

50. Cic. *in Piso* 50, *pro Clu.* 97, *in Verr.* 1.5, 12, *ad fam.* 3.2.2, *ad Herr.* 2.12.47; Ascon. p 59; Tac. *Ann* 1.72.

51. *D.* 3.3.42.1, 47.10.5,15; John Anthony Crook, *Law and Life of Rome* (Ithaca, NY: Cornell University, 1967) 107.

52. François Hinard, *Les proscriptions de la Rome republicaine.* Collection de l'École française de Rome (Paris: de Boccard, 1985) 71.

53. See above discussion; cf. also Keaveney, *Sulla,* esp. 192.

54. See above.

55. So, too, Santalucia, *Studi,* 119; Contardo Ferrini, *Diritto penale romano, Esposizione storica e dottrinale* (Rome: L'Erma di Bretschneider, 1902) 379 and n. 2; Cloud, "Primary Purpose," 258.

56. Keaveney, *Sulla,* 194; cf. Plut. *Sulla 7.7.*

EPILOGUE

1. E.g., *D.* 48.6, 7.

2. See, e.g., J. D. Cloud, "The Primary Purpose of the *lex Cornelia de Sicariis,*" zss 86 (1969) 282-286.

BIBLIOGRAPHY

Agamben, Giorgio. *State of Exception*. Trans. Kevin Attell. Chicago: University of Chicago, 2005. (Originally published as *Stato di eccezione*. Turin: Bollati Boringhieri 2003.)

Alexander, Michael C. *Trials in the Late Roman Republic 149 BC–50 BC*. Toronto: University of Toronto, 1990.

Ansuategui, A. Dupla. "El *senatus consultum ultimum*: ¿Medidà de salvación pública o práctica de depuración política?" *Latomus* 49 (1990): 75–80.

Antonini, Enrico. *Il "senatus consultum ultimum": Note differenziali e punti di contatto col moderno stato d'assedio*. Turin: Regia Università, 1914.

Badian, Ernst. "The Death of Saturninus." *Chiron* (1984): 101–147.

———. "Tiberius Gracchus and the Roman Revolution." *Aufstieg und Niedergang der römischen Welt* 1.1 (1978) 668–731.

Bauman, Richard A. *Crime and Punishment in Ancient Rome*. London: Routledge, 1996.

———. "Criminal Prosecutions by the Aediles." *Latomus* 33 (1974) 245–264.

———. *The Duumviri in the Roman Criminal Law and in the Horatius Legend*. Historia. Einzelschriften 12. Wiesbaden: Steiner, 1969.

———. "Family Law and Roman Politics." In Vincenzo Giuffrè, ed., *Sodalitas: Scritti in onore di Antonio Guarino*, vol. 3. Naples: Jovene, 1984, 1283–1300.

———. "The *Hostis* Declaration of 88 and 87 BC." *Athenaum* 51 (1973): 270–285.

———. *Lawyers in Roman Republican Politics: A Study of the Roman Jurists in Their Political Setting, 316–82 BC*. Münchener Beiträge zur Papyrusforschung und Antiken Rechtsgeschicht 75. Munich: C. H. Beck, 1983.

———. "Leges Iudiciorum Publicorum." *Aufstieg und Niedergang der römischen Welt* 2.13 (1980): 103–233.

———. *Women and Politics in Ancient Rome*. London: Routledge, 1992.

Bennett, Harold. "Sacer Esto," *Transactions of the American Philosophical Society* 61 (1930): 5–18.

Berger, Adolf B. *Encyclopedic Dictionary of Roman Law*. Transactions of the American Philosophical Society, n.s. 43.2, 1953.

Bernstein, Alvin H. *Tiberius Sempronius Gracchus: Tradition and Apostasy.* Ithaca, NY: Cornell University, 1978.

Black, Henry Campbell. *Black's Law Dictionary,* 6th ed. St. Paul: West Publishing, 1990.

Bleicken, Jochen. *Lex Publica: Gesetz und Recht in der römischen Republik.* Berlin: de Gruyter, 1975.

Bonfante, Giuliano. "Paricidas." *Labeo* 22 (1976): 98–101.

Botsford, George Willis. *The Roman Assemblies from their Origin to the End of the Republic.* New York: MacMillan, 1909.

Brasiello, Ugo. "Sulla ricostruzione dei crimini in diritto romano. Cenni sulla evoluzione dell'omicidio." *Studi et Documenta Historiae et Iuris* 42 (1976): 246–264.

Brecht, C. H. *"Perduellio." Eine Studie zu ihrer begrifflichen Abgrenzung im römischen Strafrecht bis zum Ausgang der Republik.* Münchener Beiträge zur Papyrusforschung und antiken Rechtsgeschichte 29. Munich: C. H. Beck, 1938.

Broughton, T. Robert S. *The Magistrates of the Roman Republic.* 2 vols. New York: American Philological Association, 1951/1952.

Buck, Charles H., Jr. *A Chronology of the Plays of Plautus.* Baltimore: Johns Hopkins University, 1940.

Cagniart, Pierre F. *The Life and Career of Lucius Cornelius Sulla through His Consulship in 88 B.C.E.: A Study in Character and Politics.* Austin: University of Texas, 1986.

Calore, Antonello. "La 'pena' e la 'storia.'" *Diritto Storia* 3 (2004); also published in electronic form at *Diritto@Storia. Rivista internazionale di Scienze Giuridiche e Tradizione Romana* 3 (2004), http://www.dirittoestoria.it/3/TradizioneRomana/Calore-Pena-e-storia.htm#_ftn1

Cantarella, Eva. Review of L. Peppe, *Posizione giuridica e ruolo sociale della donna romana in età repubblicana. Iura* 35 (1984): 136–143.

Cascione, Cosimo. *Tresviri capitales: Storia di una magistratura minore.* Pubblicazioni del dipartimento di diritto romano e storia della scienza romanistica dell'università degli studi di Napoli "Federico II" 13. Naples: Editoriale Scientifica, 1999.

Clark, Albert Curtis, ed. *Q. Asconii Pediani Orationvm Ciceronis qvinqve enarratio.* Oxford: Clarendon, 1907.

Cloud, J. D. "The Constitution and Public Criminal Law." *Cambridge Ancient History* 9, 2nd ed. (1994): 494–530.

———. "*Parricidium*: From the *lex Numae* to the *lex Pompeia de parricidiis.*" ZSS 88 (1971): 1–66.

———. "The Primary Purpose of the *lex Cornelia de Sicariis.*" ZSS 86 (1969): 258–286.

Cornell, T. J. *The Beginnings of Rome: Italy and Rome from the Bronze Age to the Punic Wars (c. 1000–263 BC).* London: Routledge, 1995.

Crawford, M. H., ed. *Roman Statutes,* vol. II. Bulletin of the Institute of Classical Studies, Supplement 64. London: University of London, 1994.

Crook, John Anthony. *Law and Life of Rome.* Ithaca, NY: Cornell University, 1967.

———. "*Patria Potestas.*" *Classical Quarterly* 17 (1967): 113–122.

Currie, Sarah. "The Killer within: Christianity and the Invention of Murder in the Roman World." *Differences: A Journal of Feminist Cultural Studies* 8.2 (1996): 156–170.

Daube, David. "*Nocere* and *noxa*" *Cambridge Law Journal* 7 (1939): 23–54 = *Collected Studies in Roman Law*. Frankfurt am Main: Klosterman, 1991, 71–101.

Develin, Robert "*Provocatio* and Plebiscites," *Mnemosyne* 31 (1978): 46–55.

Dignös, Georg. "Die Stellung der Aedilen im römischen Strafrecht." Doctoral Thesis, Universität München. Munich, 1962.

Dixon, Suzanne, "Conflict in the Roman Family." In Beryl Rawson and Paul Weaver, eds. *The Roman Family in Italy: Status, Sentiment, Space*. Oxford: Clarendon, 1997, 149–168.

———. *The Roman Family*. Baltimore: Johns Hopkins University, 1992.

———. "The Sentimental Ideal of the Roman Family." In Beryl Rawson, ed., *Marriage, Divorce and Children in Ancient Rome*. Oxford: Clarendon, 1991, 99–113.

Dunkle, J. R. "The Greek Tyrant and Roman Political Invective of the Late Republic." *Transactions of the American Philological Association* 98 (1967): 151–171.

Dyck, Andrew R. "On the Interpretation of Cicero, *de Republica*" *Classical Quarterly* n.s. 48.2 (1998): 564–568.

Elster, Marianne. *Die Gesetze der mittleren römischen Republik: Text und Kommentar*. Darmstadt: Wissenschaftliche Buchgesellschaft, 2003.

Ewins, Ursula. "*Ne Quis Iudicio Circumveniatur.*" *Journal of Roman Studies* 50 (1960): 94–107.

Eyben, Emiel. "Fathers and Sons." In Beryl Rawson, ed. *Marriage, Divorce and Children in Ancient Rome*. Oxford: Clarendon, 1991, 114–143.

Fanizza, Lucia. "Il parricidio nel sistema della 'Lex Pompeia'," *Labeo* 25 (1979): 266–289.

Ferguson, Yale H., and Richard W. Mansbach, *Polities: Authority, Identity and Change*. Columbia, SC: University of South Carolina, 1996.

Ferrary, Jean-Louis. "Lex Cornelia de sicariis et veneficiis." *Athenaeum* 79 (1991): 417–434.

Ferrini, Contardo. *Diritto penale romano, Esposizione storica e dottrinale*. Rome: L'Erma di Bretschneider, 1902.

Fiori, Roberto. "Homo sacer": *Dinamica politico-costituzionale di una sanzione giuridico-religiosa*. Pubblicazioni dell'Istituto di diritto romano e dei diritti dell'Oriente mediterraneo, 72. Naples: Jovene, 1996.

Flach, Dieter. *Die Gesetze der frühen römischen Republik: Text und Kommentar*. Darmstadt: Wissenschaftliche Buchgesellschaft, 1994.

Gabba, Emilio. *Dionysius and the History of Archaic Rome*. Sather Lectures 56. Berkeley: University of California, 1991.

———. "Maximus Comitiatus." *Athenaeum* 65 (1987): 203–205.

———. "Studi su Dionigi da Alicarnasso. I. La costituzione di Romolo." *Athenaeum* n.s. 38 (1960): 175–252.

Gage, Jean. *Matronalia. Essai sur les devotions et les organisations cultuelles des femmes dans l'anciènne Rome* (Collection Latomus 60) Brussels: Latomus, 1963.

Garofalo, Luigi. *Appunti sul diritto criminale nella roma monarchica e repubblicana,* 2nd ed. Padua: Cleup, 1993.

———. "In tema di 'provocatio ad populum' (a proposito di un recente saggio)." *Studi et Documenta Historiae et Iuris* 53 (1987): 355–371.

———. *Il processo edilizio: Contributo allo studio dei "iudicia populi."* Padua: CEDAM, 1989.

Gaughan, Judy E. "Killing and the King: Numa's Murder Law and the Nature of Monarchic Authority." *Continuity and Change: A Journal of Social Structure, Law and Demography in Past Societies,* 18.3 (2003): 329–343.

Gelzer, Matthias. RE 7, s.v. M. Tullius Cicero (no. 29). Alfred Druckenmüller Verlag in Waldsee (1939), cols. 827–1091.

Gioffredi, Carlo. *I principi del diritto penale romano.* Turin: G. Giappichelli, 1970.

Giovannini, Adalberto. *Consulare Imperium.* Basel: Friedrich Reinhardt, 1983.

Giuffrè, Vincenzo. *Il diritto penale nell'esperienza romana: Profili,* 4th ed. Naples: Jovene, 1989.

———. *La repressione criminale nell'esperienza romana.* Naples: Jovene, 1997.

Grant, Michael. *Cicero Murder Trials.* London: Penguin, 1975.

Greenidge, A. H. J. *The Legal Procedure of Cicero's Time.* Oxford: Clarendon, 1901.

Gruen, Erich S. *Last Generation of the Roman Republic.* Berkeley: University of California, 1974.

———. *Roman Politics and the Criminal Courts, 149–78 B.C.E.* Cambridge, MA: Harvard, 1968.

Hardy, E. G. *Some Problems in Roman History: Ten Essays Bearing on the Administrative and Legislative Work of Julius Caesar.* Oxford: Clarendon, 1924.

Harris, William. "The Roman Father's Power of Life and Death." In Roger S. Bagnall and William V. Harris, eds. *Studies in Roman Law in Memory of A. Arthur Schiller.* Leiden: Brill, 1986, 81–95.

Hengel, Martin. *Crucifixion in the Ancient World and the Folly of the Message of the Cross.* Philadelphia: Fortress, 1977.

Herrmann, Clodine. *Le rôle judicaire et politique des femmes sous la République romaine.* Brussels: Latomus, 1964.

Heuss, A. "Zur Entwicklung des Imperiums des römischen Oberbeamten." ZSS 64 (1944): 57–133.

Hinard, François. *Les proscriptions de la Rome republicaine.* Collection de l'École française de Rome. Paris: de Boccard, 1985.

Holland, Louise Adams. "Septimontium or Saeptimontium." *Transactions and Proceedings of the American Philological Association* 84 (1953): 16–34.

Hurlet, Frederic. *La dictature de Sylla: Monarchie ou magistrature republicaine?* Brussels: Institut historique belge de Rome, 1993.

Jones, A. H. M. *The Criminal Courts of the Roman Republic and Principate.* Oxford: Basil Blackwell, 1972.

Kaser, Max. *Das altrömische Ius.* Göttingen: Vandenhoeck & Ruprecht, 1949.

Katz, B. R. "The First Fruits of Sulla's March on Rome." *Acta Classica* 44 (1975): 105–115.

Keaveney, Arthur. *Sulla, The Last Republican.* London: Croom Helm, 1982.

Kelly, Gordon P. *A History of Exile in the Roman Republic.* Cambridge: Cambridge University, 2006.

Klebs, Elimar. RE 1, s.v. Aemilius (no. 72). J. B. Metzlerscher Verlag (1894), cols. 554–556.

Köbler, Gerhard. *Juristisches Wörterbuch für Studium und Ausbildung.* Munich: Vahlen, 1995.

Kubitschek, Joseph Wilhelm. RE, s.v. Aedilis. J. B. Metzlerscher Verlagsbuchhandlung (1894), cols. 448–464.

Kunkel, Wolfgang. "Ein direktes Zeugniss für den privaten Mordprozess im altrömischen Recht." ZSS 84 (1967): 382–385.

———. "Das Konsilium im Hausgericht." ZSS 83 (1966): 219–251.

———. RE 24, s.v. quaestio. Stuttgart: J. B. Metzler (1963), cols. 741–755.

———. *Über die Entstehung des Senatsgerichts.* Munich: Verlag der Bayerischen Akademie der Wissenschaften; Beck in Kommission, 1969. Also in *Kleine Schriften.* Weimar: Böhlau, 1974.

———. *Untersuchungen zur Entwicklung des römischen Kriminalverfahrens in vorsullanischer Zeit.* Munich: Verlag der Bayerischen Akademie der Wissenschaften; Beck in Kommission, 1962.

Kyle, Donald G. *Spectacles of Death in Ancient Rome.* New York: Routledge, 1998.

Lacey, Walter Kirkpatrick. "Patria Potestas." In *The Family in Ancient Rome: New Perspectives,* Beryl Rawson, ed. Ithaca, NY: Cornell University, 1986, 121–144.

Landgraf, Gustav. *Kommentar zu Ciceros Rede pro Sex. Roscio Amerino.* Leipzig: Teubner, 1914.

Lanfranchi, Fabio. *Il diritto nei retori romani contributo alla storia dello sviluppo del diritto romano.* Milan: Giuffrè, 1938.

Latte, Kurt. *Kleine Schriften zu Religion, Recht, Literatur und Sprache der Griechen und Romer.* Munich: C. H. Beck, 1968.

———. "The Origin of the Roman Quaestorship." *Transactions of the American Philological Association* 67 (1936): 24–33.

———. RE, Supplement 7, s.v. Todesstrafe. Alfred Druckenmüller Verlag in Waldsee (1950), cols. 1599–1619.

Lengle, Josef. *Untersuchungen über die Sullanische Verfassung.* Freiburg im Breisgau: Charitas-Druckerei, 1899.

Lintott, Andrew W. *The Constitution of the Roman Republic.* Oxford: Clarendon, 1999.

———. "Provocatio: From the Struggle of the Orders to the Principate." *Aufstieg und Niedergang der römischen Welt* 1.2 (1972): 226–267.

———. "*Quaestiones de sicariis et veneficiis* and the Latin *lex Bantina.*" *Hermes* 106 (1978): 125–138.

————. "The Tradition of Violence in the Annals of the Early Roman Republic." *Historia* 19 (1970): 12–29.

————. *Violence in Republican Rome.* Oxford: Clarendon, 1968.

Lovisi, Claire. *Contribution à l'étude de la peine de mort sous la république romaine (509-149 av. J.-C.).* Paris: de Boccard, 1999.

Magdelain, André. "De l' 'auctoritas patrum' à l' 'auctoritas senatus.'" In *Ius Imperium Auctoritas: Études de Droit Romain École française de Rome,* Rome: Palais Farnese (1990) 385–403 (= *Iura* 33 [1982]: 25–45).

————. "Paricidas." In *Du Châtiment dans la cité: Supplices corporels et peine de mort dans le monde antique.* Collection de l'École française de Rome 79. Rome: Palais Farnèse, 1984, 549–571.

Magie, David. *Roman Rule in Asia Minor, To the End of the Third Century after Christ.* Princeton: Princeton University Press, 1950.

Marino, E. A. *Aspetti della politica interna di Silla.* Palermo: Presso l'Accademia, 1974.

Martini, Remo. *Il Problema della "causae cognitio" pretoria.* Milan: Giuffrè, 1960.

Menghi, Angelo. *Dizionario di terminologia giuridica,* 2nd ed. Florence: Barbera, 1950.

Miles, Gary. *Livy: Reconstructing Early Rome,* Ithaca, NY: Cornell University, 1995.

Miners, N. J. "The *Lex Sempronia ne quis iudicio circumveniatur.*" *Classical Quarterly* 52 (1958): 241–243.

Mommsen, Theodor. *Römisches Staatsrecht.* 3rd ed. Leipzig: Dunker & Humblot, 1887.

————. *Römisches Strafrecht.* Systematisch Handbuch der deutschen Rechtswissenschaft Abt. 1, Teil 4. Leipzig: Duncker & Humblot, 1899.

Mommsen, Theodor, Paul Krueger, and Alan Watson. *The Digest of Justinian.* Vol. 4. Philadelphia: University of Pennsylvania, 1985.

Monaco, L. "'Veneficia Matronarum' Magia, medicina e repressione." In *Sodalitas. Scritti in onore di Antonio Guarino* 4. Naples: Jovene, 1984, 2013–2024.

Münzer, Friedrich. *RE* 3, s.v. Cassius (no. 91). J. B. Metzlerscher Verlag (1899), cols. 1751–1752.

————. *RE* 4, s.v. P. Cornelius Lentulus (no. 202). J. B. Metzlerscher Verlag (1901), cols. 1374–1375.

————. *RE* 16, s.v. P. Mucius Scaevola (no. 17). J. B. Metzlerscher Verlagsbuchhandlung, neue Bearbeitung (1935), cols. 425–428.

Mustakallio, Katarina. *Death and Disgrace: Capital Penalties with post mortem Sanctions in Early Roman Historiography.* Annales Academiae Scientarum Fennicae Dissertationes Humanarum Litterarum 72. Helsinki: Suomalainen Tiedeakatemia, 1994.

Nardi, Enzo. *L'otre dei parricidi e le bestie incluse.* Milan: Giuffrè, 1980.

Nicholas, Barry. *Introduction to Roman Law.* Oxford: Clarendon, 1962.

Nippel, Wilfried. *Aufruhr und "Polizei" in der römischen Republik.* Stuttgart: Klett-Cotta, 1988.

————. "Policing Rome," *JRS* 74 (1984) 20–29.

————. *Public Order in Ancient Rome.* Key Themes in Ancient History. Cambridge: Cambridge University, 1995.

Nörr, Dieter. *Causa Mortis: Auf den Spuren einer Redewendung.* Münchener Beiträge zur Papyrusforschung und antiken Rechtsgeschichte 80. Munich: C. H. Beck, 1986.

Ogilvie, R. M. *Commentary on Livy, Books 1–5.* Oxford: Clarendon, 1905.

Orelli, Johann Kaspar von, Johann Georg Baiter, and Franciscus Marcoduranus Fabricius, eds. *M. Tullii Ciceronis Opera quae supersunt omnia ac deperditorum fragmenta: recognovit et singulis libris ad optimam quamque recensionem castigatis cum varietate Lambiniana MDLXVI, Graevio-Garatoniana, Ernestiana, Beckiana, Schuetziana, ac praestantissimarum cuiusque libri editionum integra, reliquae vero accurato delectu brevique adnotatione critica.* Zurich: Füssli and Company, 1826.

Ortega Carrillo de Albornoz, Antonio. *De los delitos y las sanciones en la ley de las XII Tablas.* Malaga: Universidad de Malaga, 1988.

Parker, Holt N. "Why Were the Vestals Virgins? Or the Chastity of Women and the Safety of the Roman State," *American Journal of Philology* 125 (2004): 563–601.

Peppe, Leo. *Posizione giuridica e ruolo sociale della donna romana in età repubblicana.* Pubblicazione dell'Istituto di diritto romano e dei diritti dell'oriente mediterraneo, Rome, LXIII. Milan: Giuffrè, 1984.

Pesch, Andreas. *De Perduellione, crimine maiestatis et memoria damnata.* Aachen: Shaker, 1995.

Plaumann, Gerhard. "Das sogennante senatus consultum ultimum die Quasidiktatur der späteren römischen Republik," *Klio* 13 (1913): 321–386.

Rabello, Alfredo Mordechai. *Effetti personali della "patria potestas" I: Dalle origini al periodo degli Antonini.* Istituto Diritto Romano Università. Milan: Giuffrè, 1979.

Reinhardt, Tobias. *Marcus Tullius Cicero, Topica.* Oxford: Oxford University, 2003.

Resina, Pedro. *La Legitimación activa de la mujer en el proceso criminal romano.* Madrid: Ediciones Clasicas, 1996.

Riccobono, Salvatore. *Fontes Iuris Romani Anteiustiniani* I. Florence: Barbèra 1909.

Riggsby, Andrew. *Crime and Community in Ciceronian Rome.* Austin: University of Texas, 1999.

———. "Criminal defense and the conceptualization of Crime in Cicero's Orations." Doctoral dissertation, University of California, Berkeley, 1993.

Rilinger, Rolf. *Humiliores-Honestiores: Zu einer sozialen Dichotomie im Strafrecht der römischen Kaiserzeit.* Munich: Oldenbourg, 1988.

Robinson, Olivia F. *The Criminal Law of Ancient Rome.* Baltimore: Johns Hopkins University, 1995.

———. "Slaves and the Criminal Law." *ZSS* 98 (1981): 213–254.

———. "Women and the Criminal Law." In *Raccolta di scritti in memoria di Raffaele Moschella,* ed. Brunetto Carpino. Perugia: Università degli studi di Perugia, 1987, 527–560.

Rödl, Bernd. *Das Senatus consultum ultimum und der Tod der Gracchen.* Bonn: Habelt, 1969.

Rodríguez-Ennes, Luis. "La 'provocatio ad populum' como garantia fundamental del ciudad romano frente al poder coercitivo del magistrado en la epoca republicana." In *Studi in onore di Arnaldo Biscardi* IV. Milan: Cisalpino 1983, 73–114.

Roebuck, Derek, and Bruno de Loynes de Fimuchon, *Roman Arbitration*. Oxford: Holo Books, Arbitration Press, 2004.

Rotondi, Giovanni. *Leges publicae populi romani: Elenco cronologico con una introduzione sull'attivita legislativa dei comizi romani*. Hildesheim: G. Olms, 1962.

Rüpke, Jörg. "You Shall Not Kill: Hierarchies and Norms in Ancient Rome." *Numen* 39 (1992): 58–79.

Sachers, E. *RE*, s.v. *Potestas patria*. Stuttgart: Metzler, 1113.

Saller, Richard P. "*Pater familias, Mater Familias*, and the Gendered Semantics of the Roman Household." *Classical Philology*, 94 (1999): 182–197.

———. "*Patria Potestas* and the Stereotype of the Roman Family." *Continuity and Change: A Journal of Social Structure, Law and Demography* 1 (1986): 7–22.

———. *Patriarchy, Property and Death in the Roman Family*, Cambridge: Cambridge University, 1994.

Santalucia, Bernardo. "Alle origini del processo penale romano" *Iura* 35 (1984): 47–48.

———. *Diritto e processo penale nell' antica Roma*. 2nd ed. Milan: Giuffrè, 1989.

———. "Omicidio." *Enciclopedia del diritto*, vol. 29. Milan: Giuffrè, 1979, 885–896.

———. "Osservazioni sul *duumviri perduellionis* e sul procedimento duumvirale." In Yan Thomas, ed. *Du Châtiment dans la cité: Supplices corporels et peine de mort dans le monde antique*. Collection de l'École française de Rome 79. Rome: Palais Farnèse, 1984, 439–452.

———. *Studi di diritto penale romano*. Saggi di storia antica 7. Rome: L'Erma di Bretschneider, 1994.

Schilling, Robert. *La réligion romaine de Venus depuis les origines jusqu'au temps d'Auguste*. Paris: de Boccard, 1954.

Stangl, Thomas, ed. *Ciceronis orationum scholiastae: Asconius, Scholia Bobiensia, Scholia Pseudasconii Sangallensia, Scholia Cluniacensia et recentiora Ambrosiana ac Vaticana, Scholia Lugdunensia sive Gronoviana et eorum excerpta Lugdunensia*, Vienna: F. Tempsky 1912.

Stankiewicz, Antonius. *De Homicidio in iure poenali romano: Excerpta ex dissertatione ad lauream in iure civili assequendam*. Rome: Officium Libri Catholici, 1981.

Stavely, E. S. "Provocatio during the fifth and fourth Centuries BC." *Historia* 3 (1955): 412–415.

Stockton, David. *The Gracchi*. Oxford: Oxford University, 1979.

Strachan-Davidson, James L. *Problems of the Roman Criminal Law*. 2 vols. Oxford: Clarendon, 1912.

Thomas, Yan. "Parricidium." In *Melanges d'archeologie et d'histoire de l'École Française de Rome* 93 (1981): 643–715.

———. "Se Venger au forum. Solidarité familiale et proces criminel a Rome." In Raymond Verdier and Jean-Pierre Poly, eds. *La Vengeance: Vengeance, pouvoirs et idéologies dans quelques civilisations de l'antiquite*. La Vengeance: Études d'ethnologie, d'histoire et de philosophie, 3. Paris: Éditions Cujas, 1984, 65–100.

———. "*Vitae necisque potestas*: le pére, la *cité*, la mort." In *Du Châtiment dans la cité*:

Supplices corporels et peine de mort dans le monde Antique. Collection de l'École française, Rome: Palais Farnese, 1984, 499–548.

Tondo, Salvatore. *Leges regiae e paricidas*. Florence: Olschki, 1973.

———. "L'Omicidio involontario in età arcaica." *Labeo* 18 (1972): 294–332.

Tyrrell, William Blake. *A Legal and Historical Commentary to Cicero's Oratio Pro C. Rabirio Perduellionis Reo*. Amsterdam: Hakkert, 1978.

Ungern-Sternberg von Pürkel, Jürgen, Baron. *Untersuchungen zum spätrepublikanischen Notstandsrecht, senatusconsultum ultimum und hostis-Erklärung*. Beiträge zur alten Geschichte, Band 11. Munich: C. H. Beck, 1970.

Venturini, Carlo. *Processo penale e società politica nella Roma repubblicana*. Pisa: Pacini, 1996.

Völkl, Artur. *Die Verfolgung der Körperverletzung im Frühen Römischen Recht: Studien zum Verhältnis von Tötungsverbrechen und Iniuriendelikt*. Vienna: Bohlau, 1984.

Volterra, Edoardo. "Il preteso tribunale domestico in diritto romano." *Rivista Italiana per le Scienze Giuridiche*. ser. 3.2 (1948): 103–153.

Waldstein, Wolfgang. "Review of Bauman, *The Duumviri in the Roman Criminal Law and in the Horatius Legend*." *ZSS* 88 (1971): 417–421.

Watson, Alan. "The Death of Horatia." *Classical Quarterly* n.s. 29 (1979): 436–447.

———. "Roman Private Law and the *Leges Regiae*." *JRS* 82 (1972): 100–105.

———. *Society and Legal Change*. Edinburgh: Scottish Academic Press, 1977.

———. *The State, Law and Religion: Pagan Rome*. Athens, GA: University of Georgia, 1992.

Westbrook, Raymond. "The Nature and Origins of the Twelve Tables," *ZSS* 105 (1988): 74–121.

———. "*Vitae Necisque Potestas*." *Historia* 48 (1999): 203–223.

Yaron, R. "Vitae necisque potestas." *Tijdschrift voor Rechtsgeschiedenis* 30 (1962): 243–251.

Zumpt, August W. *Das Criminalrecht der Römischen Republik*. 2 vols. Berlin: F. Dümmler, 1869.

INDEX